PRAISE

for Janet Best Dart and
Tender Loving Care

"It's the slow boil that gets you -- and Janet Dart describes it well. Cult indoctrination -- step by step. While many may not know of Synanon, it was one of the most well-known in its day. And unfortunately, Dederich's teachings still ripple through "troubled-teen" programs today. Dart's memoir is well worth the read."

> Janja Lalich, PhD
> Professor Emerita of Sociology
> Author of *Take Back Your Life: Recovering from Cults and Abusive Relationships*

"Janet Dart gives her readers a factual, insightful and thoroughly chilling guide to life within a cultist structure. But her book is far more than a personal memoir that recaps the peculiarities, realities and consequences of a certain point in time. Instead, through personal experience, the book demonstrates how the cultist life normalizes abnormality and insidiously conquers and corrupts all within its grasp. Reaching across decades, its story is also very much in the here and now. Substitute MAGA for Synanon and/ or vice versa and, while the details differ, the mindset is essentially the same."

> Olivia Taylor-Young
> Creative Writing Facilitator
> Osher Lifelong Learning Institute
> University of Oregon

"Janet Dart's story asks the questions that women and men who have been recruited into and stayed for too long in cults often ask themselves: Why did I surrender so much control of my life? Why did I stand aside and remain silent as the abuses mounted? How was it that my friends and I allowed the community we cherished to turn so horribly bad?

"Ms. Dart builds her account with unflinching integrity. She never skirts a question. She searches hard for answers. She never makes excuses for herself.

"Her probing is not abstract. It emerges hand-in-hand with a briskly delivered narrative—one so richly detailed that you are right there with her as she and her community are dragged ever deeper into fear and madness.

"Ms. Dart's story is as honest a memoir as I have ever read. And it is an engaging read. Though I have been through stories of cults many times, I could not put Ms. Dart's book aside after reading the first few pages."

David Gerstel
Author of *Paradise Incorporated: Synanon*

Tender Loving Care
Escaping One of the Most Dangerous Cults in America

Janet Best Dart

LOST HILLS
PRESS

To honor the privacy of those in these pages, some names and details have been changed.

Identifiers: ISBN: 979-8-9932848-0-4 (paperback);
                979-8-9932848-1-1 (ebook);
                979-8-9932848-2-8 (audio)

Printed in the United States of America

Jacket design by Bridget Halberstadt
Author's photograph by SHE Photography, Bend, Oregon

For Robert Best IV

Author's Note

It was on Wikipedia that I first saw Synanon described as one of the most dangerous and violent cults America had ever seen.[1] I don't know about that. To me, it was home.

When I began writing, I wanted to capture the remarkable, idealistic community where I lived from 1971 to 1977. I interviewed nearly two dozen people, hoping to braid their memories with my own. When I asked what they missed most about Synanon, almost everyone said, "I miss the community."

After one long conversation, a friend turned the question back on me: "Do you believe now it was a cult?" I told him, "Maybe by the time you arrived in 1976—but not at the beginning." Now I'm not so sure. I realized I couldn't tell anyone else's story until I understood my own.

This is mine.

---

1. "Synanon." https://en.wikipedia.org/wiki/Synanon, accessed October 18, 2025.

Contents

Chapter 1: The Beginning of the End

April 1976, Santa Monica, California

I stopped crying the day Synanon stole my baby.

Arms folded tightly over my stomach, I tried to soothe the knot twisting in my gut as I watched the Demonstrators—the women entrusted with our children—buckle my ten-month-old son into a white fourteen-passenger van. This wasn't a field trip. Synanon was sending him to another compound four hundred twenty-five miles away. Without me.

I stood on my balcony like a marble statue, feet rooted to the floor, tears frozen beneath my eyelids. An ache crept into my chest, traveled through my lungs and constricted my throat. Was I even breathing?

How will Robert understand he won't see his mommy every day? How will I live without being a part of his life? What if I miss his first steps?

Still no tears.

Across the street, the sun shimmered on the gentle waves of the Pacific breaking onto the sandy shores of the promised paradise of Santa Monica, the promised utopia of Synanon.

Act as if. I repeated the mantra I had been reciting for seven years. Act as if you're happy, and you will become happy.

Demonstrators! I had already been replaced by Demonstrators who worked in shifts, ten hours a day. One week on; one week off. But at least I saw my baby every day. Until now.

I tamped down my feelings, replaced them with... nothing. Not sadness. Not rage. Hollow. My body had gone quiet, as if I'd stepped out of it, leaving my sadness hidden even from myself.

On the street below, Bobby leaned through the van's window and hugged our son. Bobby's brown eyes matched Robert's, but his skin was two shades darker, his hair three times curlier. He still had those football player shoulders that had caught my eye four years earlier. Bobby turned and looked up at me, raising his eyebrows. I slowly shook my head. I couldn't go downstairs and pretend this was a festive event, couldn't smile while I watched my baby being ripped away from me.

1

I don't know how long I stood there staring out the window that chilly spring morning. Minutes? An hour?

When Robert was born, with his curly black hair, and golden brown skin, his deep brown eyes gazed intensely into mine as if to say, "So that's who you are." He didn't nurse when I first held him to my breast as I lay on the delivery table. Instead, he turned his head and found my eyes, and I knew that even after the doctor cut the cord, Robert was still part of me. I knew he felt it, too. Our love flowed through our eyes and multiplied in our heartbeats as he lay on my chest.

All sound in the delivery room faded as we became one again—mother and son—as we had been from the moment I conceived.

There he lay, staring into my soul. I thought my heart might explode with joy in that first moment, holding him. My love encompassed my husband Bobby and this beautiful child we had created. In that moment, they were my world.

Ten months later, they were still my world. But Synanon was my world too.

I should have listened to the tug in my gut, to the whisper that said, *run*. But I didn't. I trusted Synanon more than I trusted myself.

I stood there until the van disappeared, until there was nothing left to watch but empty pavement. No sound. No footsteps. Just the waves crashing in the distance.

God, we didn't even have car seats. My baby, who wasn't yet walking, was seat-belted into a van for a seven-hour drive. Seven hours? Would they stop to feed them? Let them out to crawl? Hold them on their laps while the van barreled north on I-5? And why a van? Synanon owned a Greyhound-style bus with plush seats, a snack bar, and a restroom. They drove it back and forth between northern and southern California every day. Why didn't my baby get that small luxury?

None of these questions went through my numb mind.

The big question isn't whether Synanon drove my baby in a van or a luxury bus. The tough questions are—why did they take him? Why did I let them? Why the hell didn't I run? The details of his ride don't matter.

How much did Charles "Chuck" Dederich, our founder, our

megalomaniac leader, hate children? Babies?

All the terrible things I witnessed in Synanon after that day paled in comparison. I lived as if I were watching a play. A play with a cruel protagonist, pushing people to their limits. Seeing how far they would go. Until the only residents left would do whatever Dederich said. Including buying liquor for Dederich, who had once been destroyed by alcohol, and who formed Synanon with only two rules: no drugs or alcohol and no violence. After Dederich fell off the wagon, instead of helping him like we helped thousands of substance abusers, his inner circle reveled in his drinking parties, defying everything Synanon—my Synanon—stood for: Tender loving care.

But I am getting ahead of myself.

It's been a long road to forgiving myself. I'm not sure that I have.

I doubt that anyone knowingly joins a cult. I certainly didn't. I had never even heard of a cult and wouldn't have recognized it if I had.

What is this strange pull that cults seem to have? Maybe it's the yearning for community, the promise of a higher purpose, the lure of saving the world, or perhaps saving oneself. For me, it was all of that.

Chapter 2: Seven Years Earlier

Summer 1969, Oakland, California

The sun hung low when we parked outside the eight-story building. Gritty gargoyle statues glared down from the roofline, sending shivers through me. What the hell was I thinking—agreeing to a Saturday night party in one of Oakland's scariest neighborhoods?

It was Anne's idea, my new neighbor. "Gary and I've been working on our relationship," she told me the day we met. "We tried Esalen, but that didn't do it for us. Now we go to Synanon. It's a club. Hard to explain, but I think you'll like it." Her brown eyes sparkled through her long, straight bangs.

"Sure, I'll go," I said, caught in one of those what-the-hell-I'll-try-anything moods.

I'd already met her live-in boyfriend, Gary, the day before when he was out front, banging on the hood of his car.

"Hi—I think I'm your neighbor. Just moved in upstairs. Need help?"

He brushed his longish black hair off his forehead and looked at me under dark eyebrows. "What can *you* do? My car won't start, and I've got to get to work."

His old blue Ford Falcon sat parked on the hill in front of my faded red Alfa Romeo. "Is it a stick shift?" I asked.

"Yes," he grumbled. "God, I hate this fucking car. But my dad's buying me a new VW next week."

I rolled my eyes. *Daddy's buying him a new car.* My family had never even owned a new car.

"Well, let's try popping the clutch. If that doesn't work, I'll give you a ride."

His face told me he had no idea what I meant.

"Give me the keys." He did, and I slid into the driver's seat, rolling down the window to air out the stale Taco Bell smell. I figured I had just enough room to get the car started before it rolled onto busy Park Boulevard.

I turned the key to the on position, right foot on the brake, left on the clutch, and released the parking brake. Timing is everything. As the car began to roll, I let off the clutch and gave it gas. The engine

4

bucked to life, jolting me between the seat and steering wheel. I grinned, rolled through the stop sign, and drove half a block. Gary ran up beside me, panting.

"How the hell—? Thank you! I'll see you later! Maybe come down for dinner sometime. Gotta go!" And off he went.

A few weeks shy of nineteen, I'd just moved into my first apartment after being kicked out of my family home. Well, maybe not kicked out. Mom gave me an ultimatum.

My pulse still races thinking about that day. I'd spent my first night home from U.C. Davis with my fiancé, Kevin, in his Berkeley apartment. My first time smoking pot. We were too stoned to ride his motorcycle back to Richmond, so we slept curled in each other's arms.

When we pulled into Mom's driveway the next morning, she stood at the door, pointing. "If you want to shack up, shack up," she snapped. "But if you want to live in my house, you live by my rules."

Her eyes shot daggers. My ten-year-old brother and his miniature poodle peeked through the drapes.

My mouth fell open. No words came. I went still, thoughts swirling.

Had she been worried? I should've called. But no, she's not a worrier. I've traipsed all over San Francisco, camped with friends, driven to Death Valley with my brother. I lived away at college for a year. She never flinches.

It's the sex.

Her accusatory finger stabbed me in the heart. I lifted my chin, clenched my jaw, turned my back, and climbed onto Kevin's motorcycle. I didn't realize she was doing me a favor—shooing me away from my father.

"Let's go," I said, wrapping my arms around him. He restarted the engine, and we left my mother's rules behind.

I broke up with Kevin a week later. Ran off with his roommate. Daring to walk out on Mom gave me the nerve to walk out on my high school sweetheart.

I'm free. I don't have to listen to my parents. I don't have to get married. I don't have to have two babies. I can do whatever I want.

How coldhearted. Ending a four-year relationship on a whim. No discussion. I have no excuse. But now, all these years later, I see a pattern. When things go bad, I move on. I've always blamed Synanon. But I did it before. With Kevin.

Now I know: I was running from my father, from one awful night.

***

The air in Berkeley in 1969 was thick with restlessness: free speech, women's rights, anti-war, Black is beautiful. I breathed it all in. Change.

So, I went to the Saturday night party. Whatever it was.

Dressed in a miniskirt and ankle-high boots, I followed Gary and Anne beneath a crisp canvas awning emblazoned with "Synanon Club." I took a deep breath and stepped into a brightly lit lobby—like the Mark Hopkins Hotel where I'd gone to prom, but run-down. A wide staircase flanked by glossy railings beckoned. Laughter echoed from above. To the left, an old-fashioned elevator with ornate caged doors stood idle. I would learn that the building had been the old Athens Club, a prestigious social and cultural hub in Oakland during the 1920s and 1930s, which Synanon bought and refurbished in 1966.

A swarthy, bedraggled man—ageless, leathery-skinned, smelling faintly of homelessness—slouched on a wooden bench. I looked away when I caught him staring. He made my skin crawl. Thankfully, he returned his gaze to the floor. But what was he doing here? Were they collecting homeless people?

A chirpy twenty-something clerk ended a phone call and asked, "Here for Saturday Night Party? Mona will take you upstairs to the ballroom."

Ballroom? Sounds fancy.

We nodded and followed a stocky woman in jeans and a loose shirt. I hoped I wasn't overdressed.

Upstairs, my eyes widened. Floor-to-ceiling windows lined two walls. Marble pillars held up the ceiling, and a six-foot stone fireplace anchored one side. Chandeliers hung from the cathedral ceiling. At least a hundred people sat at tables, smoking, drinking, laughing, talking.

The room pulsed with vitality, wrapping me in its vibrant buzz.

We passed a pale man shivering beneath a blanket on a couch, a bucket beside him—like the ones Mom used to set by my bed for me to throw up in when I had the flu. A clean-cut man with glowing skin sat beside him, murmuring.

The man and the bucket unsettled me. Surreal. Like a scene from *Twilight Zone*. Mona smiled and nodded at them as if a man puking into a bucket were the most natural thing in the world, then led us to a table with two women sipping coffee and nibbling cut-up vegetables.

We introduced ourselves, and before we sat, one woman said, "Mostly ex-drug addicts live here. Chuck started this place to cure addicts. But now even squares are moving in." She clinked mugs with her friend.

"Squares?" I asked.

"People who never used drugs. Like me. I don't live here, but I'm in the Game Club. I play once a week and help out on Saturdays. I love this place."

Were there addicts in the room? I couldn't tell. Not that I'd known any personally, but I'd seen them—scrawny, scraggly, pale. No one here looked like that. Except the puke-bucket man.

"There are only two rules," she continued. "No violence or threats of violence, and no drugs or alcohol. That's it. We work everything else out in the Game."

"Then what is everyone drinking?"

Gary rolled his eyes. "Gatorade or Tab. Whatever was donated this week."

"Donated?"

"Yeah," Anne said. "Companies donate food and stuff. Synanon's figured out how to cure drug addicts, and everyone wants to help."

My mind spun. What did this have to do with Gary and Anne working on their relationship?

I sighed. "Okay then, what's the Game?"

The second woman leaned in. "We sit in a circle and talk honestly."

A booming voice interrupted.

"Welcome, everyone." The room quieted. I followed the voice to a man in his thirties standing by the fireplace. He spoke briefly about upcoming events. Something about their school moving to Tomales Bay. I didn't understand most of it, so I let my eyes wander.

The sea of people—every age, every color—captivated me. My high school was integrated, but this felt different. Blacks and Whites mingled like friends, not clustered in separate groups. Men wore overalls or jeans, women slacks or skirts. A haze of smoke lingered, the scent of stale cigarettes comfortingly familiar—home, Mom and Dad's Marlboros.

Maybe I should have seen through the smiles, seen the shadows behind them. But I didn't. I saw what I needed: warmth. A cause to believe in. A fresh start.

The speaker paused, then announced, "We have a one-year anniversary to celebrate." Heads turned as a young man in crisp overalls stepped forward.

The room erupted in cheers, like a hometown football game. The young man smiled until the noise died down.

Voice quaking, he said, "One year ago, it was me sitting on that bench in the lobby." He pointed to the couch with the puke bucket. "One year ago, it was me on the kicking couch. Today, I am one year clean."

Several people cheered.

"Before I walked into Synanon, I was strung out on heroin and barely hanging on. My family had cast me aside. I had no money, nowhere to go. Then I saw a poster: 'Go to Synanon or go to hell.' I chose Synanon."

My jaw dropped. This guy—an addict, a word that made my skin crawl—had quit drugs and looked... ordinary. Whole. All these people had helped him. He said Synanon gave him a job in food service. Now he was a cook.

His story tugged at my heartstrings.

The anniversary man paused, and the room held its breath. "The Synanon Philosophy," he said, scanning the crowd, maybe searching for a familiar face. Then, looking up to his left as if reaching for something just out of view, he continued:

8

"The Synanon Philosophy is based on the belief that there comes a time in everyone's life when he arrives at the conviction that envy is ignorance; that imitation is suicide; that he must accept himself for better or for worse as is his portion. That though the wide universe is full of good, no kernel of nourishing corn can come to him but through his toil bestowed on that plot of ground which is given to him to till."

I felt a shock of recognition. I knew those words. Emerson. I'd underlined that passage in high school. Words to live by.

"The power which resides in him is new in nature... Bravely let him speak the utmost syllable of his conviction. God will not have his work made manifest by cowards."

That reminded me of Kipling's *If*: *If you can keep your head when all about you / Are losing theirs and blaming it on you...* My best friend, Jacqui, and I used to hike in the mountains, dissecting those lines like they held the secret to becoming who we wanted to be.

What kind of place had I stumbled into? It was everything we talked about—purpose, conviction, transformation. I couldn't wait to tell her.

I did tell her later that summer. She wasn't impressed. Didn't even come to check it out. Thought the Game would mess with my mind. She was still taking classes at Berkeley, smoking pot, dropping acid. I thought the drugs would mess with hers. We reconnected twenty years later and decided we were both right. But by then, she was another person I'd left behind.

Anniversary Man was still reciting. He ended with, "God helps those that help themselves." He let out a deep breath and beamed.

The room erupted in cheers. I smiled and clapped with everyone else. Imagine—a place built around Emerson's philosophy of self-reliance.

Then guitars kicked in, and a rock band sprang to life. I hadn't even noticed them setting up. People pushed tables aside, and in seconds the room was a dance floor. Not couples swaying, but a surge of people moving in sync—choreographed steps, each adding their own flourish. Today I'd call it a blending of Soul Train and country line dancing, but neither had been invented yet. Back then, it felt like something brand new crackling into existence.

"This is the Hoopla," my neighbor Anne said, jumping to her feet. "Just follow along."

I twisted my long hair in my fingers. "Oh, I don't know. I'll watch." I hated dances. I was a klutz, and always felt like everyone was staring.

"Oh, come on. It's fun." She tugged my arm, and I reluctantly followed.

The Hoopla was simple—two steps right, two steps left, forward, back. Repeat. Easy. No one was watching. The music poured over me, pulsing through the floor, and I slipped into the wave of bodies moving separate yet together. For the first time in a long time, I didn't feel like I was performing. I felt like I belonged.

After the dancing, Gary and Ann were hugging. As I stood awkwardly beside them, a woman, maybe ten years older, slipped between us, flicking her long straight hair off her neck.

"Hi, I'm—" I didn't catch her name. "Isn't this place amazing?"

I raised my eyebrows. Why was she talking to me? "I don't know much about it."

Her eyes twinkled. "It's an experimental community. Not the same old nuclear family. A whole new way of living, of raising and educating children." She didn't wait for me to respond. "We have our own school. That's why I moved in. Instead of just two parents, kids have lots of role models. We're educating the whole child."

I leaned forward, lingering on the idea of not being under the thumb of just two parents. Of my father.

"My kid is so happy here." She crossed her arms. "The public school wanted to give my five-year-old Ritalin. That's their answer to everything."

A loud voice hushed the room. "Oh, orientation," she said. "I'll let you go."

I turned. A clean-shaven man with short dark hair—good-looking for someone my father's age—quieted the crowd. "Welcome. I'm Don. My day job is a DJ at KSFO, but I live here. I donate my salary to Synanon. Every time I get a raise, Synanon gets a raise." His blue eyes sparkled. "To you new people, we invite you to join the Game Club to see what we're all about. The Game Club meets once a week for a Game. Dues are five cents a month or whatever you can afford."

I didn't recognize the sales pitch. It didn't feel like one. These were passionate people talking about something they truly believed in. And I wanted to believe too.

Mona, who had escorted us upstairs, approached me to sign up. I wasn't ready. I needed space to think, to let the evening settle.

"I don't have any money with me," I said quietly. *That should do it.*

"Here's a nickel," Mona said, digging into her pocket and pressing it into my hand.

Excuse gone, I signed up.

I bought it. All of it. The words I chose to live by, the words I thought the community lived by:

The Synanon Prayer

> Please let me first and always examine myself
> Let me be honest and truthful
> Let me seek and assume responsibility
> Let me understand rather than be understood
> Let me trust and have faith in myself and my fellow man
> Let me love rather than be loved
> Let me give rather than receive.

I was young, idealistic, naïve, trying to find myself in the world. Wanting to be involved in something more than the free speech movement, more than the anti-war movement. Dederich called it a revolutionary community. He said we could save the world. And I believed him.

But it was an illusion. Now, having looked behind the curtain, I realize that yes, some lives were changed for the better, even saved. But many were hurt. My family was among those who paid the price of belonging.

In the beginning, I was a believer. Then the doubts began to creep in. Whispers that grew louder, then screamed. But I buried them. I'm good at burying things; I learned that growing up.

Tender Loving Care

During my years in Synanon, belonging to my community—my chosen family—was all I wanted to hold on to. The truth was blurred.

The author, age 20
Photo by Mark Cozza

Chapter 3: The Synanon Game

Summer 1969, Oakland, California

The following Wednesday evening, I sat in the back seat of Gary's new light blue VW fastback, which his dad had bought for him the day after I jump-started his Ford. Anne sat in the front passenger seat as Gary drove down 12th Street through old downtown Oakland, the street lit only by the timed red signals that threatened to stop us on every short block.

"Stop!" I shouted as Gary approached the first intersection at full speed, about to run a red light. Miraculously, the light turned green just as he crossed the crosswalk.

Gary looked at me in his rearview mirror with a glint in his eyes. "Don't worry. The lights are timed. As long as I keep steady at twenty-five miles per hour, I get all green lights."

I knew about timed lights, but I wasn't driving. I came from a family of racecar drivers and hated being a passenger. Expecting a collision at every intersection, I clutched the door handle, worrying more about being t-boned than some game I'd been talked into. After a few miles, I glanced left, recognizing the twenty-two-story Tribune Tower with its illumined clock and green roof—my mother's landmark for anywhere in Oakland.

Gary turned right and parked across the street from the eight-story Synanon building. Even in the dim light of the streetlamps, I could tell it was dingy white and in need of sandblasting. The gargoyle statues stared down at me. Warning me?

I climbed out of the back seat as Gary complained about his dad having bought him a VW sedan instead of a Bug. I bit my tongue instead of saying, *Your daddy bought you a car and you're complaining?* I'd saved for two years to buy my barely running 1956 Alfa by working as a Camp Fire Girl summer camp counselor and working part-time for a local florist after school. My dad had rebuilt the engine for me.

I followed Gary and Anne into the club and waved at the front desk clerk. The wooden bench where the homeless guy had been sitting was vacant, revealing an ornate carving that looked something like an S inside a circle.

We climbed the stairs into the same ballroom where we'd been for the Saturday Night Party. The tables were gone, replaced by worn couches scattered haphazardly. Fifty or so people milled about, mingling, chattering, and laughing. Gary and Anne stopped to greet a few, but I hung back, nerves prickling, caught between curiosity and the urge to bolt. The only familiar face was the DJ from Saturday night.

The DJ's voice cut through the chatter. "Okay, let's get started. Listen up for your Game groups." One by one, names were called, and clusters of people peeled away. Relief washed over me when I heard I'd be with Gary and Anne—at least I wouldn't be facing this with complete strangers.

Our group of fifteen followed the DJ into a brightly lit room, the chairs waiting in a perfect circle—faded blue, yellow, and tan canvas stretched slack, worn from use. Black-and-white photographs lined the walls, their subjects with frozen smiles. I took a seat, my pulse quickening. This was the Game. I told myself it would be like the encounter groups in college—controlled, polite, careful not to hurt anyone's feelings. But the words from Saturday night echoed in my head. *We work everything out in the Game.*

Outside, buses hissed and rumbled. Headlights swept briefly across the building opposite us, then were gone. A traffic light cycled—green, yellow, red—flashes of color pulsing through the window.

"Welcome newcomers. I'm Don. Ex-square. I live here now." His gaze traveled the circle, stopping on each of us in turn. When his eyes caught mine, I looked away.

"There are only two rules," he said. "No violence or threat of physical violence and stay in your chairs. Other than that, say what you want."

DJ Don asked the newcomers to introduce themselves. When it was my turn, I clasped my hands in my lap so no one could see them shaking. Warmth spread from my neck to my face and I hurried through my words to get the spotlight off me. "I'm a student at U.C. Berkeley and live in an apartment in Oakland." Pointing to Gary and Anne, I continued, "Gary and Anne are my neighbors. They brought me down here last Saturday night, and I joined."

A few people nodded, muttering, "Welcome," before being interrupted by a handsome twenty-something guy sporting an ironed, button-down shirt tucked into creased slacks. He leaned forward, face red, and started screaming at a guy across the room.

"I wanna talk to my fucking roommate." His hands gripped the wooden chair arms like he was about to leap out of his seat.

What in the world? Definitely not an encounter group.

The guy across the room sat back with an incredulous look on his face. "What?"

"You're a fuckin' slob. You leave dirty dishes everywhere. Your crap is all over the living room. The bathroom is disgust—"

"Screw you and your fancy neatness. It's my house and I'll live how I want. You're just payin' rent. And you can't even do that on time! Maybe it's time you found your own fucking place!"

"Whoa, whoa! All I'm sayin' is I wanna bring a girl home and it would be nice not to have to fuckin' clean the toilet before I let her in."

"What's with guys and dirty bathrooms?" A woman who looked like she'd just arrived from an office chimed in. "If I walked in that house, I would turn around and walk out."

Neatnik sneered at her. "Well, you haven't been fuckin' invited. All I need is my quote landlord to clean up his shit."

She put on a schoolmarm voice. "Guys! Make a cleaning schedule. Pay your rent on time. Good Lord, how hard is that?"

I felt like I was at a soccer game, watching the ball bounce in all directions. One person would accuse another; that person would defend; a third person would interject their two cents. A tight knot twisted in my stomach as voices exploded around me. *This isn't what that woman described Saturday night. Where's the honest conversation? This is just people screaming obscenities at each other.*

Words ricocheted across the room like a WrestleMania match, only seated. And not choreographed. People competing to talk. Raw emotion, punctuated with the word *fuck*—a word I'd only ever seen scrawled on bathroom stalls. Here it was tossed around like candy, and every time it landed, my gut clenched. Laughter burst out here and there, cutting through the tension like sparks.

This wasn't the tame honesty that woman promised on Saturday.

15

It was an avalanche of rage and energy. And somehow, it was exhilarating.

Then DJ Don turned to me. "Well, Janet, you've been pretty quiet. Do you have anything you want to say to your friends?"

The room went silent as all eyes focused on me. My face grew hot. *I don't want these people screaming at me.* "Actually, Gary borrowed fifty dollars from me a couple of weeks ago and hasn't paid me back. I need the money for rent."

DJ Don turned to Gary, his deep voice booming. "You're mooching off this college student? Why haven't you paid her back? This young lady helps you out, and now you're fucking stealing from her!"

Gary quietly responded, looking at his feet. "I'm not stealing. Of course, I'll pay her back. I just forgot." Others joined in; I don't remember the specifics, things like "you're a scumbag," "you're as bad as a drug addict."

Gary looked forsaken while Anne remained silent.

Never in my life had anyone stood up for me. I felt powerful and energized. Looking at Gary, I felt a pang of guilt. I didn't enjoy getting someone into trouble, but I needed my money back.

"Okay, folks," DJ Don announced, looking at his watch. "This has been a great Game. Let's all go grab some coffee. Remember, out of the Game is just as important as in the Game." Getting up from his chair, he remarked, "The Game is our time to vent. Outside the Game, we smile and treat each other respectfully."

Like a switch turned off, everyone smiled and chattered, several hugs and claps on the back. Gary muttered, "Sorry, Janet. I'll give you the money tomorrow."

I didn't realize I had been part of a session of emotional catharsis, something I would learn to both dread and crave. I would feel as if a boulder had been lifted, my emotions unblocked leaving me mental clarity once I stopped ruminating. I would experience the stimulation of intense concentration and learn to speak on my feet. I would learn to defend myself, to listen to criticism.

Until they took my baby. Then everything changed.

But that first Game Night, it was all new. Exciting.

Gary paid me back the next day but never returned to Synanon.

On the other hand, I dove into this Game Club I'd joined. I thought I'd found where I belonged.

Instead, I lost myself.

A Game
Photo by Laurie Pepper

Chapter 4: Chuck and The Birth of Synanon

Summer 1970, Oakland, California

My friend Elizabeth invited me to hear chamber music at the Club. I had met Elizabeth in the Game Club. She was my age and looking for an apartment to share. Elizabeth was tall like a basketball player, but she stood with rounded shoulders as if trying to make herself short, maybe invisible. She had moved in with me, splitting my seventy-five-dollar-a-month rent. Six months later she moved into Synanon as a Lifestyler—someone who moved into Synanon for the communal lifestyle. I was still a Game Player.

Elizabeth explained Synanon didn't hold church services, but she still enjoyed a Sunday morning gathering. I joined a dozen people in the living room to listen. The sun bathed the room in a warm glow. Elizabeth wore a long dress and cradled her violin between her chin and collarbone. She placed her bow on the strings and emitted sweet music with rich, warm tones, so different from the guitar that I played.

I sat transfixed; I hadn't known she played the violin. Afterward, she told me how disappointed she was that so few people had shown up. "Give them time," I suggested. "Maybe no one's heard this kind of music before." I hadn't. As a teen, I was a Beatlemaniac and then drifted into folk music. I only encountered jazz at the Club.

"I'll think about it. I'm going downstairs to change. Let's go eat after."

I agreed and followed her. She ducked into the restroom, and that's when I saw Chuck for the first time.

I felt his presence before I saw him, like an energy force blowing through the hallway. Stopping mid-stride, I turned to look. Until then, he had only been a photo on the wall. His crooked face, one eye sagging, and his mouth in a half-grin looked exactly like his pictures. He wore baggy overalls, a loose shirt covering his expanded belly, and comfortable, non-descript shoes. He had a presence like he owned the place—well, he did own the place.

I knew his sagging eye was from meningitis when he was thirty-one. It lent an impression of thoughtfulness, adding to his aura of philosopher-king. Seeing him in person was like seeing a movie star in a restaurant. Continuing my childhood fear of authority figures, I stepped back into an alcove, averting my eyes, hoping he wouldn't notice me. He didn't.

"How are all my dopefiends in Oakland today?" he bellowed heartily, his face creasing. "What have you cooked up for lunch? I'm starved." And up the stairs he went toward the dining room, followed by a procession including the Oakland Director, Tribe Leaders (community leaders who looked after twenty to thirty people), old-timers who had known him for a decade, and his dog robber—personal assistant. I love the term dog robber, borrowed from the military for an officer's aide-de-camp. The aide is expected to rob anyone, including the family dog, to get his general what he wants.

Elizabeth returned in her usual jeans and loose blouse. We went to the dining room for lunch which consisted of leftovers from the night before. We talked a little, but mostly, we watched the show in the corner where Chuck dined with his entourage.

Chuck sat at a large dining table reserved for directors, regents, and the Synanon elite. The table was set Emily-Post-style, with chinaware, napkins, two forks, a knife, a spoon, and water glasses, evenly spaced. Waitresses took their orders and served them food like they were at a fine dining restaurant instead of a common dining room in a drug rehab community. The rest of us grabbed our food from the buffet line.

Chuck, sitting with his back to the windows, watched over the dining area like a king surveilling his court. He bellowed with laughter over something spoken at the table.

Then Chuck glared at a guy the next table over. I sat transfixed as if watching a car accident.

Chuck shouted at him. "Hey! You in the overalls! Who taught you to eat? Why are you talking with your mouth full, spewing food all over our table? If you want to eat like an animal, go live somewhere else!"

Gulping his mouthful of food, face flushed, the guy in overalls answered, "Sorry, Chuck. You're right. Thank you!"

Chuck turned his attention back to his table like nothing had happened.

"Jeez," Elizabeth whispered. "I can't imagine getting a pull-up from Chuck."

"What's a pull-up?" I asked, taking small bites and chewing all my food.

"You know, when you see someone do something wrong, like leaving a coffee cup in the living room." She pointed to an empty plate on the table. "Or a dirty dish on the table. You say, 'hey, take your plate back to the kitchen', or 'pick up that piece of trash you dropped.' Something like that. You see someone do something wrong, and you tell them. They answer with a thank you."

"That sounds so civilized," I responded, remembering my father hitting me with a butter knife when I reached across the kitchen table.

"It's one reason I like living here," she mused. "Everyone is polite. Any arguments are saved for the Game."

I turned my attention back to Chuck, feeling his energy permeate the room. The black and white photos adorning the walls didn't do him justice.

I've never seen a photograph capture charisma, that magnetic charm oozing off someone, their confidence, their passion and eagerness to share their ideas. It's something you feel, a gravitational pull.

After seeing Chuck in person, I wanted to learn more about him, so I spent a Saturday afternoon in a small windowless room in the Synanon Club perusing the Tape Library, a collection of recordings of seminars and chalk talks. A tall bookshelf crafted from one-by-eight planks stood against one wall, filled with dozens of small boxes, each adorned with hand-printed labels:

- Ten Years Sober • Love as a Creative Tool
- Acting As If • How to Play the Synanon Game
- How to Be a Synanon Fanatic

The other library walls featured black and white photos of Chuck and various people I didn't recognize. The photos weren't labeled. An African American with her hair worn short and natural, her gleaming skin and bright smile contrasted with Chuck's stern face.

That must be Chuck's wife, Betty D.

I grabbed the Ten Years Sober tape and settled in one of the comfortable chairs next to a table with a reel-to-reel tape machine that played six-inch spools of half-inch tape. Several more comfortable chairs dotted the area, each beside a table holding a tape player and an empty ashtray. Not a speck of dust in the room, not even in the ashtrays.

Chuck's gravelly voice on the tape mesmerized me. He was obviously speaking to a group, as the audience's laughter was sprinkled throughout the speech.

It was 1956. Dederich was forty-three and had been on a drinking binge for a month. He was so sick his wife took him to the hospital to detox and then when he was sober, she dragged him to Alcoholics Anonymous in Santa Monica. He listened to others address the group, and then it was his turn. After he spoke, people laughed and clapped. "This is for me," he decided.

Chuck became a fanatic, living and breathing AA.

He found a job and went to AA after work to speak to the compassionate crowd. He went home, ate a can of chili, and returned to AA.

His wife divorced him. "She took the inside of the house, and I took the outside," he snickered, to the merriment of the listeners.

That's an old line, but it was new to me. Chuck's audience seemed to identify with all his misadventures.

Someone walked into the Tape Library and nodded. "What're ya listening to?"

"Ten Years Sober."

"I love that tape. The beginning of Synanon. Enjoy."

He walked out.

I leaned back in my chair and kept listening. *What a storyteller! What a story!*

About nine months after Chuck joined AA, his company transferred him to Santa Barbara, about ninety miles north of Santa Monica. He continued to spend his evenings at AA. Suddenly, he felt impending doom and stayed in his motel room, terrified, for a week. Then, the feeling went away.

What the hell does that have to do with anything? Maybe he was just lonely. Oh, well. Let's see where this goes.

Chuck was living out of a suitcase containing all his belongings. Mixed in with his clothes and junk was Ralph Waldo Emerson's essay, "Self Reliance," which he had read in college. In the tape, Chuck said, "It meant something to me. It seemed the most practical thing I had ever read."

Chuck gave his company two weeks' notice, moved back to Santa Monica, and decided to sober up every drunk he could find.

He invited alcoholics to his house and sobered them up. He had no money, but sometimes people would invite him to dinner. The bank repossessed his car. "They relieved me of my car," as he put it.

Someone told him about unemployment, and he collected a thirty-three-dollar check every week—enough to rent a room in the Ocean Park area of Santa Monica for fifty dollars a month. He lived on candy bars and a pot of perpetual soup made of canned beans. He decided to devote a year to reading and surrounded himself with library books.

People began to drop in, and his home became a gathering place. As Chuck put it, they sat in a circle and had a conversation with "a line of no line," a conversation that might veer off in any direction. When Chuck spoke, he yelled, accused, ridiculed, and cursed, venting all his pent-up hostility. "I felt great," he told the audience.

He was surprised when people kept coming back week after week. That was it—the birth of the Synanon Game.

Being able to yell, curse, cry, and let go of emotions. That sums up my feelings about the Game.

In those early days, someone who had been attending the after-AA talks brought along a friend addicted to heroin. Chuck had never met a drug addict. The addict participated in the bull sessions, as Chuck called them, arguing into the night. The addict stopped using drugs.

More and more people began moving in, sleeping on the floor, and taking part in the talk sessions. The talk sessions soon became known as "small s synanons" when a newly arrived addict garbled the words "symposium" and "seminar" and blurted out "synanon." A synanon may have been the first of many words which became part of the Synanon jargon.

Chuck realized he was onto something, something that cured addicts, and determined to turn it into a business.

Chuck incorporated in 1959, wanting to call his company Tender Loving Care, the name that hung above his door: "Tender Loving Care Club." That name had already been taken. On a whim, he incorporated under the name Synanon. He appointed himself chief executive officer and chairman of the board, titles he never relinquished.

The story of the birth of Synanon still gives me chills. A group of addicts, led by a recovered alcoholic, came together and figured out how to keep each other clean.

I, along with hundreds of squares—non-substance-misusers— thought Chuck had figured out a better way to live, attained through hard work and honesty. He asserted that if society was producing so many substance abusers, suicides, and homeless people, there was something wrong with our society. I believed him when he insisted we could change the world, and I wanted to be a part of that.

I thought this was it: I had discovered Utopia.

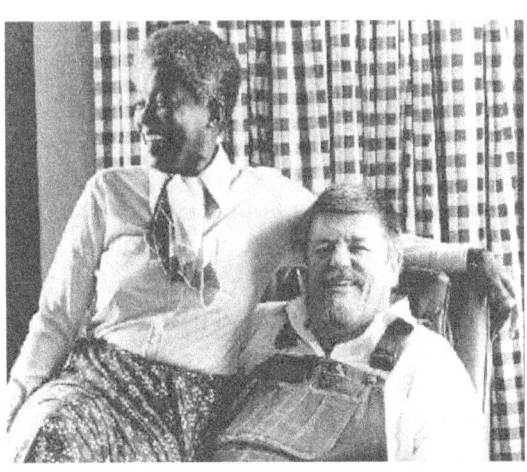

Chuck and Betty Dederich.
Photo courtesy of Synanon.com

Chapter 5: One Foot In; One Foot Out

1970, Oakland, California

First, I dropped out of college. It was only going to be for a semester, maybe a year. The admissions clerk asked me to reconsider. "So many kids take a break then never come back."

"Oh, I'll come back," I assured her.

No one else in my life said a word. Not my parents, not my siblings, not my childhood friends. No one at Synanon. And if someone had taken me by the shoulders, looked me in the eye and said, "Education is the one thing no one can take away from you; it will follow you your whole life," would I have listened? Probably not.

Who needed an education when I was living life, helping cure addicts, changing the world?

I found a full-time job in the office of an Oakland shipping company, then landed a better position in the credit department at Sloan's Furniture in San Francisco, and eventually worked my way up through the accounting office at Stauffer Chemical Company.

Synanon was my oasis amid the chaos of Vietnam, Altamont, and Kent State. Believing the Synanon Game could bring people together, Synanon arranged Games—using the same circle seating I sat in—where Black Panthers played the Game with police, and jailers played it with inmates.

I, too, believed the Game could heal people, maybe even the world.

Synanon distributed its excess donations to the Panthers, to Chavez's farm workers, and in later years to People's Temple. We opened our doors to teens on the edge, pulling them from the streets into the Notions program—part mentorship, part salvation—saving dozens, maybe hundreds of kids.

My small part—paying dues and volunteering—made me feel woven into that goodness.

Every Saturday night, we gathered in the ballroom to celebrate sobriety milestones and preach to the public.

If only people could understand each other. How did this not make sense to everyone?

After a year of being a member of the Game Club, I considered moving in as a Lifestyler.

A couple of incidents pushed me over the edge.

One Game night, I stayed until midnight and then drove home in my Alfa with the convertible top down. Glancing in my rearview mirror, chills ran up my back when I noticed a car following me. With my heart in my throat, I turned onto a side street to see if the car would follow. It did. I wound through the side streets, foregoing my turn signal and squealing around the corners. My James Bond moves weren't working. Turning back onto 14th Street, I frantically searched for a police officer. The streets were empty except for me and the car behind me. Not knowing where the police station was, I sped through red lights, hoping to attract a policeman, keeping one eye on the street and one eye on my rearview mirror.

A siren.

I took a deep, shaky breath when a policeman pulled me over and shined his flashlight in my eyes. As tears streamed down my face, I haltingly said, "Someone was following me." I sobbed. "I ran the light, hoping you would see me."

The policeman looked around. "I don't see anyone."

No words came out of my open mouth. Was he going to arrest me?

"I'll follow you home to make sure you're safe," he said. "You shouldn't be driving around at night with your top down."

My hands shook all the way home. The policeman watched until I locked my front door.

I only felt safe at Synanon.

One evening, after a Wednesday night Game, an older man wearing khakis and an ill-fitting tweed jacket sidled next to me. He wore his thick, dark brown hair short like he had missed the Beatles hairstyle revolution.

"Hi, I'm Martin," he said, shaking my hand. More holding my hand than shaking it. A waft of aftershave couldn't overpower the smell of cigarettes. His touch sent warm tingles up my spine. I had been on a few dates since Kevin, but none serious. I shuddered, remembering how they all wanted sex after a first date.

"Want to grab some coffee?" His brown eyes danced.

"Sure." I followed him into the dining room.

Martin worked as a process server and rented a room in San Francisco. Living in the city seemed so sophisticated to my nineteen-year-old self.

Thrilled with the attention of an older man—nine years older I would discover—I began hanging out with him after our Wednesday night Games.

In spring, our Game Club Tribe planned a picnic at Samuel P. Taylor Park in Marin County. It was a crisp, sunny Saturday when we gathered at the Synanon parking lot and formed carpools. Donning my jacket and carrying a brown bag lunch, I jumped in a car with three other people and drove to the park, smiling and laughing, remembering my annual Camp Fire Girl camp-outs.

Martin sat by me at the picnic table, slightly leaning into me. After lunch, he whispered, "Want to take a walk?"

"Yes. That's the best part of this place."

Martin held my hand as we walked along trails through the redwoods, breathing in the moist, woody smell, the sun peeking in and out of the treetops. Holding my hand and touching my shoulders, he sent electricity tingling through me, from my fingertips to my shoulders to my heart to my privates. There's something about simply holding hands that gets me every time.

After the walk, Martin asked, "Want to get out of here?"

"Yeah," I answered, "but we carpooled. We'll have to wait until someone with a car wants to leave."

"We can always hitchhike," he suggested. I remembered my grandparents picking up hitchhikers, a habit they had developed during World War II.

"Sure, why not?"

We bade farewell to the group and walked along Sir Francis Drake Boulevard, thumbs extended. A VW van stopped for us.

"Where ya' headed?" a dreamy-eyed girl in the passenger seat asked, her long straight hair held in place with a tie-dyed headband.

"Oakland."

"Groovy, man. Hop on in," the hippie chick offered, the tattooed flowers on her face crinkling as she smiled. "We're on our way to the Haight, but we can swing by Oakland first. It's just one more bridge."

The side door slid open. Three guys in their late teens sat on the floor in the back of the seatless van, all with long hair and clouded eyes. One of them, wearing worn jeans and a shirtless vest, waved us in, then offered a joint. Without taking a hit, Martin passed it to me, and I passed it to a guy with a peace symbol painted on his face. Hippies. The van, in a cloud of pot, took off down the winding road. I leaned into Martin at every curve, seeing only the treetops against the sky.

We could crash, and I could die in this van.

Martin sat carefree, jabbering to the guys like they were old friends. I silently prayed I would get back to Oakland alive.

I breathed a sigh of relief when they dropped us off at the Synanon parking lot. Reeking of pot, we didn't dare go into the Club. Martin gave me a light kiss as we drove our separate ways. "See you Wednesday?" he asked.

"Sure." My heart fluttered.

I don't remember when we first made love. Even in that era of free love, I still held tight to my Protestant guilt about sex before marriage, not wanting to admit that I liked it. Maybe that was part of my attraction to Martin: the handholding, hanging out, and making friends.

We became a couple; our lives wound around Synanon.

Two or three months later, I got a frantic call from Martin.

"I'm in jail. Can you bail me out?"

Horrified, I asked, "What happened? Why are you in jail?"

"I came home after serving some warrants and got in a fight with my roommate. He ran after me with a hammer." His breath rattled. "I ran to my car and locked the door. Then he hit my windshield with the hammer. I thought he was going to kill me! I called the police." A pause. Then indignantly, "They arrested me instead of him! For outstanding parking tickets."

I didn't stop to wonder how he called the police while trapped in the car. We didn't have cell phones back then. But it didn't matter; I thought I was in love.

I called my mom. Mom never held it against me after I moved

out. She stayed a part of my life, visiting me in my apartment and inviting me to family events. Martin and I had been together long enough that he knew my family. I liked that about my parents—they treated any boyfriend or girlfriend of us kids as part of the family.

"That's awful!" Mom exclaimed. "I'll go with you. I'll pick you up in the morning." She was a bleeding-heart liberal like me, positive the police were at fault.

We drove to San Francisco and found the court. The courtroom was windowless, overhead fluorescent lights giving everything a sickly bluish hue. An empty jury box was off to the side, the judge's seat in the front. The air smelled of stale bodies. Mom and I sat in one of the middle rows of hard wooden seats, watching tensely as arrestees paraded before the judge.

"People versus Martin." I leaned forward, my stomach clenching, and grabbed my mother's hand.

Martin walked in, head down. His tweed jacket hung forlornly over his hunched shoulders. He clasped his hands in front of him and looked at the floor. "Guilty," he pleaded.

The judge released him on a five-hundred-dollar bail. Which I paid.

He walked out of the courtroom with us, looking despondent. He smelled of stale cigarette smoke, body odor, and bad breath. Mom drove us back to my apartment with the windows open.

Martin obviously couldn't move back to his rented room, so I let him move in with me. He kept his job as a process server. For a while.

At first it was fun playing house. Martin helped with the rent until he lost his process-serving gig. After a couple of months, he still didn't have a job. The rent was due.

I came home from work one day and he was still in his bathrobe. I cringed.

"What the hell? You aren't even dressed?" I put my purse down and went into the kitchen, not wanting to be near him.

"Hey, I'm looking at the want ads," he muttered.

"You could have at least cooked dinner!" I wanted to throw his stuff on the sidewalk, but where would he go? Like it was my problem.

I waited for a Game to confront him, wanting the support of my friends.

"What the fuck, Martin?" I began. "I came home from work, and you were still in your bathrobe? Why don't you have a job yet? We need to pay the rent!"

Martin shrugged. "I look in the want ads all day! There are no jobs."

The Game turned to me: "Why are you with a loser like him? Why are you supporting him? You're smart, you're pretty, you're respected."

I had no idea people saw me that way.

I hadn't even admitted I was supporting him. The realization hit me like a punch in the stomach.

"I'm not gonna support you, Martin. In fact, you need to move out and find your own place."

"Aw, c'mon. I'll get a job," he whined.

But I was done with him. I asked him to leave the next day. A week later, he still hadn't left, so I moved out. I didn't want a screaming argument; it was easier to leave.

I left him in my funky, hippy-decorated first apartment and moved into a studio apartment a mile away. It was one tiny room, maybe two hundred square feet, with a bathroom the size of a closet. Along one wall was a small kitchenette with a window overlooking Park Boulevard. A second wall held a Murphy bed. There was barely room for my great-grandfather's dresser when I swung the Murphy bed open. At least there was a carport where I parked my Alfa and locked my ten-speed to a pillar.

I was living alone again—riding the bus to San Francisco, working in an office, spending every spare moment at Synanon. Moving in felt less like a question and more like the next step waiting for me.

That's what I told myself. But I also remember the Games with the relentless probing of "When are you going to move in?" It had already started, the drumbeat that would follow me throughout my days in Synanon: *Be one hundred percent committed or leave.*

By now, all my friends were there. I wasn't ready to leave them.

Chapter 6: Lifestyler

1971, Oakland, California

Elizabeth asked me in a Game: "So, Janet, when are you going to move in? You spend more time here than you do at home."

Tonight, she sat straighter, her blue eyes sparkling.

My breath caught in my throat. "I haven't thought about it," I lied, face burning red. It was all I thought about. Squares were moving in right and left. Almost everyone I knew from my first days in the Game Club had moved in as Lifestylers, shunning society, and working for Synanon. All in.

Another person, an ex-addict, joined in. "You're just a hanger-on-er. Drinking our coffee. Eating our food. Banging our dopefiends. Either you're all in or all out."

"I'm not banging the dopefiends. That was only one guy I dated." I paused. "Okay, two." *Followed by Martin, and look where that got me.*

Elizabeth cut in. "That's not the point. "Why are you still in that tiny apartment by yourself?"

Am I just a hanger-on-er, one of those people who refuses to make a commitment?

Deep breath. "God, you're right." I looked around the room, at all the people I knew. Thought of the smiles, the laughter, the camaraderie. "My apartment is so fucking quiet, I can't stand to be there. Every day's the same. Eat alone. Catch the bus to work. Do my boring job. Come home alone. Will the phone to ring." I grimaced.

She looked straight into my eyes. "Any decision is better than no decision."

Was that a line from Chuck or Emerson? The quotes were beginning to blur.

I drew a deep breath, ran my hands through my hair, and grinned. Almost breathless, I exclaimed, "Why the hell not?"

The room clapped and cheers washed over me as I felt a boulder lift from my shoulders. I sat, lightheaded. "You're right! This is where I want to be!"

The Game moved on.

Afterward, Elizabeth and I sat in the dining room. She drank coffee from her metal Sierra cup, I from a Styrofoam cup. "Were you serious?"

"Yes!" I couldn't sit still. "How do I go about it?"

"It's simple," she explained as we sat back in our mismatched chairs. The scent of fresh coffee wafted over me as the kitchen staff refreshed the coffee setup. "Just go see Bill in the Director's office and let him know."

"Okay, I'll go see him Saturday." I drove home and pulled down the Murphy bed. Sleep wouldn't come as my mind raced. I can't wait to tell Mom. I'll have to give notice to my landlord. Thank goodness she let me live here month by month. When can I move? How will I get to work from there? Am I really doing this? Should I do this? Yes! I'll never have to cook another meal! I'm moving in!

Saturday morning was gloomy as I drove down Park Boulevard past my old apartment. Spotting Martin's sometimes-running car on the side street, my blood boiled. "Fuck you!" I shouted to no one. "Are you still in your fucking bathrobe, pretending to look for a job?" Driving past Lake Merritt, bright blue reflecting the morning sun, made me smile.

Today is the first day of the rest of your life. Chuck's words rang true.

I parked my red Alfa in Synanon's parking lot next to an off-white van and skipped in through the lobby. Waving to the woman working at the front desk—the Connect, they called it. I was learning the jargon. I beamed, "Hi, I'm going to see Bill about moving in!" I ran up four flights of stairs to the Director's office.

I peeked my head in. It was a small, windowless office with pictures of Chuck and Betty on the wall and an Emerson Book on the Desk: "Essays: First Series." Bill sat behind an old, beat-up desk, talking on a black rotary phone, the tangled cord pulling his head toward the desk. He looked up and waved me in, pointing to a worn visitor chair, his blue eyes looking relieved at the interruption. I had seen him around. He was one of those old-timers (not old, but had been living in Synanon for over ten years) who always had a smile and took the time to talk to someone in distress. I had never met him face-to-face, though.

"Gotta go," Bill said, hanging up the phone. Looking up above his glasses, he asked, "Hi, what can I do for you?"

"I'm in the Game Club," I began, rattling off my memorized speech. "All my friends are here; I spend most of my time here. I believe in everything Synanon is doing, so I'd like to move in."

"Great, we probably have room for you. Tell me a little bit about yourself."

Probably? It seemed like everyone was moving in. Why probably for me? My stomach clenched.

"I'm Janet Holdaway, and I have been a Game Player for two years." *God, I'm talking too fast.* But I couldn't slow down. I repeated my spiel.

"How much can you contribute?" he asked.

I took a sharp breath, collecting my thoughts. This is an interview! Why do I have to justify myself? When Elizabeth moved in last year, all they asked her was, "When are you coming?"

Taking a calming breath, I told him, "My take-home pay is about three hundred dollars a month. I can contribute all of that."

Tilting his head back, he considered. "That might be enough. I'll talk to the other Directors and let you know. What's your phone number?" I knew my paycheck was nothing compared to the lawyers and architects who had moved in, but I believed my enthusiasm was enough. Refusing to be discouraged, I reminded myself, *Elizabeth lives here and still makes minimum wage.*

I wrote down my number. "Okay, thanks," I stammered, getting up. "I really think I will be an asset to Synanon," like I would end any job interview.

A little disheartened but determined, I waited for the reply. *What will I do if they say no?* A few days later, I got the call. I could move in. I squealed and called my mom.

"I'm moving into Synanon!"

"I'm not surprised," she told me. "You spend all your time there." She paused. "I'd move in if I could."

I gave thirty days' notice to my landlord.

The day before moving in, I went to the Director's office for my room assignment. Bill wasn't there, but Don, the DJ in my first Game, sat in his chair. He had grown a mustache and gained some weight. He looked at me with a raised eyebrow.

"Where's Bill?"

"Oh, he got reassigned. I'm the new Director."

"Cool. Well, I'm moving in tomorrow and need to know what room I'll be in."

DJ Don leaned back in his chair. "You're moving in? When did this happen?"

I cowered at his deep, booming voice.

What the fuck?

I quietly explained. "I met with Bill a month ago. He said I could move in tomorrow."

"First I've heard of it. How much are you contributing?"

"My paycheck. Three hundred dollars a month, plus my car."

"No down payment? What kind of car?"

I felt sick as a twinge of doubt seeped in, but I ignored it and stuttered, "A… a 1956 Alfa Romeo."

"We don't want that. You'll have to sell it, and you can use the proceeds as a down payment. Let me know when you've sold it." Gone was the grinning DJ who stood up for me in my first Game, berating my friend for not paying me back. I wished Bill was still the Director. At least he seemed like he wanted me there.

I blinked back tears and wrung my hands. *You're not good enough,* my baby gut tried to tell me. Then I straightened my shoulders. *This is where I want to live! This is where I belong.*

DJ Don looked back down dismissively at the paperwork on his desk. Feeling invisible, I stood. "Okay, thanks, I'll get back to you."

And now what? I have to move out of my apartment tomorrow!

Elizabeth was waiting for me in the living room. "Whose dorm will you be in? My roommates are all ex-addicts, but it doesn't matter." Her eyes sparkled. "I'll help you move. Then we can have dinner tomorrow…"

"I have to sell my car first. And now I have no place to live."

A Game Club friend, Kathy, piped in. "You can sleep on my couch. I'm sure your car will sell fast." Short and plump, Kathy fit perfectly in her Datsun 1500 sports car. Our love of sports cars had made us fast friends, but she wasn't considering becoming a Lifestyler.

I had naively thought it would go into Synanon's fleet, not considering that Synanon's cars were mostly bland four-passenger sedans and eight- and fourteen-passenger dull white vans we called jitneys.

My Alfa wasn't only a car; it was one of my few happy memories of my father.

Dad had gone with me to look at the twelve-year-old Alfa with faded red paint, door locks that didn't work, and no convertible top. He walked around it, lifting the hood, inspecting the brakes, and looking underneath for over an hour, finally agreeing to rebuild the engine so I could have my own sports car. "I'll work on it for you," he had offered. He only knew how to give attention via sports cars.

I had lost Kevin. I had lost my best friend Jacqui, who had begun smoking weed and dropping acid. Now I was losing my car.

But a car wasn't as important as saving lives.

I packed my few belongings and drove over to Kathy's apartment. As I lay sheets on her couch, she reminded me of a Game a few months back. "Remember our backpacking trip? I'm not going to live someplace where someone has so much say over my life. And I'm not going to give up my Datsun."

Earlier that year, Kathy and I had gone on a backpacking trip—my first—to the Hetch Hetchy area in Yosemite. We hiked three miles through towering granite cliffs over well-worn trails, meandering in and out of shade and finally ending at a primitive campsite. Pulling off my heavy, over-the-ankle hiking boots and thick red socks, I sucked in my breath, seeing the blisters that had made me wince with every step

"Look at my feet!" I still had to hike back.

"I brought some moleskin," Kathy said, reaching into her pack. "Stick your feet in the water, and then I'll patch them up."

The icy stream fresh from the snowpack numbed my feet with instant relief. Kathy set our sodas in the stream to cool.

The ground was soft enough to walk barefoot as we set up our tents on a flat spot of dirt near a ring of blackened stones. We cushioned our sleeping bags with pine needles. Surrounded by glaciated granite cliffs, green meadows, and wildflowers, breathing in hints of citrus and rose floating in the breeze and hearing the constant gurgle of the stream, I was at peace. I felt like I could stay forever.

It was only a long weekend trip; we hiked back two days later.

We had shown up as usual for our Game the following Wednesday night.

There were the usual arguments back and forth, and then someone who knew we had gone backpacking spoke up.

"What the hell are you two teenagers doing hiking alone in the wilderness?" shouted a dopefiend city slicker from New York who probably had only lived in a concrete jungle. "That's so irresponsible."

"Don't you know the Zodiac Killer is still loose?" a Bay Area native chimed in.

"He's not in the Sierras!" I said. "I grew up walking all over San Francisco—through Golden Gate Park, China Town, and Market Street with my girlfriends." My voice rose; I felt heat rising to my cheeks. "The Zodiac didn't get me. I camped with my friends in Samuel P. Taylor without adult supervision. The Zodiac Killer hasn't found me yet!" I leaned back, glaring, arms folded across my chest.

"This is ridiculous," Kathy added. "First of all, we're not teenagers. Second, I've been camping my whole life. It's safer there than in the streets of Oakland!"

The Game moved on.

Lying on her couch, remembering that Game and reflecting on the events of the last week, a seed of doubt tried to sprout, but I tamped dirt on it and refused to nurture it. Maybe Kathy was right. But no. I had made my decision. I wanted to live in Synanon. They had figured out a better way to live. Kathy thought her car was more important than living in this revolutionary society.

What is a car but a possession?

I put my Alfa up for sale. It didn't dawn on me I could get a down payment some other way or that I should even need a down payment. The wealthy Lifestylers kept their cars, but I didn't consider doing that. I took DJ Don's word as law without questioning it.

While sports cars were popular in the early 1970s, not everyone could fit in them. My first buyer willing to pay five hundred dollars, was six-foot-two and couldn't get his legs in. Others' torsos were too long, their heads hitting the canvas roof. After two weeks of sleeping on Kathy's couch, I accepted an offer for three hundred dollars, the same amount I paid for it.

Back I went to see DJ Don. "I sold my car. I'm ready to move in."

Raising his eyebrows like he hadn't expected me to return, he conceded, "Okay, we can make room for you in a dorm at the Clumps. Just bring your check by every month."

"Thanks, Don! I'll be here tomorrow!"

I'm in! I now live in Synanon!

I ran to the living room and plopped on a couch, arms spread wide. My lips hurt from grinning. I couldn't sit still. I walked over to a handful of musicians jamming in front of the fireplace and gushed over their sounds. I had to go to Kathy's and pack. This was now my home.

I didn't own much, so I brought everything: my work clothes, my jeans and t-shirts, my dresser that had followed me around since childhood, a few albums (but no turntable)—Bob Dylan's *Nashville Skyline* and *New Day*, Joni Mitchell's *Clouds* and *Ladies of the Canyon*. And my acoustic guitar. I even brought my baking supplies: cake and cookie pans, flour, sugar, and vanilla. I don't know why I brought my baking stuff; I knew the kitchen staff would cook all my meals.

I don't remember who helped me move—probably Mom. She seemed determined to remain part of my life.

The dorm DJ Don assigned me to was in an apartment complex across town called the Clumps. Synanon owned a city-size bus that shuttled us back and forth to the Athens Club, where I would eat in the dining room. *No more cooking and washing dishes*, I thought, excited about immersing myself in this communal lifestyle. I had been cooking meals for my family since I was twelve.

Opening the door to my new apartment, I expected to meet my three roommates, however only one was home. She was about five-foot-five with creamy white skin that looked like she had spent her life applying Estee Lauder products. Her blue eyes and long blond hair hid her steely demeanor.

"Hi, I'm Lydia," she said, flipping her hair over her shoulder. "You must be our new roommate." She pointed to a twin bed in the living room and said, "You're sharing the living room with me. Sarah and Lucy share the bedroom. I'll show you around."

It was a one-bedroom apartment on the second floor overlooking a parking lot on a busy four-lane street. A three-foot wide concrete walkway/balcony with a wrought-iron fence ran along the edge of the apartments. There was no common interior space, no landscaping, only concrete and pavement. It didn't matter; I knew most of my life would be spent at the Club.

The front door opened into the living room—my bedroom. The walls were bright white, and beige curtains hung on the window. A small kitchen and dining room with nondescript linoleum flooring were off to the side, and a short hall led to a small bathroom and the bedroom.

"We have two towel racks, so you can share mine," Lydia pointed out as she opened the bathroom door. "And there's Sarah and Lucy's room."

Excitement bubbled through me. I'm here! I'm in a dorm! Tonight, I'll have my first meal at my new home.

"The bus picks us up right across the street. You can see the schedule at the Connect." Like a front desk at a hotel, the Connect was our hub, where we could reserve cars, bus rides, and guest housing. I had seen the bus in the parking lot at the Club. It was blue and silver, the size of a city bus, with "Synanon" emblazoned along the side and a marquee reading, "Synanon, The People Business."

"I've got to catch the bus to get to work," Lydia exclaimed, tucking her hair into a stocking cap made from old nylons. Her blond hair disappeared, but her eyes still glistened, defiant. "Oh, I'm on a contract. Smoking." She ran down the stairs.

A contract. Someone was put on a contract when they were busted for breaking a rule. A man shaved his head, and a woman stuffed her hair in a nylon stocking for two weeks. Sometimes, they wore signs like, "Ask me why my head is shaved." Often, they were sent to work washing pots and pans. The wrongdoer was making a new commitment to Synanon—a contract to live by the rules. I can see now that humiliation was a tool for keeping people in line. But back then, Synanon could do no wrong in my eyes; they knew how to cure drug addicts.

I sat on my twin bed and grinned. Then, I hung up my work clothes, put my jeans, t-shirts, and underwear in my dresser, and went outside. The sun warmed my heart along with my body. Kids were running and laughing on the balcony above me. A woman my age leaned over, her wavy brown hair glistening in the sun.

"Hi! Did you just move in? I'm Angie. Sorry for all the noise. The School is up here, and it's free time for the six-year-olds. Welcome!" She turned back to the kids.

A guy sat on a chair a few doors down, strumming a guitar. He grinned. "You must be Janet."

Community. I'm home.

About an hour later, the Synanon bus stopped across the street, and people poured out, heading to their apartments. Two women came into my apartment.

"Hey, I'm Sarah," she said, nodding, not quite unfriendly, but not friendly either. "This is Lucy."

Lucy smiled, and then they both walked into their room and closed the door.

Sarah came out and headed into the bathroom. She was naked and covered in tattoos, from neck to shoulders to arms to chest to back and down her legs. Blue ink. I tried not to stare, but the blue tattoos covering her like a bodysuit were all I could see when I looked at her. The only people I had known with tattoos were hoodlums, and here I was, living with one. *She's not a hood anymore. We're in Synanon.*

Lucy was my height but heavier, with short, light brown hair. She dismissed me as if sharing an apartment with this 'square' was barely worth her time. What I remember most about her is that someone drank my entire bottle of cooking vanilla, and I was sure it was Lucy. I couldn't prove it and never confronted her in or out of the Game, but it was a realization that I was, indeed, living with ex-drug addicts who still craved getting high. I knew I should challenge her, thinking this might save her life. But it felt so stupid. Vanilla? Was she that desperate? Maybe it had evaporated. Perhaps it spilled when I packed it up. I kept quiet.

Sarah came out of the shower wrapped in a white towel, contrasting with her blue tattoos. Shaking her short hair dry, she laughed. "Did you see Lydia in her stocking cap?"

"Yeah. She said she was on a contract for smoking."

"She got busted," Sarah explained, shaking her head. "Crazy, you get in trouble for that now. We used to get a pack of cigarettes a day, but now it's just as bad as using drugs." She shrugged. "Whatever. I kicked heroin, and that's all that counts."

I didn't care that I was living with three ex-addicts. Everyone in Synanon got a clean slate when they moved in. "Character is the only rank," a quote from Ralph Waldo Emerson, was gospel. Still, it was weird knowing I was living with someone in trouble.

When Lydia got home, she was carrying an extra towel. "I had to beg for a second towel," she groaned. "How am I supposed to dry my hair with only one towel?"

How audacious! I would never think of asking for more than Synanon gave me, even though I donated my entire paycheck to live there. I didn't want to be demanding. I was a square, but I was still a newcomer to Synanon and didn't want to make waves.

We four roommates approached each other warily. I had spent little time with actual drug addicts; they had spent little time with Lifestylers. *I need to be a role model*, I thought, but mostly, I wanted to fit in, hoping I could make my bed as well as they did in the Marine Corps bounce-a-quarter-off-the-bed style that Synanon demanded. I had hardly ever made my bed growing up.

We kept the place spotless and scrubbed the room weekly. Tribe Leaders did random daily checks of residents' rooms, and if they found a bed that wasn't military-tight, they ripped the sheets off the bed and left them in a heap. Dust on a dresser? The Tribe Leader would sweep everything from the top of the dresser onto the floor. Messy bed, messy head. I had heard this for two years, and here I was, living with ex-addicts whose lives could depend on this! I certainly wasn't going to be the one with my bed tossed or responsible for my dormmates being gamed for being unappreciative slobs who didn't know how to live like human beings.

Once a week, we all cleaned the dorm together. I volunteered for the bathroom. On my hands and knees, I scrubbed the floor with a rag rinsed in bleach, as my mother taught me.

"How did you get the floor so clean?" Lydia asked, her blond hair tied in a ponytail. Her two weeks were up, and she no longer had to stuff her hair into a nylon stocking.

"Bleach and a rag!"

"Oh, that's what I'm smelling. I've never been able to get the floor that clean. Thanks!" I finally felt accepted.

Lydia was a server in the dining room and was often called upon to serve Chuck when he came to town. She encouraged me to become a server, suggesting it might be a path toward working for Synanon instead of working for an outside company. I tried it once and immediately knew it wasn't for me. Petite Lydia could carry four loaded plates and gracefully serve a table while I could barely walk across the room without tripping over my own feet.

When I left my parents' house eighteen months earlier, I had wanted to avoid defining myself solely as a good worker, daughter, mother, and wife. I had wanted to make a difference in the world. And here I was, helping drug addicts get off drugs and alcoholics stop drinking, helping build a new way of life—free of drugs, violence, alcohol, even smoking—while living and working in a tight-knit community with friends and family.

Moving into Synanon was my final break from my family, and a chance to make a difference.

I was one of over thirteen hundred Synanon residents in 1971, a mix of addicts and squares. Chuck embraced the squares, who I believe both saved Synanon and destroyed it. Lifestylers came with jobs, education, and money. The money kept Synanon afloat; the Lifestylers shared their skills and knowledge. I think we became more important to Chuck than the addicts he was saving. A recovered alcoholic, he was now surrounded by professionals who all looked up to him, listened to him, and acted on his whims.

I kept only five dollars a week in WAM (walk-around money),

the same amount Elizabeth received and the same amount long-time residents were given. I remembered DJ Don saying he kept fifty dollars a month, and I assumed he deserved more because he had donated so much money as a DJ. By the time I moved in, he was also a Director. Other Lifestylers who worked for Synanon collected fifty dollars a month as well. I'm still not sure why I felt so undeserving. Maybe it was because I had to beg just to be allowed to move in; I felt lucky simply to be there and didn't dare make waves.

Those who arrived with money lived on the upper floors of the Athens Club, in rooms that felt a world apart, while those of us with almost nothing were placed in the dorms. I saw the divide—how could I not?—but I pushed it aside. I told myself it didn't matter. In truth, I felt more at home among the "little people," grateful simply to belong.

Living in my dorm with three ex-addicts, I remembered my first glimpse of exclusivity—and how I was excluded. Back in the Game Club, a U.C. Davis graduate and artist my age had joined as a Game Player. She delighted in showing us how to dye fabric with vegetables—carrots, onions, and beets—and taught us tie-dye and batik techniques. Then, one day, she vanished from our Games. She had been invited to Directors' Games and dinners. I heard Chuck say, "What is she doing hanging around the Game Club? Take care of her—she is the type of person we want to attract." Soon after, she moved in as a Lifestyler but didn't stay long. Today she is a well-known artist in New York, living life on her own terms. I wonder what spooked her.

Obviously, I wasn't the type they wanted to attract. A twinge of doubt tickled my spine, but I ignored it. I was happy there, even if I wasn't part of the top echelon.

Moving in was my first step toward true believer status, adopting the attitude of being all-in or all-out. It was the first time I ignored misgivings, consciously deciding my love of the community outweighed my doubts. I pulled back from my Game Club friends, including Kathy, who wouldn't move in. I had long ago lost touch with Jacqui, my best friend since seventh grade. She had turned to psychedelics, and I turned to Synanon.

Jacqui and I had spent two summers at the Camp Fire Girl

overnight camp in the Mendocino Mountain Range in Northern California, looking after girls from second grade to high school. We taught the kids star gazing, swimming, backpacking, and fire building. We led the campers in songs and comforted them when homesick. We planned to buy houses in the same neighborhood and raise our kids.

The last month of summer counseling before starting college, Jacqui and I walked along a starlit trail after the campers were asleep. The air was crisp after two days of thunderstorms. We smelled bay laurel trees and pine needles as we walked along the damp trail, spotting the Big Dipper and Seven Sisters. "I've been smoking pot with Darlene," she casually mentioned. Darlene was another camp counselor, a few years older than us. "I'm going to take LSD with her."

My heart sank. My best friend was choosing drugs, something we both were adamantly against, or so I thought. She was choosing a new best friend.

Jacqui and I had one last discussion when I told her I thought LSD was bad for her mind. She felt the Game was bad for my mind. We were both intellectuals; our minds were vital to us. We had gone our separate ways.

After moving in, my Games were only with residents. I saw my family for birthdays and holidays, but the rest of my life was at Synanon.

I wasn't alone in being all-in. The Lifestyler Business—squares moving in and paying a monthly fee, brought in $1.3 million annually by 1972.[2] Chuck wooed wealthy squares. A woman donated substantial funds—I've heard it was $100,000 and I've heard $1 million—to help develop the community's properties. I thought she was an heiress, but she may have been self-made. Either way, she was instant royalty and married the attorney and ex-alcoholic who led the legal department.

Chuck postulated that as Synanon got rich, we all got rich. I was not rich monetarily, but I lived richly. People cooked for me. In Oakland, I swam in an Olympic-size swimming pool. I took a jitney

---

2. David U. Gerstel, *Paradise Incorporated: Synanon: A Personal Account* (Presidio Press, 1982), 130.

to Tomales Bay to hike and ride horses. I rode the Synacruiser, Synanon's private Greyhound-size bus, to Santa Monica to body surf off Synanon's private beach, and to Badger to hike in the Sierra foothills.

The rich life for me was the people—the friends.

The rich life for Chuck was opulent living, supported by unpaid laborers, me included. He had a fleet of cars and motorcycles, a personal driver, secretary, private cook and housekeepers, people to wash and maintain his cars and motorcycles, carpenters and tradesmen to expand his living quarters, even groundskeepers.

Plus hundreds of acolytes, striving to work for him.

I didn't see the dichotomy. I bought the bullshit.

The author next to a 1956 Alfa Romeo at a car show in Malibu

Chapter 7: Sleep Deprivation

1971, Tomales Bay, California

They scheduled me for a Stew.

I rode a jitney—one of Synanon's white fourteen-passenger vans—to the Tomales Bay property, arriving on a Chamber of Commerce day: an ice blue sky matching the blue water of Tomales Bay, a gentle breeze off the water bringing scents of seaweed. The jitney dropped me off in front of the Inn, a two-story building Guglielmo Marconi built in 1914 to house the workers of his Marconi Wireless Telegraph Company. I wanted to walk up the path through the expansive lawn and sit on the veranda, watching the bay and breathing in the salty air. Yearning to live surrounded by this beauty, I daydreamed. *Maybe I can get rotated here one day.*

But I wasn't there to visit—I was there for my first twenty-four-hour Stew. I was always nervous before Games, but this was twenty-four hours. Twenty-four hours of being awake, and it was already two in the afternoon. I had been awake since six.

Pacing, I worked up the nerve to walk into the Stew Room housed in another building on the property. What will people ask me about? Will I be yelled at? Will I be in trouble for something? How will I stay awake all night?

The Perpetual Stew—affectionately called the Stew—was a nonending Game. It was another brilliant play on words, reminiscent of the perpetual soups and stews the residents lived on in the early days. Like a mix of ingredients left to stew overnight, the Perpetual Stew was a mix of people left to stew for twenty-four hours. Similar to a relay, a new person joined every hour, and one person left every hour. Not only was there a mix of newcomers, old-timers, squares, and dopefiends, but everyone was in a different state of alertness—from wide awake to bleary-eyed.

Twenty-four hours was enough time to get beyond blowing off steam. In the wee hours of the night, when you're so sleepy you need toothpicks to hold your eyelids open, you're too tired to keep up your emotional guard. This is when I really learned about the people who lived in Synanon.

Finding my way to the Stew Room, I sat in a chair outside the Game Circle, a gallery that anyone could drop in on to watch, like an audience at a live television taping. The Stew wasn't being broadcast yet, but it was riveting to watch in person. Reality television before reality TV.

Looking around, I thought, Thank goodness they're comfortable chairs, not the canvas director's chairs. I couldn't sit in one of those all night.

My stomach fluttered when I realized I only recognized about half the people in the circle. My Games had always been with people I knew. Even after living in Synanon for three years, I was still shy, and meeting new people was one big act-as-if.

I felt better when I saw Fred, who lived in Oakland. He had been a trombonist in the Johnny Carson Show, although he was older and grayer than when I had seen him on TV. His eyes still had a twinkle, especially when he played his trombone.

Fred turned to a newcomer who had been talking about splitting. "You're full of shit. You'll never make it outside."

The newcomer looked at Fred defiantly, but before he could answer, Fred interjected. "You can't tell me you just waltzed in here because you heard it was a cool place to live. I know you dragged yourself in here because it was the only place that would take your low-life self." Fred leaned forward, elbows on his knees, looking directly into the newcomer's eyes. "Like me. I literally crawled up the steps in Santa Monica. I was so strung out I was near death and had to be carried inside."

My mouth tried to drop open. I only knew the dopefiends after they had cleaned up and become citizens of Synanon. I hadn't grasped how horrible their lives were on the street.

A man with a New York accent chimed in. "You're a dopefiend, just like me. You wanna quit when things get hard. But tell me, why do ya' think you should split? What's out there for you?"

"I'm just tired of all this bullshit, man," the would-be Splittee answered, his face turning red, his voice rising. "Everyone's always telling me what to do. I just want to go buy a hamburger and kick back." He brought two fingers toward his lips. "And smoke a cigarette. Damn!"

The New Yorker leaned forward. "So ya' go back to your old hood, get that hamburger, light up a cigarette?"

The newcomer sighed. "Yeah, man."

"And how long before you're smoking weed? And your so-called friends bring you heroin? Where ya' gonna live? Where ya' gonna work? You gonna start robbin' again to pay for your fix? How long before you end up back on the street?"

The newcomer looked at the floor. "I don't know, man. I haven't figured all that out."

Fred looked him in the eye. "Don't be a quitter. You stay here, and we show you how to live. Yeah, there's rules. That's called being a grown-up. Try being a little positive. Act as if. Smile. See what happens."

The New Yorker added, "How about makin' a motion to act positive for a month? See where it gets you. Grab me anytime you wanna talk."

The newcomer nodded. "I'll give it a try."

I took a deep breath. It was time. Someone stretched, muttered goodbyes, and left. I grabbed the empty seat. The Stew continued seamlessly, like a living entity unfaltering in its rhythm. I let the voices wash over me as I got my bearings.

An oversized easy chair sat empty across the room, with a small table in front full of pieces of wood and a whittling knife.

Oh, my God! That's Chuck's chair. I wonder if he'll drop in. My body tingled at the thought of sitting in the same room with him, hearing his wisdom. Part of me hoped he wouldn't drop in, fearing his wrath. I realize now that was precisely how I thought of my father—the same craving for attention but fearing his rage. I never knew which side of my father would show up, so I avoided him as much as possible.

A young blond woman with sparkling blue eyes walked into the Stew Room to replenish the coffee, sodas, and snacks on a table across the room, interrupting my reverie. I didn't think anyone else noticed her, but as soon as she left, people moseyed up to the food table, stretching and refilling their coffee cups. I didn't know she would become a friend I have kept all my life, a friend who would help me heal after I left. I didn't realize she volunteered to service the

Stew to avoid playing Games, which she hated. The Game was the price she paid to live in our community.

I don't remember everything we talked about during that Stew and future Stews. I remember pieces of conversation. I remember the stories.

In the evening, the Stew moved to Kenny, a Latino jazz cellist with short black hair and kind eyes. "Why aren't you playing in the jazz band?" someone asked him. "There's lots of musicians here, but I never see you jammin'."

"I'm afraid if I pick up the cello, I'll want to put a needle back in my arm," Kenny almost whispered. "I don't even know if I can play without drugs. I don't want to find out."

Fred the trombonist joined in, commiserating. "I get it. Music and drugs were all mixed up for me, too. I didn't know how to do one without the other. Don't you think we all felt that way?" He leaned back, stretching out his legs. "I'll tell you what. You grab your cello and come jam with us, and we'll see how it goes. Music is part of you. You have to figure out how to play your music without the drugs."

Dopefiend A helping Dopefiend B: Here's how to live, and here's the Game to blow off steam - the essence of Synanon and what I liked best about living there. I bought the party line believing we could change the world with the Game. Perhaps we accomplished nothing more than a therapist could achieve. Yet, for the first time, drug addicts were kicking their addiction. Was it the Game or the community?

Hearing the stories and the struggles made my childhood angst seem minuscule.

A few hours passed, and the young blonde snack-bringer tip-toed in with soup and sandwiches, sustenance to make it through the night. I stretched my legs, grabbed some food, and returned to my seat.

Someone asked a pretty brunette with an upturned nose and round cheeks to run her story. She leaned back and curled her feet up in the chair.

"I joined when I was about twenty-two. I was working at the phone company in Hollywood, and there was a Game Player, and she mentioned Synanon, and she was going to move in."

Another one who worked for the phone company, I thought. She was the third one I knew, counting me.

"It caught my eye 'cuz when I was twelve, there was an article in *Life Magazine* about Chuck and the gas station, and he had a house that he would let people live in and work at the gas station."

Pretty Brunetty uncurled her legs, her stocking feet now on the floor. "Then my dad took me and my friend to a ball game; on the way back, we stopped at the gas station on Pico. I said this is that gas station where they help people! Then, when I ran into this gal at the phone company, it fascinated me."

She took a couple of swallows of soda and looked at the floor. "My husband and I had separated—he had beaten me, I had to hide. It was a horrible life. I got divorced and was living in an apartment in L.A. I was about ready to hitchhike across the country with my child on my back and see the U.S." She nibbled on potato chips. "I knew it was a bad idea. My friends were smoking dope and using pills. I smoked some pot, but I wasn't even good at that. Everyone would fall asleep, and I'd get horny."

I laughed with everyone else, remembering my last night with Kevin when we smoked pot and made love. And the next day, when my mother threw me out, hurtling me on my path toward Synanon.

Pretty Brunetty continued. "I went to a Saturday Night Party, and I met people my age. I liked it a lot, so I started volunteering and moved in after six months. But I couldn't put my kid in the School right away. I lived in and drove out to work. When Synanon hired me in, I went to work at the Connect and then worked in housekeeping making beds."

I noticed several women nodding. They must have worked in housekeeping, preparing rooms for visitors, cleaning toilets, and making beds, but not only for visitors—for the elites. I never questioned that the elites had unpaid housekeepers while the rest of us made sure we made our beds military-tight and left no speck of dust in our rooms.

Brunetty laughed. "I got together with Phil about that time. There was a coffeehouse at the Cloverfield Apartments. Phil and I hung out and made out. I got banned from seeing him because he was a newcomer. Ha! I ended up marrying him!"

In the wee hours of the night, a young, chubby Black woman who appeared to be seventeen or eighteen couldn't keep her eyes open. "Charlene, wake up!" someone shouted. I would have sat straight up in my chair at that, but Charlene barely opened her eyes, yawned, leaned back, and applied eye drops.

"How am I supposed to stay awake so long?" she moaned.

"Come on, you can do it," someone encouraged, like a verbal embrace. I felt like I was at a slumber party with my best friends.

"I think those eyedrops are making your eyelids slippery. Maybe get some coffee," I suggested.

No one gamed her. We all had trouble staying awake.

Sometime after, when I could barely keep my eyes open, Bill, a skinny Black man in his forties, finished his story with, "By the time I got here, I had no veins left. I shot up so many veins there was no place to shoot—not my hands, not my legs. I finally shot into my neck. Now that's one crazy dopefiend."

Run your story. That's what we did. The stories were told in the Games, the Perpetual Stew, in the living room, and around the dining room table. The stories were Synanon.

But I didn't run mine. Not all of it.

A beautiful young woman wept about what she had done to her daughter. "I got so bad when I needed a hit, I couldn't move. My six-year-old would rummage through my purse for money, then go score me some heroin." She looked down at her lap. "Now she's growing up in the School, and she's so happy."

Mona, who gave me five cents to join so many years ago, related her childhood in a monotone, like she was reading a book. She had run her story many times, but it was the first time I heard it. "My parents tied me to a chair in the basement for weeks at a time to punish me. I only saw them when they would bring me oatmeal and water."

No wonder she used drugs. Who wouldn't want to blot out that memory? I thought I'd sound like an idiot complaining about my father spanking us or about my parents arguing so loudly we could hear them a block away. Of my yearning for attention from my father yet continually fearing him. *It wasn't so bad growing up, was it?* But comparisons don't work for self-healing.

Belinda, stocky with a round face and short curly hair, almost whispered early in the morning. "I still wake up from nightmares," she lamented, her arms folded across her stomach like she was trying to hold in her feelings, her legs curled under her, "but I can't remember the dream."

Jordan, the blue-eyed Tribe Leader I knew from Oakland, asked softly, "Can you tell me what you see?"

A stillness fell over the room, a deep hush that felt like reverence.

"A closed door. With an old-fashioned keyhole."

"Look through the keyhole... what do you see?"

Pain crossed Belinda's face in waves, washing up from some dark place inside. With tears running down her cheeks, she looked through that keyhole and, as we bore witness, saw her uncle making love to her mother. She felt betrayed. She never spoke of it, having blocked it out from her memory.

Others in the room started to speak, but Jordan quieted us. "Not now," he cautioned. "This is what we wanted, to find out what was eating at her." It was as if he cradled her from across the room. "It's not your fault. You were just a kid."

"Wow," Belinda sobbed. "I had no memory of that. And I think it affected my whole life."

As I listened to Belinda, the vault at the back of my mind burst open and suddenly I was reliving the night I promised never to tell.

1967, Richmond, California

At midnight, I jolted awake, my body buzzing with fear. I held my breath, trying not to move, until my sister's voice shattered the stillness: "Go to your wife!"

Her doorknob rattled. Her door clicked closed. Then, my doorknob slowly turned. I kept my head motionless on my pillow, my body frozen. Distant streetlights dimly lit my room. Through slit eyes, I watched my father's towering silhouette approach me. As he stepped closer, I closed my eyes, pretending to be asleep, wanting to bury my head in my pillow but too afraid to move. My mattress dipped, tilting me toward him. I stifled a scream. He bent down and rubbed my shoulders, his lips nuzzling my neck. My body trembled.

Why is he here? What should I do?

His rough-shaven face scraped my cheek like sandpaper, and his hot breath with the stench of stale alcohol and cigarettes enveloped me.

I prayed. Please, God. Make him leave.

Mimicking my sister, I pleaded, "Go away! Leave me alone!"

Silence. His hands left my shoulders. My bed creaked as he stood. His footsteps receded. My door closed.

I lay awake, still holding my breath, waiting for his steps to return. They didn't. My heartbeat slowed. My last thought before drifting off to sleep was, *He went to her first. He loves her more.*

The next day, my sister, Julia, and I walked down the street to a small pocket park. "I heard him go into your room," she said. "Did he do anything?"

I shook my head. Shivered at the memory of his heavy breathing. Banished the picture from my mind.

"We can't tell Mom," she insisted. "She'll divorce Dad, and it will be all our fault." I nodded.

How would we even tell her? Would we go to her while she was sitting on her kitchen stool peeling potatoes and say, "Guess what happened last night?" If Julia wouldn't tell, I wouldn't.

I had always followed my sister's lead, and that day was no different. I pushed the memory into the locked cupboard in my mind. I never said a word.

The next day, Dad was silent, sulking. Mom wondered out loud, "What's bugging him today?" It wasn't his first time sulking around the house, slamming doors, hiding out in the garage. Julia and I merely exchanged glances, then looked at the floor.

I went away to college at U.C. Davis the following fall, putting my family behind me. Or so I thought.

I should have stayed at Davis longer than my freshman year instead of transferring to Cal Berkeley, where all my friends were. I had a full four-year scholarship, but that only paid for tuition, not housing and books. I planned to move back home and go to Cal.

What made me think I could live in my father's house again? I hid that night in a steel locker, sealed so well I thought it wouldn't leak out. But it did leak. Every time I came home for three-day weekends and semester breaks, he rubbed my shoulders when no one else was around. *Does he think he's showing me he loves me?* Wanting to puke, I held my breath, squirmed away, never confronting, never telling. My father. My father had never showered me with love; he had only showered me with fear.

I thought I could live there. Stay out of his way. Julia still lived at home, commuting to U.C. Berkeley, and then to Hayward State when she ran out of money. My parents wouldn't—or couldn't—help. I don't know how Julia did it. Probably avoided him like we did our whole lives.

I came home but didn't stay long.

Back then, I thought you could walk away and start a new life, pretending your past didn't exist.

Someone stood up and stretched, jolting my out of my memories. "My time's up. You all have a good Stew."

He left and someone took his place, like a relay.

Fred the trombonist turned to me at some point.

"What's your story?" There were no windows, but I knew it had to be morning. My eyes felt like sandpaper; I leaned forward to stretch my back; I curled my legs under me until they fell asleep and then stretched them out and wiggled my toes to stop the tingling. Only the stories kept me awake.

"I had a pretty normal childhood. I have two brothers and a sister. I graduated from high school in 1968. We lived on a short street with a creek at the end, with blackberries growing wild." I recalled the sweet smell of the ripe blackberries we picked, returning with our arms bleeding from the thorns, delivering a bowl of berries to my mother, which she would bake into a pie.

All I said was, "I used to go camping all over California with my best friend and her parents. It was all pretty fun."

"But why are you here? I can't figure out why you squares live here."

"I like the community. I never did drugs, so I like being in this drug-free place. I think nuclear families are fucked up. I think society is fucked up. This makes much more sense."

Synanon derided nuclear families: one father, one mother, and their children living in one household, where the children learn about life only from their parents.

52

That seemed to satisfy him. My sad memories were nothing compared to others' stories.

Hearing the stories during that Stew, I gained an appreciation for the life my parents gave me. It wasn't perfect, but it was much better than those who came to Synanon to save their lives.

I didn't appreciate that my childhood grievances hurt me as much as the dopefiends' grievances hurt them. It's all relative.

Sometimes I wonder if dredging up the past and talking about it helps or if it's better to keep it buried. But the pain never goes away, even if you talk about it. It comes back in the middle of the night.

At last, my twenty-four hours were up. Walking outside, my body was so tired that it ached, but I felt like every one of my senses was on alert. The wind rustled in the redwood trees and the birds chirped. The brilliant green grass smelled as if freshly mowed, and the sun reflected like sparklers on the deep blue bay. I leaned over and touched a delicate yellow flower, and it felt like silk. Most of all, I felt a warmth in the pit of my stomach, a deep connection to everyone in the room.

I left the Stew convinced Synanon was better than any nuclear family. It was another step in disavowing my past and wholeheartedly becoming a loyal follower of Chuck.

The Inn at Tomales Bay (now part of Marconi CoLnference Center State Historic Park in Marshall, CA). *Photo from Tripadvisor.*

Chapter 8: Bobby

Summer 1971, Oakland, California

When I saw Bobby stroll into the enormous ballroom we called our living room, the noise dulled, the faces blurred, and I felt as though a spotlight shone on him. With the broad shoulders of a linebacker tapering into the narrow hips of a wide receiver, and a smile of pearly teeth set against soft, inviting lips, Bobby took my breath away. Dark-skinned and about my height, he lit the room with his dazzling smile.

He never noticed me.

My skin tingled every time I saw him: on the bus, in the dining room, hobnobbing with Tribe Leaders and Directors. His infectious joie de vivre drew people to him. I needed to work up the nerve to say hello.

"Why don't you take his dance class?" Elizabeth asked over leftovers soup. Elizabeth's crystal blue eyes peered at me through her bangs. We were enjoying a Saturday lunch in our communal dining room. Like every other twenty-one-year-old single female, we wanted to fall in love.

I had watched Bobby and his friends take over the Hoopla with their choreographed routines, their moves and energy foreshadowing the break-dancing craze that would sweep the seventies.

Bobby had started a dance class, convinced everyone could learn to dance like him.

I rolled my eyes at Elizabeth. "That'd be embarrassing… I'm too left-footed." I loved dancing the Hoopla with no one staring and no pressure to move the right way. But a class with everyone watching?

I signed up anyway.

About a dozen of us showed up to his class and formed a loose cluster in front of him. I stayed in the back, not wanting him to see what a klutz I was. The only dance moves I knew were the Twist and the Swim, but Bobby's dance was a full aerobic workout. Swinging your hips side-to-side in the Bump was easy—and sexy. The Electric Glide tripped me up: bending my knees to the music, all the way down to the floor, sliding and swirling, hips moving in all directions, hands up and out and around. I couldn't get the rhythm.

Bobby didn't seem to notice me, and then the class fizzled out after a few weeks.

My next maneuver was the bus. Like me, Bobby lived in the Clumps and rode the Synanon bus back and forth to the Club.

When I hopped on the bus one Saturday morning, there he was. I sat gingerly on the blue, cushioned seat next to him, catching a whiff of patchouli oil. My entire body tingled when his shoulder touched mine.

"So, you moved in?" he asked, as the bus eased into traffic.

Oh, my God. He noticed me, after all.

"Yes, a few months ago. I live with Lydia, Sarah, and Lucy, but still work out in San Francisco."

"I thought I was seeing you around more."

So, he knows who I am. I secretly rejoiced, my heart pounding. It wasn't like me—the old me—to pursue a man. Moving into Synanon had buoyed my confidence.

As the streets of Oakland blurred by, I noticed a new store. "Have you seen that 7-Eleven? It's open twenty-four hours. Who would shop at two a.m.?"

"There's a lot of night people, ya know." He looked like he was mentally noting its location. Turning back to me, he asked, "Do you wanna grab lunch today? I don't have much going on."

My insides vibrated as the bus pulled up to the Club. "Sure," I chirped, hoping to sound nonchalant. "See you at noon?"

Bobby nodded as I got out of the seat and sashayed down the aisle, trying not to bounce on my toes.

A little after noon, I wandered toward the dining room, hoping he would be there. The sun flooded the room, and there he was, illuminated like he was on a stage, talking with a few teenagers. "I gotta' go... catch you later," he said, walking toward me.

"Hey, Janet. You came. Let's grab some food."

I still wasn't used to the buffet smell, a mixture of steaming water, coffee, and canned vegetables. Plus a pizza aroma from pizza rolls, a donation the Hustlers had procured. Hustlers—another Synanon idiom—solicited donations of everything from food to clothing to lumber. Grocery stores donated unsold food; Levi donated jeans overruns; Baskin-Robbins donated ice cream failures.

We went through the line, and I filled my plate with pizza rolls, a novelty for me. I grew up with home-cooked meals and brown-bag lunches. A home-cooked meal sounds healthy and nourishing, but my family had little money, and Mom stretched it. Some weeks, we had hamburgers every night and fried chicken on Sunday for a fancy meal. Mom could stretch spaghetti into three meals: first, traditional spaghetti with ground beef and homemade marinara; second, throw together a meatloaf with leftover spaghetti, frozen peas, and stale bread; third, another round of spaghetti with "meatballs" made from the meatloaf, complete with pieces of spaghetti.

I turned my attention back to the buffet, grabbed some salad and pizza rolls, and Bobby and I wandered over to an empty table.

"So, how long have you lived here?" Bobby asked in Synanon's typical start to a conversation.

"Since last spring." I took a few bites, sipped some Cyclamate-loaded soda, and asked, "How about you?"

"A couple of years. I was in the Notions and was here more and more, and then I was here all the time. I just kind of moved in."

"I've heard about the Notions. In fact, when I was a Game Player, someone suggested I volunteer with them, but I had no idea what I'd do. Play folk songs on my guitar? I thought you were all kind of scary delinquents."

"We were! Or at least I was headed that way." He spoke matter-of-factly, like he had told this story many times. "My mom sent me to live with my dad in Oakland when I was sixteen. We were living in Virginia, and I was a wild child. I used a little cocaine." He looked quizzically at me, but I didn't react. *Another life saved by Synanon.* It didn't matter; more than half the people in Synanon were ex-addicts. Now they were clean. We all had a chance to plop ourselves in our mini-society and start fresh with no judgments about our past lives. Or so I believed. Judgments were always there, I would find out. Judgments to remind us of our bad life choices; judgments to demand gratitude for all Synanon did for us.

Bobby smiled, back in the present. "Then I met friends at school who were going to Synanon in the afternoons, and they brought me along. I've been here ever since. I'd probably be dead if I'd stayed in Virginia. All my old friends back home are into hard drugs."

"So, you must have joined the Notions about the same time I joined the Game Club. How old are you?" *Why did I ask that? No one asks that question.*

"I just turned twenty-one in October," he boasted, picking up a pizza roll.

"Me too, but my birthday was in August. Funny thing about turning twenty-one in Synanon is you can't drink milk anymore!"

He swallowed the pizza roll in one bite. "I never drink milk, anyway. Why can't you drink it?"

"Someone donates it, but it's only for children. Once you turn twenty-one, you can't have it." *What a stupid thing to talk about. Why did I even bring it up?* I sipped on my soda, something I never had at home.

We finished eating and carried our dishes into the waiting bins, as I had done at the U.C. Davis cafeteria.

"Are you going to Saturday Night Party tonight?" he asked, not quite inviting me out on a date.

"Yeah. A bunch of us will be cutting up vegetables all afternoon, but I'll be there after I go home and clean up."

"Okay, see you tonight."

I think he likes me!

Bobby was a refreshing change compared to the men I'd known. In the Game Club, I had dated a few Synanon residents and then was attacked in a Game (being gamed, we called it).

"You and your square friends are just here to find a boyfriend. Go look somewhere else! Leave our dopefiends alone!"

I had felt sick. Is this what they thought? Didn't they see how much I loved Synanon?

"That's not why I'm here," I had defended, but where else would I find a boyfriend? I spent all my time at Synanon.

I wasn't doing well in the romance area. Until now, I hoped.

Bobby sat with me at Saturday Night Party. I had attended almost every week for two years and now helped with the setup. We were supposed to mingle with guests, sharing information about Synanon and persuading them to join. Instead, we sat by ourselves, drinking coffee.

Everyone who walked by greeted Bobby and stopped to chat; Bobby always included me in the conversation. "This is Janet," he said, beaming. "She moved in a few months ago."

By Bobby's side, I met most of the Oakland residents. He seemed to revel in meeting new people while I had to force myself. "Hey, I haven't met you before. I'm Bobby. Is that a New Jersey accent I detect?"

One guy sat at our table for a while, and Bobby asked him, "How's it going with your job? I heard your boss was giving you a bad time?"

"It's okay. We worked it out in a Game. Big misunderstanding, ya' know?"

Was there anyone he didn't know? Directors went out of their way to say hello. "How's it going, Bobby?"

"All good, all good," he said, shaking their hands. "What's not to like? Have you met Janet?"

Bobby was the personification of out-of-the-Game, but it wasn't just an act. After being sent away by his mother and after trying to live with his alcoholic father, he seemed to have adopted Synanon as his family.

When the band started, Bobby grabbed my hand and pulled me to the dance floor. For once, he didn't join his dance troupe; he stayed by my side as we danced side-by-side, eyes locked, hands brushing, eyes eating each other up.

This was my first Saturday Night Party that felt like a romantic date rather than an obligation.

Dating in Synanon differed from dating in the outside world. Bobby and I met for dinner after work and danced after Games. We were the same height, and his eyes gleamed when I towered over him in my three-inch heels. We sometimes rode the jitney to Tomales Bay and rode horses. I'm sure we played Games with each other, but I remember nothing about them.

On one trip to Tomales, Bobby held my hand as we hiked over the golden hills toward the Bay property. While catching my breath at the top of the hill, the wind tangling my hair, Bobby grasped my shoulder, turned me toward him, and gazed into my eyes. My body melted. He pulled me toward him and leaned in for a kiss. His soft lips explored mine; his hands slid down my body. I lost myself in that kiss. My entire body tingled, and I wanted him inside me. But he made me wait.

I hoped he would ask me to go to the Guest Room.

The Guest Room was a one-bedroom apartment furnished with tacky second-hand furniture that couples could reserve to spend the night. Those lucky enough to have private rooms had a place for sex; those who lived in dorms had to use the Guest Room. I had been to the guest room once. First, I had to reserve the room. The night of, I walked to the room carrying a set of clean sheets, my face bright red when people gave knowing nods, recognizing where I was headed. Then, the tacky motel-look of the place—but not a motel, an apartment with a kitchen, table, couches, chairs, and a bed, a throwback to life before living in dorms and eating communally. I went early and cooked dinner like I was playing house before bed. Talk about taking the spontaneity out of sex.

Tired of waiting for Bobby to invite me to the Guest Room, I took his roommate aside and asked him to spend the night somewhere else. Then I went into Bobby's room and lay on his bed, waiting for him to come home after his Game. Instead of sexy lingerie, I wore an ordinary blue dress that I had found in the General Store (Synanon's store for clothing, usually hand-me-downs from residents) and plain underwear. I should have put on something slinky and alluring, but I was in hippie-commune mode, living simply with what I had.

Bobby caught his breath when he walked in and saw me lying on his bed. Then he smiled, unhooked his overalls, and walked over to me. He gently lay beside me, smothering me with kisses. Turning me on my side, he slowly unzipped my dress, kissing my back every few inches. My body tingled with each kiss, and I yearned for him inside me. Taking his time, he undid my bra and slipped me out of my dress in one smooth movement, his hands and lips never leaving my body. I arched my back. *Please, I can't wait any longer.* Slowly, gently, he entered me, his firm body enveloping me, and he gazed into my eyes, reaching out for my soul. I matched his slow rhythm, moaning in anticipation. At last, I cried out as he allowed me to release my passion. We collapsed, his sweet sweat mixing with mine. We slept. We made love again. And again. I stayed all night.

My dormmate, Lydia, was dating Bobby's roommate, Eddie, a wiry,

Black man who looked like a shorter version of Don Cheadle.

One Friday during lunch, Eddie leaned his elbows on the table. "You know what I miss? Soul food."

Bobby chimed in. "Me too. I know a great place. What d'ya think?"

Eddie's face brightened. "Let's go! How about tonight?" He invitingly looked at Lydia and me. "I've got WAM."

I grinned. "Sounds fun!" I had no idea what soul food was, but I loved the idea of a double date.

Lydia shrugged. "Sure. I'm game."

The shadows outside were long when Bobby checked out a car. Bobby and Eddie sat in the front; Lydia and I were in the back. Bobby drove through parts of Oakland I had never seen. Along the darkening streets, we passed run-down homes with weed-filled yards. I felt like I was in a foreign country.

Bobby warned as we approached the rib and soul food joint, "Duck down in the back seat. We can't be seen here with white women." Not questioning, Lydia and I ducked, trying to cover her blond hair that sparkled in the sparse streetlights. Bobby parked the car in the dimly lit parking lot. He and Eddie went to order food while Lydia and I huddled in the back seat, trying to breathe without moving our chests. Muffled words floated through the closed windows. "Hey, man, how's it goin'?" "Not bad, not bad."

What's going to happen if someone looks in the back seat? Is someone going to pull us out of the car, or beat up our guys? I didn't want to find out.

Bobby and Eddie returned with a bulging brown paper bag, liquid oozing out from the bottom, filling the car with the aroma of barbecue sauce. We drove a few blocks before Lydia and I unfolded our backs. "God, Eddie, don't ever make me do that again!"

Back home, we dove into the food, barbecue sauce covering our hands and faces. My tastebuds awakened with new-to-me spices of cayenne, coriander, and curry. Every bite of black-eyed peas, collard greens, and tender ribs made me crave more.

For some of our dates, we went to the movies. I took Bobby to see "Woodstock." My best friend, Jacqui, and I had wanted to go to Woodstock, but she hadn't wanted to defy her parents, so we stayed home. Plus, how would we get there? The movie was my chance to at least experience the music.

Bobby and I walked into the theater hand-in-hand. The audience was glow-in-the-dark White—probably eighty percent White with a few Blacks and Asians sprinkled throughout. I glanced at Bobby and saw him staring straight ahead, studiously ignoring the stares. I stared right back at people in a silent challenge.

Afterward, I asked, "So, did you like it?"

"Eh, interesting, I guess. Not something I would have ever gone to. Not my type of music. But I liked Jimi Hendrix."

"I loved it! I wanted to go but couldn't figure out how to get there."

He looked at me like I was crazy.

"C'mon," I suggested. "While we're out, let's go to the Body Shop in Berkeley. They've got all these natural oils."

We drove down Telegraph Avenue and parked across the street from the Body Shop, jaywalking during a break in traffic. It was a warm summer day filled with the same mix of people I had seen at the peace march when I was teargassed in 1969: Shirtless men with long hair held down by a woven headband, Blacks sporting Afros up to six inches high, women with long, straight hair. Some wore short shorts; some wore jeans belted with scarves. The air was a mix of car exhaust, cigarette smoke, and marijuana.

Walking into the Body Shop closed off all the sounds and smells of Telegraph Avenue. The walls were a soothing dark green; the sun filtered through the windows, and intermingled aromas of incense and oils immersed us. My eyes were drawn to shelves filled with lotions. We leaned over tables laden with tiny bottles with handwritten labels: vanilla, lavender, musk, rose, and more.

"Here, try this one," I said, dabbing sandalwood oil on Bobby's wrist. It smelled earthy, like the forest. "I kinda' like it."

He sniffed. "Nah. Not me. Look for patchouli. That's what I wear."

I found it and dabbed it behind his ear. I leaned in; the musky scent aroused me. "Let's buy this and get outta' here."

"Not yet. Let's find an oil for you." He leaned over the table. "How 'bout Satsuma? I like the sound of that." He placed a drop on my wrist.

"Oh God. I smell like oranges. No way."

"Okay. Let's try vanilla." Another dab.

I breathed it in. "Chocolate chip cookies!"

"That's it. I love how you smell with that." He put a drop on my neck, breathed it in, and nibbled on my ear.

A few weeks later, Bobby took me to see "Shaft," the first movie starring a Black action hero. Ninety percent of the audience were African Americans. Several men gave Bobby nods, but the women glared at me. I felt their eyes on me, acutely aware of my whiteness. I felt like I didn't belong and had walked into someone else's world. *This must be how Black people feel all the time.*

"Great movie, huh?" Bobby gushed on our way home.

"I really liked the music. I've never listened to anything but folk music and the Beatles. And jazz at the Club."

He turned on the radio to a soul station with Marvin Gaye singing "What's Going On." "Now, this is music."

Marvin Gaye and Al Green became the background of our lives while Synanon wove through our relationship. He was my rock. He was always there for me, and I was always there for him until gradually Synanon became more important to me.

I wanted to introduce Bobby to my family, so I invited my parents to dinner, reserving a table for six or eight so some friends could join us. We never considered having dinner with the four of us—Mom, Dad, Bobby, and me. We traveled in packs. My parents knew about Synanon, and they knew about Bobby, but they didn't know he was Black.

In a Game a few days before the dinner, someone asked me, "Are you ready for this dinner with your parents? Do they know he's Black?" I hadn't told my parents he was Black; it wasn't something I thought about after being in this integrated community for two years.

"Well, no, but my high school was half Black, and my dad works on the railroad with Black men, so they'll be fine," I lied, twisting my hair. I really had no idea.

I called Mom before the dinner to warn her. Taking a calming breath, I launched right in. "Hi, Mom. I'm calling about dinner Saturday night."

"Yeah, we'll be there. Can't wait to meet this Bobby."

"Well, there's something you should know…. He's Black."

Not missing a beat, she chuckled, "So what? But I'll tell Dad."

My parents arrived, and we had that awkward meet-your-daughter's-boyfriend moment. Then we went through the buffet and settled at our table. It was dark outside by then, hiding the shabby downtown area that was our usual view. Accepting everyone as part of his extended family, Bobby led the conversation, told jokes, and even got my dad to laugh, winning his heart.

A few months later, one evening in early 1972, I was getting ready for bed when I heard singing. I crept outside onto the balcony in my bathrobe. It was dark, but in the parking lot below, illuminated by the glow of the streetlights, was a group of about fifteen people grinning up at me.

Bobby was in front, crooning an Al Green song, *Let's Stay Together.*

Bending down on one knee, he looked up and called out, "Will you marry me?"

"Say yes! Say yes!" his friends shouted.

"Yes!" I exclaimed. *I'm engaged! I'm not going to be a spinster after all.* While today it is common for women to wait until their thirties to marry, if they marry at all, back then we were still getting married right out of high school. I was already behind the curve.

Only one person, Wilma, thought we were too young to get married. Wilma was an older Black woman who had been a prostitute and then had run a house of ill repute. She had taken Bobby under her wing, and her wingspan had extended to me.

"Come here, you two," she implored as we walked by her in the living room. She was sitting next to a grizzled white man who, in an earlier life, was a KKK branch treasurer, who had come to Synanon to get off heroin. We stood by them, waiting for Wilma's words of wisdom. "You're too young to be getting married. What are you thinking?"

That took us by surprise. "No, we're not," Bobby defended. "We're adults. Besides, we live in Synanon. We don't have to worry about jobs and family and houses. We get to live together. We won't have to use the Guest Room."

"Ahh, let 'em do what they want," the KKK man added, "they're going to anyway."

Wilma shook her head, and we walked away hand-in-hand, ecstatic, thinking about planning our wedding.

Before we had picked a date, there were rumors of a wedding festival. "What do you think that is?" I asked Bobby.

"I heard they had something last year when ten or twenty couples got married, and they all had a big party. Must be something like that."

"That sounds cool! Elizabeth told me she and Jim are getting married, and you said Eddie and Lydia are getting married. Maybe we can all be in the ceremony."

"I love it! I'll talk to Eddie."

Including my mother in my wedding plans never crossed my mind.

Within weeks, more and more couples jumped on the bandwagon to get married. The festival would be at the Ranch in the warm August sun.

Synanon had purchased the old Maggetti Ranch in Marin County in 1970, about a mile inland and up some rolling hills from Tomales Bay. A year later, they bought a nearby ranch with Walker Creek Stream running through it. The two ranches totaled about five square miles. Chuck and Betty moved into the two-story ranch house on the Maggetti property after setting Synanon's carpenters and artisans loose on renovations. Everyone referred to the Maggetti property as Home Place—where Chuck and Betty lived.

The Ranch is where we would have our wedding.

Instead of sending wedding invitations, our graphics department made a poster: Synanon Wedding Festival 1972.

First, we had to get married in the eyes of the state, which required a premarital blood test. Synanon's medical department had a lab that could run the tests, and they returned negative.

They tested me for Rh antibodies to make sure I could have a healthy baby and tested Bobby for sickle cell anemia. I guess the assumption in 1972 was that you were getting married for popping out babies. They also tested us for syphilis. The public health officials had decided that the only way to curb syphilis was to mandate testing, and the best way to order testing was to require it before issuing a marriage license.

I took a day off work so we could get our marriage license. Bobby and I met early for breakfast, but I was too nervous to eat, too excited to notice anyone but Bobby. We ran downstairs to the Connect. We picked up the keys to a nondescript car and drove a few miles to the County Recorder's office to get our license.

My heart skipped a beat when we came across the sign pointing us to marriage licenses. Bobby held my hand as we followed the signs and got in line.

"Next," the clerk said, looking bored.

"We're here to get our marriage license," Bobby announced to her and the world.

She looked at us indifferently on this, the biggest day of my life. "Paperwork and blood tests?"

Bobby grinned and held me by the waist as we handed over our blood test results in exchange for a piece of paper. A piece of paper that would allow us to marry.

"When are you getting married?" Maybe the clerk finally picked up on our excitement. "Or do you want to go before the Judge and get married today?" she asked.

"No, we have our own minister," Bobby explained, eyes sparkling. "And we're getting married with all our friends in a huge joint marriage."

"Well, good luck. Next?"

We went home and filled out the paperwork, then sent it via

inter-department mail to Dede Harvey, a minister who had moved into Synanon as a Lifestyler. It came back to us, signed, a few days later. My body tingled when I realized I was legally married.

With the paper, Bobby and I could live together, but I still wanted to be married in the eyes of my Synanon community. That meant waiting four months, giving me time to sew my dress.

At work, I told my boss, "Today, I am Janet Best," and displayed a photo of Bobby and me on my desk. A Black woman stopped talking to me. We had always been cordial, but now she gave me a disdainful look when I was near. This must be what I had heard about—Black women resenting White women who married all the good Black men. *If only she knew my good Black man lived in a drug rehab facility.*

In early summer, before the Wedding, Mom put together a reception for us at her house. Bobby and I checked out a car and drove north on Highway 880 as I rattled off the names of my high school friends who would be there—friends from another life. As the sun burned through the fog, it lit the artwork on the Emeryville mudflats—windmills made of driftwood, smiley faces made of old tires, figurines made of discarded metal, like a mini city on the sparkling bay.

Arriving at my parents' house, I held Bobby's hand as we walked up the brick stairs. Bobby was dressed in a casual blue shirt and jeans, while I wore the prettiest hand-me-down dress from the Synanon store. It had a black bodice with a black-and-white checkered skirt. I hadn't finished sewing my wedding dress and had no money to buy a new one. My sister told me years later, "I wondered why you wore black to your reception, instead of something white or spring-like."

My old friends trickled in, giggling, showing off engagement rings. I didn't have a ring, but I didn't care. I waited for the room to quiet.

"Everyone, this is Bobby!" I announced, standing tall. "We got married in April, but we're having a big wedding in August. Thanks, Mom, for inviting everyone!" I felt like I had stepped into a past I had left behind, but Bobby greeted everyone effortlessly, as if he had known them forever. My friends didn't blink at our mixed marriage; we had all attended the same integrated high school and our minister had marched in Selma with Martin Luther King, Jr. No one asked about Synanon. Did they know? Did they care? To them, it was simply another wedding reception.

On a table in the formal dining area of the living room (where a table had never stood) was a three-tier wedding cake decorated with red piped flowers—my favorite color. Red and white carnations encircled the cake. Lace wedding bells topped the cake. Mixed-race bride and groom toppers weren't available.

Bobby held my waist and placed his hand over mine as we ceremoniously cut the cake. So traditional and quaint.

That was the last time I saw my high school friends. I felt as if they lived in another world I had left behind. My life revolved around Synanon.

By the big day on August 7, 1972, two days before my 22nd birthday, seventy-five couples had legally wed.

Each couple could only invite two people because of size and water constraints at the Ranch. Bobby's family were all back east, so we invited Mom and Dad.

The Wedding theme was country. I designed a dress of white muslin with an orange undercoat and sewed a matching shirt for Bobby, which he wore with white overalls—Synanon's de facto uniform.

For my dress, I asked my friends to embroider five-inch squares with a design they chose. Twenty-one friends jumped at the offer. When I wore it, I felt enveloped in love; my wedding dress was made in my style yet enhanced by my community with an overskirt of squares embroidered by my friends.

I still have the dress, but I only remember three or four people who embroidered squares. I thought I would know who was part of my dress forever. I wish I had written their names on the back of each square.

Tender Loving Care

For months before the Wedding, the Hut buzzed with sewing machines as bride after bride sewed her dress.

Unique to Oakland, the Hut was a room on the fifth floor next to the swimming pool. No men allowed. Windows looked out over Oakland and the Berkeley Hills, letting in the day's gloom or sunlight. We had a sauna, comfortable couches, sewing machines, tables, and makeup stations. We held women's Games and retreats there, or simply hung out. There was an easy, unguarded comfort in sharing stories and laughing, freed by the knowledge that no man was listening.

It's funny to think that in 1972, as women were staging sit-ins and protests challenging systemic discrimination and launching Ms. Magazine—the first national magazine run by women and for women—we in Synanon were sewing our wedding dresses, about as domestic as you can get. We talked about women's equality, but men ran Synanon. Betty D. was on the Board of Directors, but no women ran the facilities.

Bobby and Janet 1975

Chapter 9: Wedding with a Few Friends

August 1972, Marshall, California

It was my first time at the Ranch, near the heart of Synanon, where Chuck and Betty lived. I rode there in a jitney with a dozen other brides. We turned off the Marshall-Petaluma Road onto a graded dirt lane. It was a perfect Marin County day, a day Frank Lloyd Wright must have imagined when he designed the Marin County Civic Center: the sky a deep blue, the rolling hills golden with the grasses dried by the summer sun. To the left was a hillock covered in a luscious copse of trees concealing the original ranch buildings.

Elizabeth had been there before. "Look past the trees," she said reverently. "That ranch house is where Chuck and Betty live." I glimpsed a gleaming white, two-story farmhouse with an attached, roofed veranda. "It was ramshackle when we bought it, but our carpenters fixed it up. That's what I want to do, be a carpenter. Maybe at the Home Place."

In her wedding attire, face glowing beneath her makeup, she didn't look like a carpenter. "Huh," I shrugged. Lydia rolled her eyes.

Elizabeth pointed to small outbuildings and a large barn sprinkled among eucalyptus, oaks, maples, and tall shrubs that earlier ranch owners had planted. "Their staff live in those other buildings."

The road turned toward the right, obscuring the view of Chuck and Betty's compound. We drove past a half dozen tan, utilitarian Butler barns and a dozen wooden bunkhouses separated by dry grass and narrow sidewalks. A few white, army-style tents sprinkled the hillsides. No trees. No shade.

"Everyone else lives over here," Elizabeth said.

I should have noticed the dichotomy between the haves and the have-nots. Chuck, Betty, and their entourage lived in splendor while the workers lived in bunkhouses. I didn't blink an eye, though; I thought how wonderful it must be living so close to Chuck and Betty.

A few minutes later, we pulled up to an asphalt parking lot just as people poured out of the Synacruiser.

Couples arrived from all the Synanon facilities. The Synacruiser transported couples from Santa Monica, five hundred miles south. In Oakland, already dressed in our wedding attire, we had piled into jitneys, nervous men in one jitney, giggling women in another, a nod to the tradition of brides and grooms not seeing each other before a wedding. There had been no rehearsal, so Elizabeth, Lydia, and I had read the script as we drove, wanting the day to be flawless.

We exited the jitney into a parking lot filled with laughter. Our bright wedding attire contrasted with the dry hills.

The air was still. I breathed in the scents of dry grass and roasted pork. Men in overalls unburied a pit, revealing roasted pigs. Tears filled my eyes as I gazed at the long row of tables, one adorned with three-tiered wedding cakes. *My wedding day!*

My old friend Jacqui and I had dreamed of a joint wedding. And here I was, sharing my wedding with all my friends. I beamed.

We lined up as couples and walked over a small wooden bridge. Bobby clasped my hand as we walked behind Elizabeth, striking in her long yellow dress, and her husband, Jim, in white overalls. Behind us were Eddie in crisp blue overalls and Lydia in a simple white dress. We promenaded into a field enclosed by a bright white ranch fence and gathered in rows, with an aisle down the middle. The music of Burt Bacharach's *Raindrops Keep Fallin' on my Head* filled the air.

Most brides wore long, colorful dresses, with only a few white ones here and there. All our dresses were tight at the waist, modest at the breast, and set off with summery hats. The grooms wore overalls of different colors, all with long-sleeved shirts, some white, some checkered, some patterned. A few broke the mold and wore jeans with a Western vest. A mass of colors filled the field, contrasting with the dry golden grasses on the hillside. Guests sat and leaned on the fence surrounding the field.

I looked for Mom and Dad. I had expected to see them before the ceremony. Finally, there they were along the fence, Mom leaning forward, smiling, Dad standing awkwardly beside her. Dad was still as handsome as in his wedding photo, with sandy hair that would have been blond had he lived in sunny Southern California, square jaw, and movie star blue eyes. I had never known Mom without short curly hair and glasses, but in that wedding photo, she had long, black curly hair with blunt bangs. Still those glasses, though. I caught Mom's eye and waved, tears of joy springing from my eyes.

I am sad that Mom was merely an onlooker at my wedding. She didn't get to walk down the aisle after the guests were seated; she didn't help me pick out a dress, send invitations, or invite her friends, relatives, or even my siblings. She didn't help pick a venue or plan a reception or a honeymoon. We didn't even have a honeymoon, nor, by the way, did we have rings. Mom had thrown us that pre-wedding reception, but that's it. She took it in stride like she did everything life threw at her.

We all quieted as Chuck and Betty walked down the aisle, holding hands. Chuck was out of his overalls for once, wearing black pants, a crisp, white short-sleeved shirt, and a black vest with a straw cowboy-style hat; Betty wore a long-sleeved ruffled blouse and a long, plaid cotton skirt and held a parasol above her head. They took their place on a stage erected for the occasion.

Instead of adding solemnity to the occasion, our resident minister, Dede, broke the tension when he walked in wearing loose white pants tucked into black cowboy boots, a black vest and black topcoat, a red bowtie, and a top hat. He waved and bowed to us.

A marching cadence sounded from behind us. At first, I couldn't make out the words, but they got louder and louder.

> Your left, your left. Your left right left.
> Everywhere we go-o, people want to know-o, who
> we are.
> So we tell them.
> We are the boot camp... left, left, left right left!

The young women of the Boot Camp, wearing blue jeans and white sleeveless blouses, paraded in, their voices booming in unison as they marched to the cadence of their squad leader.

> Pick 'em up and put 'em down.... 40 inches all around... That's the boot camp boogie...it's a crazy sound...left, left. Left right left.

The Boot Camp men followed, wearing crisp, snug-fitting denim overalls, blue denim shirts, and black boots.

> Your left, your left. Your left right left.
> Now pick up the step, your left your right your le-eh-eft.

Your left, your left, your left right left. Left my
mother and forty-eight children alone in the kitchen
in starving condition without any gingerbread left.
Left. Left right left.

This is the best of our community, I thought, chill bumps tickling my
arms. I'm a sucker for drill routines.

The women and men of the Boot Camp lined up in front of the
stage at parade rest like Marines, hands clasped behind their backs,
eyes looking forward at nothing.

The Boot Camp, formed earlier that year, was a small, elite group
of newcomers (dopefiends there less than a year), the cream of the
crop, who lived at the Ranch. This latest experiment in teaching
people how to live without drugs had them dressing in matching
overalls, shirts, shoes, socks, and bandanas. They rose before dawn,
ran before breakfast, performed calisthenics, and had to adhere to
the highest standard of neatness and cleanliness. For work, they
helped build out the Ranch and Walker Creek properties at Tomales,
erecting buildings and pouring concrete for sidewalks.

I held hands with Bobby alongside my friends, with the sun
lighting our dresses and brightening our faces. Chuck and Betty were
on the stage in front, Dede in front of them, with the Boot Camp
lined up at attention. A hush fell over the gathering.

I don't remember what was said. I remember every word spoken
at my second wedding over forty years ago, but I can't remember my
first. I'm sure Chuck spoke; he wasn't one to stay quiet before a
crowd. Dede led us in vows, something about committing to both
my husband and my community.

After the vows, we recited the Synanon Prayer, something I had
repeated nearly every day for the last year and a half.

Please let me first and always examine myself
Let me be honest and truthful
Let me seek and assume responsibility
Let me understand rather than be understood
Let me trust and have faith in myself and my fellow man
Let me love rather than be loved
Let me give rather than receive.
"I now pronounce you man and wife."

We cheered like a baseball stadium after a home run. Bobby and I kissed and hugged as he swung me around. We joined the couples in a short square dance, which morphed into a line dance. Our wedding dance differed from the Hoopla. This time, we all held hands, an inner circle of brides facing an outer circle of grooms, moving in opposite directions, swaying to the music, beaming, with the dried grass crunching underneath our feet and the sun shining upon us.

When the music stopped, Bobby kissed me and ran to the stage. He and his dance troupe were part of the entertainment. I had known that, but I didn't expect him to leave me so abruptly.

Suddenly, I stood alone among one hundred forty-nine brides and grooms, hugging and kissing. Tears stinging like tear gas, I sought Mom and Dad along the fence. I hadn't realized how much I depended on Bobby's gregariousness to be comfortable in a group, even a group of friends. No matter our past, Mom was somehow there for me.

It's all right, I told myself. *Of course, he ran to the stage. He's part of the entertainment. It's his joy.* Still, I felt alone and wanted Mom to hug me and tell me everything would be okay. I instead put on my best face, refusing to admit that I had a seed of doubt about my marriage. *I'm married!*

I wove through the couples toward Mom and Dad, who were still waiting at the fence. Mom gave me a big hug. "That was marvelous! What a wedding! Where's Bobby?"

Dad gave me an awkward hug. I didn't want him to touch me.

"Bobby's up on the stage." I pointed.

"Ooh! I didn't know he could dance like that!" Mom loved music, dancing, and singing.

We joined the buffet line. I remember heaps of roast pork, bowls of potato salad (not as delicious as my mom's), green salads, and rice. And those elegant wedding cakes. Bobby, exuberant, joined us, and my feeling of abandonment vanished.

Now, I know that our first commitment had to be to Synanon, not each other. But in August 1972, my first commitment was to Bobby.

Wedding dance 1972
Photo from author's collection

Janet and Bobby Best 1972
Photo from author's collection

Chapter 10: Only One of Us Can Work for Synanon

Fall 1972, Oakland, California

A couple of months after my wedding, an envelope awaited me in my mailbox—a manilla interoffice envelope with names scribbled out as the envelope passed from person to person. "From Director's Office."

Fingers shaking, I opened it.

"Please stop by the Director's office." It had to be good. I would have been called out in a Game if I had done something wrong.

I had been petitioning to work for Synanon since I moved in. Working for a company on the outside instead of working for Synanon felt like I had "one foot out the door," as was often drummed into us working-out Lifestylers. We were not one hundred percent part of Synanon.

I rode the 1920s elevator to the fourth floor, working the controls myself. Sliding the scissored elevator door closed, I was encased in wood paneling smelling of furniture polish. A dim light cast a yellow tone over the worn beige carpet. Turning the brass lever left for up, I felt the elevator rise, accompanied by a hum, and watched the brass floor indicator until it almost reached four. The unhurried ascent calmed my nerves. Slowing the elevator, I eased the lever, so the floor lined up with the outside hallway—another perfect landing.

It was only a few steps to the Director's office; it was the same office where I had applied to move in: windowless, photos of Chuck and Betty on the wall. DJ Don had moved up the corporate ladder. Lenny, a short, curly-haired man I had seen around, often playing the piano, greeted me. He was about ten years my senior, both age-wise on the earth and age-wise in Synanon. He seemed more comfortable sitting on a piano bench than sitting behind a desk.

"Oh, hi Janet," he began, beckoning me in, looking over his glasses. "We'd like to offer you a job working for Synanon."

So matter of fact. My heart raced. Wanting to jump out of my seat and cheer, I instead leaned forward, attempting dignity while still babbling. "I'd love to! Where? When do I start?"

"Hold on, lemme finish," he said, his brown eyes gazing at me.

"We're a nonprofit corporation curing drug addicts. We have to justify every square who's hired in."

I nodded. I didn't know that. No wonder it was so hard to work in.

Lenny went on. "We can't ever find enough secretaries; we need you in Office Services."

I grinned, barely containing my excitement, my eyes asking him to go on. I wasn't a secretary. Sure, I had held two office jobs, but all I had ever typed were college papers. Maybe I was on management's radar when I applied to work in the legal department.

"Here's the thing, though," Lenny continued. "To hire one square, we have to send another out to work. Bobby's going to have to go find a job." I felt the blood drain out of my face. This was so sudden.

"We're all adults here," he concluded, staring at a piece of paper on his desk. "I don't think we need to have a Game about this. You can let him know."

In my typical fashion, I accepted Lenny's authority, and simply replied, "Um, okay," like this was a condition of employment. In my mind, I was screaming. *Are you crazy? How am I supposed to tell Bobby?*

I crossed my legs and air-tapped my toes to the beat of my racing heart. My dream had come true, but Bobby would have to go out to work. And I had to tell him.

Uncrossing my legs, I stood to leave. "Thanks, Lenny. I have to give two weeks' notice at work." I almost skipped out of his office. *I'm in! I get to work here! No more taking AC Transit over the bridge. Oh, God, how do I tell Bobby? This doesn't make sense. I get to work in!*

I found Bobby in the living room singing in accompaniment to some musicians jamming. There wasn't a day that I didn't hear someone plunking out a tune on a piano or guitar or playing a flute, cello, or sax. Today was jazz, and I felt the melody seep into my soul, calming me.

The fog was rolling in outside, painting a gray hue over the city.

"Hey, Beest." Bobby waved to the group and walked over to hug me. He endearingly called me Beest the day we married, his play-on-words, Best to Beest.

Now's the time, I thought, avoiding Bobby's eyes, focusing instead on a bus stopped at a light outside on 12th Street. Turning back toward him, I took a deep breath. "Guess what? I just got hired to work in!"

Whooping loudly, he grabbed my waist, but before he could swirl me around, I had to continue. "But... you have to go out to work. Only one of us can work in."

I watched his face turn from delight to distress, then his act-as-if kicked in, and he put on a happy face. Act as if you are happy, and you will become happy. "That's okay, Beest; I'll find a job."

How could he be so calm? I cast my eyes about to look anywhere but Bobby's eyes. Being sent out to work was worse than a man having to shave his head for penance. A shaved head only lasted a couple of weeks. Being sent to work outside of Synanon was as close as we came to throwing someone out.

How cold-hearted. Lenny fired Bobby without explanation. He didn't even tell him face-to-face. I didn't have enough work experience to know how to fire employees appropriately, but we weren't employees, were we? We were unpaid labor. Lenny didn't call a Game; I didn't call a Game; Bobby's bosses didn't call a Game. We marched forward believing that Synanon was our family and Chuck knew best.

A few nights later, we met Eddie and Lydia at dinner, sitting at a spool table for six. The Tribe Leaders sat at the Director's table with the servers serving them. The city outside was darkening as the sun set, streetlights reflecting off the fog, amplifying the feeling of living in a separate world. Residents came in, loaded their plates from the buffet, and sat at the tables sprinkled around the room. There was no specific dinner time, just a few hours when food was available.

"Why don't you apply to the Sales Team?" Eddie asked Bobby.

Bobby bristled and fiddled with his overalls buckle. "I don't know anything about sales."

"Well, it's worth a try. They're always looking for people. I heard they're bringing in so much money we hardly need Hustlers anymore."

"Oh, I tried to work there once," Lydia said, putting down her fork and brushing her blonde hair off her eyes. "I didn't sell one pen, but Bobby'd be good at it."

"What exactly is this sales team?" I asked.

"ADGAP. They sell pens and stuff," Bobby explained. "The sales team goes to different areas around here and talks to business owners, getting them to buy pens and mugs with their company name on them." He shook his head. "I don't know if I could do it, but it might be fun." His eyes brightened. "I know they started sending people on sales trips all over the country."

Lydia added, "Buy a pen and save a life. That's the pitch." She rolled her eyes. "I tried that. I hated it. I had to walk into a business and ask for the owner. First, I had to get through the receptionist. We had some script for that." She took a few bites of salad, then continued. "I would hold out a sample pen and say, 'We'll engrave your company's name on this, and you can give them away to your customers as a promotion.'

"You could totally do that, Bobby," I said.

Lydia continued to frown. "Then I talked about Synanon and how it saved my life. By buying pens, the company could save lives as well."

She shrugged. "I didn't sell anything."

I would have thought her blond hair alone would have sold pens.

Advertising Gifts and Promotions (ADGAP), sold promotional items in bulk: pens, mugs, coasters, and such imprinted with a company's logo and phone number. Synanon had acquired a hot-stamping machine in the early sixties, imprinting "Synanon" on pencils as giveaways. In 1967, Chuck recruited his younger brother, Bill (known as Bill D. in our community), a salesman with thirty years' experience, to move in and run ADGAP.[3] Bill hired and trained Synanon members for the sales team who received the same WAM as the rest of us. Synanon kept all the profits. I don't know if Bill D. made a salary. I thought management received fifty dollars a month, but I was probably wrong. In my first Game, when DJ Don said he received fifty dollars a month, I assumed that was the other Directors' pay forever. I was so gullible back then.

Bobby found Bill D. the next day and asked to work for him. "He asked me when I could start," Bobby told me later. His smile was

---

3 . Gerstel, Paradise Incorporated, 131.

back, his eyes sparkling. Synanon wanted him. *What a relief.*

Bobby, with his outgoing personality, had a gift for sales. He and the other salespersons cold-called companies, driving in jitneys to various business locations, knocking on doors, telling the Synanon story, and selling pens.

I should have seen this as a red flag that Synanon would send Bobby out to work to crunch the numbers. And he didn't come in as a Lifestyler; he came in as a troubled teen dabbling in drugs, so it wasn't even a fair trade. Ignoring the red flag may have been my first step over my moral code, a turn toward selfishness. I would be one hundred percent immersed in Synanon while Bobby would have one foot out the door.

What happened to the me who quit my first part-time job in a florist shop because the boss started giving me more hours than the single mother of two simply because my hourly wage was lower?

As I think back, I'm sure being asked to go out to work was the beginning of a downward spiral for Bobby. I don't remember his job in Synanon; maybe he was a dog robber to one of the bigshots. I can now imagine how it hit him, but I didn't see it then. He seemed to take it in stride, yet I doubt he ever recovered. He, like I, had adopted Synanon as his family, but being told to go out to work was a sign that he was no longer the golden boy. He shrugged it off. "Whatever's good for Synanon." I wasn't worried.

Now working for Synanon, I started my day by making my bed drop-a-quarter-on-it military style, except on Sundays when we could leave our beds unmade for some unknown reason. Bobby and I lived in an apartment at the Clumps and rode the Synanon bus across town to the Athens Club, where breakfast awaited: oatmeal, scrambled eggs, toast, cold cereal, and perhaps orange juice, depending on our donations that week. On Sundays, we could special order eggs, like the omelet stations you see at hotels, as our food service staff hustled up breakfast for hundreds.

One ex-addict told me his first job was as a cook in Santa Monica. "We used to have over five hundred for breakfast during the week.

Sundays, when it was grazing—it was something else. Because breakfast ran to noon on Sunday, and it was fifteen hundred people. Seven hundred wanted eggs to order. People would say, 'Do you know how long I've been here? I want this done to my eggs.' Everyone wanted to be treated special."

I never asked for special treatment. I had cooked meals for my family since I was twelve; I was grateful to have someone else cook. And plan the meals. And clean up afterward.

We kicked off each weekday with a Morning Meeting. Everyone attended. In Oakland, my friend Emma, a natural storyteller, ran it. Emma was probably in her thirties, plump, with dark curly hair. She had a kid in the School. Emma had become hooked on prescription drugs after her husband committed suicide by shooting himself in their bedroom. Knowing she took too many drugs and was just plain unhappy, she found her way to Synanon to start a new life. Emma took me under her wing.

Emma started Morning Meeting with a group recitation of the Synanon Philosophy. I can see how one might say, aha—indoctrination. And maybe that's true. Yet I stood tall reciting the Synanon Philosophy, certain those around me were striving for the same ideal.

A man is relieved and gay when he has put his heart into his work and done his best, but what he has said or done otherwise shall give him no peace. As long as he willingly accepts himself he will continue to grow and develop his potentialities.... God helps those who help themselves.

Emma then told jokes to loosen everyone up while our coffee kicked in, announcements of Synanon birthdays—the anniversary of when someone moved into Synanon. Department heads gave updates, and we all scurried off to our respective jobs.

It sounds trite, this feeling of community, of belonging. Our miniature society, our commune, gave me the gift of family. I mattered. I cared about everyone in the room and felt like they cared for me. All these people with assorted backgrounds were my family.

A Morning Meeting highlight was a report from one of the Hustlers about the latest donations they had procured: pizza rolls, weird Baskin-Robbins' ice cream flavors, beef stroganoff, chicken cacciatore, meatballs, and Ghirardelli chocolate.

Morning Meeting ended with the Synanon Prayer.

Then, I headed downstairs to work in Office Services. It was my first time working on a Cubic Day, one of Chuck's better experiments in living. I worked ten hours a day for seven days, then had seven days off. Seven days off every other week! We called the work period Motion, where we had to be in constant motion working our butts off. Teeth and fuzz, we called it: smiling and moving at the speed of light. We called the off week Vacuum: a time for leisure, reading, and socializing. Motion was easy for me. I developed a strong work ethic from both parents, who never missed a day of work. My father even worked back-to-back shifts for months when my younger brother was born, and we desperately needed cash. The Cubic Day only worked because we had a food service department to cook our meals and a school to take care of the children.

The only downside to my Cubic Day was that Bobby worked the typical five-day work week, so now we only had a weekend together every other week. As our marriage went on, we had less and less time together rather than more. It didn't strike me as unusual. We built our life around the Synanon community. While a typical married couple in larger society might go to work and hang out every evening and weekend, we filled our evenings and weekends with community life.

A cool thing about Synanon was that there was no unemployment and no homelessness. Everyone had a job, and every job was important. There were no addicts or alcoholics. A utopian dream.

I didn't think about the fact that if someone didn't make the cut, they were forced out. We didn't throw anyone out; we merely made their lives miserable. Lifestylers could easily get another job. But what about substance abusers? Did we merely force our rejects onto larger society?

Synanon propaganda was that any addict who left would go back on drugs, but that wasn't true. It was another legend to keep people from splitting (leaving Synanon). Some Splittees started drug rehab facilities. Some became counselors. Some were hired as cooks in fancy restaurants. Many started businesses.

*
**

One morning, John, the head of the transportation department, called me into his office. He was the department head for one week of the Cubic Day schedule; he had a counterpart on alternate weeks. "What do you think about driving the bus?"

"Why? Is that my new job?" I grinned and my insides tingled.

"It could be. We need a new driver, and I think you'd be perfect. You would drive the bus back and forth to the Clumps and take a jitney run to Tomales once a day."

Oh, I wanted this. It would put me back on the road, not in my Alfa, but at least driving. It would take me to Tomales, the place I loved. But a bus?

"But I don't know how to drive a bus," I said, hoping it wasn't a job killer.

"I'll train you. You'll have to get your Class 2 license, and I'll teach you how to drive the bus." Deal done.

I studied for a Class 2 driver's license, which was required for driving over eight passengers. All I remember from the test is that the only things that could fall on the highway from commercial vehicles were water and feathers from live birds.

I met John in Synanon's back parking lot for my first driving lesson, where the silver and blue city bus loomed before me. I hopped on for my first lesson. John drove us to a large, empty parking lot by the docks. The sky was overcast, matching the neglected concrete buildings that were gray with age and grime. He stopped the bus, stepped out of the driver's seat, and motioned me into it.

Sitting on the soft, cushioned leather seat, I placed my hands on the steering wheel, perhaps twice the size of my Alfa's wheel. I couldn't reach the top without leaning way forward. To turn the wheel, I had to lift my butt off the seat.

I could see forever. The bus was about forty feet long and eight-and-a-half feet wide. The driver's seat, about level with a sedan's top, left me feeling above the world. Large mirrors on the left and right gave visibility down the length of the bus and into the next lane. The

82

rear-view mirror reflected a wide view of the parking lot behind us. I had three-hundred sixty-degree vision. I imagined this was how my father felt sitting in the engineer's cab of a train: peering down at the world, high visibility front and sides, ready to follow the tracks into the distance. He wasn't an engineer; he worked the tracks. But he got to sit in the engine cab to help with mechanical work. *I wonder if he ever dreamed of riding off into the distance, following the tracks toward an unknown adventure.*

"It's so big! How do I know where the sides are? How do I fit in the lane?"

John drove most people crazy with his detailed training, indicating the best time to change lanes to get off the freeway, when to start signaling, and things like that. But it didn't bother me. I wanted to know every detail.

"You know where the left side of the bus is," he explained. True, the left side was about six inches from my elbow. "And you know the bus fits in the lane, so as long as your left side is close to the white line, don't worry about the right side." It made perfect sense. "Plus, look in the mirrors."

I drove the bus forward and braked. "Notice how long it takes to stop, much longer than a car. And the more people in the bus or jitney, the longer it takes to stop." I nodded. "Leave more following room than you do in a car."

There wasn't a soul in the parking lot, so I had free rein. I drove forward and made turns, using the parking lot stripes as a lane guide, getting a feel for the bus.

Then, I had to back up the behemoth. "To pass the driving test," John said, "you have to back up alongside the building." Without hitting the building, he didn't need to add.

Practice, practice, practice.

After a couple of weeks, John gave me the driving test. The Department of Motor Vehicles had authorized him to sign off on Class 2 licenses. Thus, I started my short bus-driving career.

No longer on the Cubic Day, I worked the swing shift, driving from about two in the afternoon until ten at night. Being off in the mornings felt like the entire world was working for my pleasure. I jogged at Lake Merritt before work and enjoyed leisurely breakfasts and lunches. I relished the freedom of the road, even if it was only on city streets and a few freeway miles. I met almost everyone who lived at the Clumps, half-listening to snippets of conversations while concentrating on driving. When someone on the freeway drove erratically, my passengers' conversations faded as if someone lowered the radio volume while I fixated on the traffic. Danger averted, the background volume cranked up.

Better than driving the bus was shuttling residents in our fourteen-passenger jitney over fifty miles to Tomales, a nearly two-hour drive across the Richmond-San Raphael Bridge. Driving north on the top-level toward San Raphael, I could see the San Francisco Bay stretching to the left past Oakland, almost to San Jose, with views of the San Francisco Bay Bridge, Treasure Island, Alcatraz, San Francisco, a quick glimpse of the Golden Gate, finally ending in a view of San Quentin. Off to the right were old whale processing docks with a backdrop of the Marin County hills. I always cracked the window open to smell a mix of seaweed and salty air. Sometimes the water was gray, reflecting the overcast. On other days, it was a dazzling blue, mirroring the cerulean sky.

The last jitney left Tomales at 8:00 p.m., and passengers got sleepy on the dark drive back to Oakland. In my rearview mirror, I watched them drift off and then pop their eyes open. "I don't want you to fall asleep," they told me.

Please just sleep, I wanted to respond. You're interrupting my radio show. You're interrupting the joy of knowing every curve and every bump on the road. This was my favorite route: the peace of driving over winding roads, practicing perfect acceleration out of the apex of every curve, and listening to the radio.

I drove the bus and jitneys for about six months. Bobby and I were on different schedules; he worked days while I worked the swing shift. He always waited for me when my shift ended. We slept in on our days off; we often jogged three miles around Lake Merritt. I was living in my utopia: in love, working, and living with friends in a stimulating environment, feeling like I was making the world a better place, having no inkling of how Synanon would change.

I have dreams about those jitney rides now.

I drive the jitney to Tomales Bay and drop off my passengers, but then I miss the turn. The road narrows into a mile of dust and gravel, the wheels rattling beneath, the scorching sun beating down on dry hay fields. The air is thick with the dry, choking smell of grass and dirt. There's no place to turn around. My chest tightens. How do I get back to the pickup spot? I'm going to be late. I can already see them waiting, angry, suspicious, imagining I've stolen the jitney and split.

I glance left, right, behind. Nothing looks familiar. Then, looming out of the wavering heat, a compound rises. Kerry's place. Chuck's daughter. My pulse races. I grip the wheel with sweaty hands, wanting to sink down, vanish, anything but be seen.

A cluster of women gather there, my age but untouchable, their circle closed tight. The princesses. I catch a glimpse of them through the dust, sharp outlines in the sun. My stomach knots. I hope they don't see me, hope the jitney doesn't betray me with its noise and dust. I don't belong here.

Over the years, my mind has played tricks on me. I yearn to be back in my community for the connectedness, the kinship, and the hugs that lasted forever. Yet, in a way, I was always an outsider, never part of the elite group. I tried to join a few times. I applied for the second Academy. Chuck and Betty had started an Academy for teenagers and twenty-somethings, always the best-looking youth, to apprentice under them. Chuck was grooming the Academy group to be the next leaders. I had applied to the second Academy, and they turned me down. My insecure self whispered, *you're not smart enough. You're not pretty enough.* Next, I applied to be the seamstress for Betty D. Another rejection.

Maybe they didn't want me. Maybe I didn't want them.

The Synanon bus that I drove through Oakland.
Photo courtesy of Synanon.com

Chapter 11: They Have to Hit Rock Bottom

Spring 1973, Detroit, Michigan

My bus-driving career ended when Synanon sent Bobby and me to Detroit for a six-month sales trip. As Bobby and I packed our meager belongings, we broke into grins, twirling around the room. I had never been out of California. I had never flown on a plane. Neither of us could stand still.

I barely had enough time to see Mom for a quick goodbye. "You're so lucky," she marveled. "Moving into Synanon was the best thing you ever did." She was so supportive of my communal life that I sometimes wondered if she would move in if she had the chance. But maybe she was simply keeping a lifeline open—she would be there if I needed her.

The Detroit facility was a large two-story house fronting Shaeffer Road, with traffic whizzing by day and night. Instead of entering through a lobby as in Oakland, we walked into a living room with cozy couches and chairs. A bluish snowfield twinkled through the windows. A large kitchen with a built-in dining room opened off the living room. Homelike.

The Director and his wife lived in one upstairs bedroom; the second bedroom served as Office Services, where I would work as an administrative assistant. The rest of us stayed in apartments a few miles away.

I felt more married in Detroit, maybe because living in a home setting with only a couple dozen people instead of five hundred gave us more time together. Maybe it was because we worked the same hours and drove a car home to our apartment instead of taking the bus. Maybe it was because Bobby wasn't preoccupied with helping newcomers and glad-handing directors. I had all his attention. At the end of our workday, I ran to the door when the sales team returned from their cold calling, welcoming him home like a scene out of *Leave It to Beaver*. His touch electrified me, and we made love almost every night.

We started the weekdays with Morning Meeting, and I beamed watching Bobby energize the sales team with his infectious joie de vivre. The team drove off to sell, and I walked upstairs to my job as an administrative assistant.

I excelled at office work—corresponding with the California facilities, typing letters, fielding phone calls, and setting up tickler files. Synanon had put me through a "How to Drive a Desk" course, and I used all of it. Only three of us worked upstairs: the Director's wife, our one Hustler, Serena, and me.

Serena spent her day calling companies to ask for donations. She told them about her heroin addiction and how Synanon saved her. A sign on her desk read: "Perseverance Furthers."

"What's with the sign?" I asked, thinking it was probably something about if you asked and asked for donations, something would come through.

Leaning on her elbows and looking up through her straight brown bangs, she explained, "A couple of years ago, a bunch of us were reading the I Ching." I remembered doing that in the Game Club but didn't take it seriously enough to do more than dabble.

She went on. "Someone said perseverance meant the reaping of rewards, like a harvest, that you persevere, then harvest your crops, and that creates a new beginning." She sat up straight, her smile lighting up her face. "And I thought, that's me in Synanon. My new beginning. The sign reminds me to keep going, take the next step and keep going forward."

Serena, quiet and serene, was a perfect example of someone ridding her body of addictions to find her true self. It is still amazing to me that we took hope-to-die drug addicts off the street, helped them rid their bodies of drugs, gave them a job and respect, and then remarkable, intelligent, talented people emerged.

"That's deep. I thought it had to do with asking for donations. I would hate to do that." I was content typing letters to help Synanon in my own way.

"It's fun," she laughed. "People love to give us things. And I meet interesting people. Did you know that Sam Walton said if I ever needed a job to just give him a call?"

Sam Walton was the founder and CEO of Walmart. I've often wondered if Serena looked him up when she left Synanon. Serena was one of the threads of friendship I carried in Synanon. These connections wove through my life as I moved from facility to facility, job to job—drifting in like fog, lingering for a while, then dissolving without a trace.

Soon, reality hit. Right when we were enjoying so much time together, Bobby and the sales team left for a six-week sales trip to Chicago. Alone again, I displayed a false bravado by hanging out at the house until everyone went to bed, jabbering with residents and Game Players. Back at my apartment, I reached for him across the bed and buried my head in his pillow, breathing in the lingering scent of patchouli. Then he came home, and I was married, and we laughed and made passionate love. Then he left for a two-week sales trip. Then single, then married.

On weekend days off, when Bobby was gone, a bunch of us explored Detroit, passing neighborhoods still decimated from the 1967 riots five years earlier, solidifying my belief in Synanon—we would never leave a building or a neighborhood in shambles. Then one day, I said, "Hey, why don't we drive to Canada? It's right across the bridge." We didn't need passports in those days.

Serena checked out a jitney, and four of us piled in.

Soon, we reached the Ambassador Bridge, a suspension bridge reminding me of the Golden Gate but not painted orange. Canada sparkled on the other side of the river. We drove across the bridge and up to the Canadian checkpoint. A border patrol officer looked at our driver's licenses and walked around our van. He returned, grim-faced, leaned over toward Serena, and looked us each in the eye.

"Why do you have packages of brand-new shock absorbers in the back of your van?" He didn't carry a gun, but I had no doubt he could detain us. "Are you planning to sell them?"

Serena exhaled, trying not to laugh while she explained. "We live in Synanon. The shock absorbers are a donation that I picked up yesterday. I didn't have a chance to take them out of the van."

His stony expression told me he didn't believe her. "Let me see your purses." We passed them all to Serena.

The officer first rummaged through Serena's purse and pulled out a bag of loose tea.

Eyebrows raised, he demanded, "What's this?"

I tried not to giggle at the absurdity of our drug-free group being arrested for stolen goods and drugs.

Oh, my God, he must think it's pot. We're going to jail.

He opened the bag and took a whiff. Earl Grey.

Not finding anything in our purses more exciting than tea, he waved us forward.

We crossed the bridge and drove around for about an hour, too spooked to even walk into a store. We rolled down our windows and drove through neighborhoods of two-story, well-kept houses with perfectly groomed, emerald-green lawns bordered with flowers bursting in color: reds, yellows, pinks, whites, their scents mixing with freshly mown lawn, perfuming the inside of our jitney. I didn't see one piece of trash.

As we approached the Ambassador Bridge to return home, I looked across the river to Detroit, spewing black smoke from its factories, the buildings gray with soot.

I breathed a sigh of relief when we returned to Synanon, my island of sanity.

Perhaps it was the contrast with the bustle of the Oakland facility that brought me peace, deepening my sense of belonging. I jogged along the avenues almost every morning. Sunday mornings we ate bagels and cream cheese, something I had never tasted, having grown up with Grapenuts and day-old bread. While others dove into the fresh lox, I smothered my bagel with cream cheese and strawberry jam. Biting into the bagel, jam dripped down my chin. One bagel became two, and by the time I returned to Oakland, I had gained ten pounds.

Some evenings, I went on speaking engagements to tell the story of Synanon, the miracle of curing substance abusers. An ex-addict and I spoke to a women's business group. My heart almost stopped when they greeted us with a board filled with samples of drugs from heroin to cocaine to weed. I half expected my co-host to drool over it, but she calmly handed the board back and said, "We won't be needing this."

When the snow melted, the Director's wife and I dug up the lawn and planted a vegetable garden.

And I interviewed my first addict.

After one Morning Meeting, Director Dave asked me to help with an interview. Not a job interview—an interview with a substance misuser who wanted to move into Synanon.

I stepped back and avoided his eyes. My stomach roiled, and I broke out in a sweat. Me? What could I say to this addict? I hadn't even smoked cigarettes, let alone used drugs.

Looking at the floor, I replied, "I've never done an interview," hoping he would realize how foolish it was to have me—a square—interview an addict.

"You've lived in Synanon a couple of years. It's time you learned to do interviews. Come on." He walked with me into the study and motioned for me to sit next to him.

The snowfield outside the window no longer looked like a sparkling wonderland. The gray sky turned the world into a cold, uninviting ice planet. I was happy to be inside.

After we were seated, Director Dave's wife escorted in a scruffy-looking man, maybe in his early twenties, wearing tight jeans and a baggy hoodie. He had long, scraggly, mousy blond hair and looked like he should stink, but the stench of cigarette smoke masked any other odors. The young man slumped into a chair opposite the three of us, eyes looking defiant.

"I'm Dave, and this is Janet. What's your name, and what brings you here?"

"Uh, Lewis."

"Well, Lewis, what can we do for you?"

"I gotta' get off drugs, man."

"Well, we can help you if that's what you want to do."

Lewis nodded, looking a little more interested.

Director Dave looked him square in the face. "Up until now, the end point of your life is here. All the values you accumulated brought you here. What you thought you learned from everyone, teachers, parents, brought you here. You missed the boat."

Lewis sat up straight, thrusting his chin forward. "That's not it, man. It's just the drugs. They say you can get me off drugs."

Director Dave interrupted, his voice stern. "It's not the drugs, Lewis. The drugs are your excuse. You don't know how to live. I know that because here you are."

Lewis gulped.

"Here's the deal. We'll take you in and feed you and clothe you and get you off drugs. We'll teach you to be a decent human being. You just have to act as if you believe we know what we're doing and do everything we say. If we want you to mop the floor, you mop the floor."

Lewis nodded.

"You do what we say, and we'll teach you how to live without drugs. We'll start by cutting your hair."

"I'm not cutting my hair, man. What does that have to do with getting clean?"

I bit my lip, wanting to tell him his hair wasn't important. We could cure him! I let Director Dave do the talking.

"It has everything to do with getting clean. You're a dopefiend. That's all you've done with your life." Director Dave's voice rose. "I can take one look at you and see you're a failure. And I'll tell you what." He pointed at Lewis. "We know how to fix you. We know how to turn you into a man. But if you won't even cut your hair, we can't help you."

Lewis scowled, looking from Director Dave to me like he was weighing his options.

"I'm not cutting my hair." He got up and strode out of the room, leaving the door open.

I started to go after him, wanting to rescue this young man. "Listen, Lewis…" Everyone who came to Synanon to get off drugs followed instructions. That was the first step to getting clean. Why would Lewis turn his back on us?

Director Dave cut me off. "Let him go. We can't help him if he won't help himself."

I followed Dave back into the living room, where a forty-ish-looking woman stood watching Lewis stomp out the front door, slamming it behind him. She looked ordinary, dressed in slacks and a winter coat, like my mother and friends' mothers. Her strained face intensified her deep, premature wrinkles. Mouth hanging open, she looked questioningly at Director Dave.

"There's nothing we can do for your son, Ma'am," Dave told her matter-of-factly.

The mother's body slumped. She grabbed the back of a chair to hold herself up. With a long sigh, she looked sorrowfully at the closed door and asked, "What am I supposed to do? You were my last hope."

"There's nothing you can do for him. We can't help him if he won't help himself. He has to hit rock bottom, and then maybe he'll come back."

I wanted to hug her and let her cry on my shoulder, but I knew I had to demonstrate tough love, even to the mother. I merely stood with my hands at my sides with what I hoped was a stern look.

I have watched this play out over and over in my life—the furtive attempt to fix those we love. The realization that change or rehabilitation has to come from the person in trouble; that he or she may not change until there is nowhere else to turn. I'm thankful I have not had to make that decision in my life. I don't think I could do it—let my child sink. Still, for any problems my children encounter, I hold out a lifeline, like my mother did for me.

We never saw Lewis again.

I like to think Lewis tried an alternate drug rehab program. Today, there are over seventeen thousand treatment programs, but few existed in 1973.[4] I was vaguely aware of other rehab centers—many had been started by Synanon Splittees. Nixon had declared a war on drugs and enacted policies to encourage drug treatment.[5] But in 1973, Synanon was still regarded as the best.

Nixon's reputation for fighting drugs was lost with the Watergate hearings. As the snow melted from the streets of Detroit and the field of snow behind the house gave way to a not-yet-green lawn, Director Dave implored us to watch the Watergate hearings on the nightly

4. Jenny Yang. "Total number of substance abuse treatment facilities in the U.S. from 2003 to 2023." https://www.statista.com/statistics/450281/total-number-of-substance-abuse-treatment-facilities-in-the-us/#:~:text=In%202023%2C%20there%20were%2017%2C561%20substance%20abuse%20treatment,notified%20via%20email%20when%20this%20statistic%20is%20updated, accessed December 24, 2024.

5. The Editors of Encyclopedia Britannica, revised and updated by Adam Augustyn. https://www.britannica.com/topic/war-on-drugs, accessed March 15, 2025.

news.

"This is huge. Pay attention," he said every night, gathering us around the television. "The President could be impeached over this."

I tried to watch the hearings, but they were so boring—old men in suits droning on and on. They needed a Game to get to the truth.

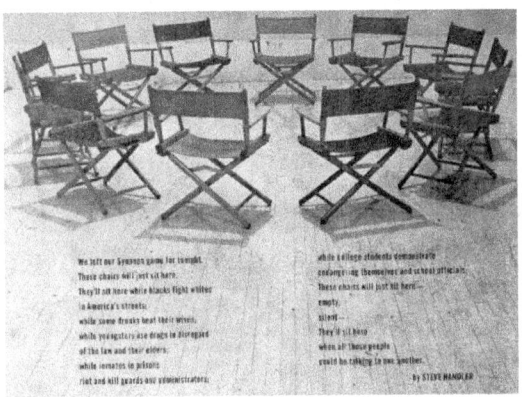

A Synanon poster, words by Steve Handler.
Photo courtesy of Synanon.com

We left our Synanon game for tonight.
These chairs will just sit here.
They'll sit here while blacks fight whites
in America's streets;
while some drunks beat their wives;
while youngsters use drugs in disregard
of the law and their elders,
while inmates in prisons
riot and kill guards and administrators,
while college students demonstrate
endangering themselves and school officials.
These chairs will just sit here
empty
silent —
They'll sit here
when all these people
could be talking to one another.

Chapter 12: Mandatory Aerobics

1973, Oakland, California

Aerobics. Healthy—right?

I always held my head high. I had joined a community that gave up drugs, alcohol, and violence. And then one day—before I moved in—they quit smoking. Wow! Ahead of their time! How proud I was to live in such a wholesome community. And now, aerobics! Another plus.

How did I not see how wrong it all was?

Shortly before my twenty-third birthday, Bobby and I moved back to Oakland. A summer hot spell pushed the temperatures into the nineties, sweltering for Oakland, where no one had air conditioning. The heat waves wiggled through the air, and the smell of sweat mingled with the scent of perfume as we rode the Synanon bus to our apartment across town. Beads of perspiration broke out on Bobby's forehead. We slept naked, our bodies wound around each other like black and white braided bread.

We settled into our old routines: Bobby selling pens locally for Synanon's ADGAP business and me working in Office Services. Someone else drove the bus. It was as if we hadn't even been gone.

Except things were shifting in degrees so subtle I didn't notice, like the frog that doesn't realize it's being boiled alive.

One cliché we spouted to each other was, "The only constant in the universe is change." So, when Chuck demanded changes, I embraced the universal constant. Met the changes with enthusiasm instead of seeing them for what they were: compliance demanded by an authoritarian leader.

Chuck made a rare visit to Oakland, so I joined the rest of the community in the living room to hear him speak.

"We're all going to start doing aerobics," Chuck announced.

He started running in place. "Look how easy it is." He panted. "We're all going to get healthy." My mouth hung open as I watched this larger-than-life man jogging, going nowhere, knees raising waist high, belly bouncing up and down, sweat dripping down his face. I tried not to laugh. He must have worn shorts and tennis shoes, but in my mind, I can't picture him wearing anything but overalls. "All you do," he huffed, "is raise your right leg." His breathing came in waves, and he could utter only a few words with each breath. "Then your left leg." Another breath. "Waist high." Breath. "Every day."

He stopped after a few minutes. "And that's how you do it. I've never felt better in my life." We cheered.

Chuck's doctor had warned him: lose weight or risk a heart attack. If it was good enough for Chuck, it was good enough for all of us.

Chuck latched onto Dr. Kenneth Cooper's 1968 book *Aerobics* and declared running-in-place our new communal ritual. No equipment needed. Each facility set up an aerobics room so we could all bounce in place—publicly, of course, so everyone could see you were   obedient.

Chuck asked—well, demanded—our live-in doctors to create stretching routines to follow the fifteen-minute sessions.

I thought it was a healthy plus. I'd been on the cross-country team in high school. Bobby and I jogged three miles around Lake Merritt. What's wrong with asking everyone to be healthy?

What was wrong was that it wasn't a community decision. It was a command. Run-in-place or leave. Another decree. Like no smoking. It's almost like he was preparing us for what was to come. Maybe he was.

Chuck had ordered everyone to quit smoking in 1970, while I was still in the Game Club. It was the third rule—after no violence and no drugs. His best friend had lung cancer. Chuck quit smoking to support him—or maybe he quit out of fear of cancer.

When Chuck quit, everyone quit.

Sounded healthy. Revolutionary to my twenty-year-old mind: An entire community quit smoking.

But what was it really? A leader demanding that they quit smoking or leave.

Before Synanon quit smoking, it housed close to two thousand residents—most of them smokers, each receiving a free pack of cigarettes daily. The day before the ban, Synanon was offered a donation: enough cigarettes to supply every resident for a year. They turned it down on the eve of its arrival.

Hundreds left instead of giving up cigarettes. They were branded

Splittees. Quitters.

The population shrunk. It would never recover.

Chuck, who once considered naming his fledgling empire *Tender Loving Care*, enforced the smoking ban with no hint of tenderness. No compassion. No grace. No easing off. No tender loving care like heroin addicts received when they kicked.

Just quit smoking or leave.

No one split over aerobics. I've learned that some skipped their aerobics—something I never contemplated. One guy even started his running-in-place a little before midnight, technically finishing the next day. He counted it as two days' worth of aerobics.

I used to boast that we were pioneers—giving up cigarettes, doing aerobics before it was trendy. The truth is, none of it came from us. We were following Chuck, the "benevolent dictator" he claimed to be.

I never thought to question Chuck, unaware of how the smallest steps can carry you into the abyss.

Synanon members running in place
Photo courtesy of Synanon.com

Chapter 13: The Voice of God

1973, Oakland, California

I didn't see it coming. The creeping normality.

Like everything in Synanon, the Wire was fun in the beginning. It began when DJ Don kicked off an in-house radio broadcast: KSYN.

I first heard the Wire reverberating through loudspeakers when Bobby and I returned to Oakland in 1973. At first, the light-hearted show aired a few hours a day, like DJ Don's old talk radio show on KSFO, where he threw out a topic, and people called in to comment.

One sunny afternoon, with DJ Don's show broadcasting in the background, I sat typing at my desk, bright sunshine filtering through the daffodil-colored curtains I had sewn to screen us from pedestrians. Someone must have donated the fabric to Synanon; it was the only piece long enough to cover the floor-to-ceiling windows. "Thanks for the curtains, but now our office looks like a bumblebee," my boss had remarked. My face turned red, but he was right. Someone had painted the walls black, and we were now working inside a beehive.

"That's the only fabric we had," I defended. "At least people walking by can't see us."

DJ Don, speaking on the Wire, interrupted my thoughts. He was ranting about Synanon needing to rein in its spending. "Do you know how much we spend on tampons?" He had a dollar amount. "You women should think about how many tampons you use."

Really? A man is telling me how many tampons to use?

I called in. "Don, sometimes my period is so heavy that I have to use two tampons at once. How am I supposed to cut down?"

"Uh, let's move onto another topic," he snapped.

That's when the Wire was fun, back when I had a boisterous laugh and made witty comments.

Soon, like a glimpse into the Internet future, our electronics whizzes connected the radio to all the facilities via telephone lines.

Weren't we amazing! Now we were all connected to Chuck and to each other. I reveled in our interconnectedness.

Tender Loving Care

KSYN grew from announcements and light banter to broadcasting Games and Stews, making them public. I don't think any of us knew the Wire would change the Game, the bedrock of Synanon. It would become a megaphone for Chuck. It would introduce twenty-four-hour, seven-days-a-week indoctrination.

Chuck spoke to us over the Wire. He no longer needed to visit facilities; he merely called DJ Don during his show or dropped in on Games that were being broadcast from Home Place.

When Chuck spoke on the Wire, the background chatter of life diminished. Now, even I, who had never lived in the same facility with Chuck nor had ever met him, could listen to him preach or rant as if I were in the same room.

It was like the voice of God.

Chuck was on the Wire talking to one of the live-in architects. I stopped what I was doing and listened.

Chuck yelled in his gruff voice: "What the hell do you call those apartments you designed? The walls are so thin you can hear the person next door fucking!"

The architect, defending himself: "I won architectural awards for those apartments. You don't have any sense of style."

Chuck: "Style? I'm talking about being able to live without hearing your neighbor flush the toilet! What are you going to do about it?"

Architect: "There's nothing to do, they're done. People are already living there. They love it."

Chuck: "You fuckin' Lifestylers have your heads up your ass. One of my dopefiends could have done a better job. You're all fucking character disorders. Why else would you live in this nuthouse?"

His words stabbed me in the gut. I'm a Lifestyler. I have to prove myself worthy.

And on it went—the background of my life.

The Wire. It changed everything. I believed the Game was our iconoclastic tool. In Games, we learned to understand each other emotionally. I was sure that through the Game, we could teach the world how to break racial tension and appreciate and love each other. The Game worked mainly because of the dichotomy of in-the-Game and out-of-the-Game. The Game was almost private, like a therapy session. We were venting feelings. But we were also coercing members into how to think, how to behave.

With Games broadcast over the Wire, I lost the distinction of in- and out-of-the-Game. Somehow, my privacy felt safe when I was in a closed room. I wasn't alone. We began donning Mobius loops before each Game—an infinity scarf sewn with a half twist so there is neither an inside nor an outside. We ceremoniously removed the scarves when we left the Game to signify returning to real life.

Games echoing over the loudspeakers morphed into reality, even though the snatches of conversation—like the soundbites of today— were out of context. Chuck's words booming through the hallways seeped into my soul.

Chuck: "You're a fucking deadbeat. Go the hell out and get a job. The days are over when you get to lie around sucking off the teat of Synanon."

He wasn't talking to me. I don't know who he was talking to, but I was determined not to be a deadbeat. I doubled down with my enthusiasm.

Another Game over the Wire:

Random Person: "You have a bad fuckin' attitude. All I want to see out of you is teeth and fuzz. If you can't do that, go scrub pots until you figure it out. Or get the hell out of here."

The words reverberated through my mind without me even realizing it. Don't be a deadbeat. Work your ass off. Smile. Don't show negativity.

Another random Game in the background:

A resident: "Why did you toss my room? My bed's made. There's not a speck of dust. What the fuck?"

A Director: "You have too much glut!"

My reaction: Glut means owning too many belongings. Do I have too much stuff?

I lived simply. It wasn't hard. Growing up, we had little money. When school started every year, Mom bought me two new dresses, and my sister gave me her hand-me-downs. I learned to sew when I was eight and sewed all my clothes. I owned one pair of shoes, which I held in my hands while walking to school in the rain to protect them. Accumulating glut wasn't something I had to worry about, but

I did.

With Games and discussions reverberating through the hallways, I absorbed the words and made them my own. Was it peer pressure? Programming? Indoctrination? Brainwashing? Today, academics refer to "coercive persuasion"—a broadly a controlled program of social influence to bring about substantial changes in behavior and attitude in members of a group (e.g., military recruits, cult followers).[6]

If asked, I would have told you there was no peer pressure; I simply agreed with everything Synanon had to say. I learned early in life to follow the rules to avoid getting spanked or having my mouth washed out with soap like my sister did. I made sure that didn't happen to me.

Everything we did reinforced the party line, from Saturday Night Parties to Morning Meetings to the Game. I parroted Chuck without realizing it: Follow the rules or leave. You're a character disorder; you can't make it in society. If you're not happy here, leave, but you'll probably fall down a manhole (get back on drugs). I believed that, and I was a square.

I see that now. There were signs of a cult from the beginning, but I didn't notice them. It felt normal.

The Boot Camp marching at my 1972 wedding. *Photo courtesy of Synanon.com*

6. American Psychology Association. "APA Dictionary of Psychology." https://dictionary.apa.org/coercive-persuasion, accessed April 18, 2025.

Chapter 14: Betrayal

1974, Oakland, California

I jumped out of the jitney in the Oakland parking lot on a spring afternoon. Shade from tall buildings cooled my sunburned face. I had spent the morning hiking on the Ranch property, my below-shoulder-length wavy hair rubber-banded into a ponytail. *Maybe I'll take a swim and a sauna. Then dinner with Bobby.* My heart skipped a beat, thinking of seeing Bobby. Too bad he had to work and couldn't come with me today.

As my feet touched the asphalt, a man called out to us, gesturing earnestly. "Hurry into the dining room. There's a General Meeting just starting!"

"What? Where? Now?" I stammered, my mouth going dry. I wanted to run the other way, but I followed him. I had heard of these General Meetings, community gatherings that originated in the earliest days of Synanon when the first residents copped out—confessed—to using drugs.

What happened? Did someone get busted for drugs? Stealing? Too much glut? Oh my God, I had heard about General Meetings, but I thought they were something from the old days. Not something for 1974. Butterflies filled my stomach.

I took deep breaths as I approached the dining room, trying to conjure a happy image of assemblies from grammar school when we quietly amassed in the auditorium for announcements. The lights were blazing like spotlights, even though it was sunny outside, sending a chill down my spine. People sat in rows of folding chairs as if they had gathered to watch a play. The welcoming coffee urns, snacks, and dining tables were gone. An eerie quiet had settled in, replacing our community's ever-present background chatter.

Jeez, I think every single person in our Oakland facility is here. Bobby sat stone-faced across the room, looking straight forward. Most people looked at the floor, hands clasped on their laps. The butterflies in my stomach swarmed.

I tiptoed in.

DJ Don stood at the front of the room, glaring at the assemblage like a lord looking over his serfs, counting heads to ensure no one was missing. Alongside him were Tribe Leaders and department managers, arms folded across their chests, eyes narrowed, and jaws jutting forward.

I belong up front. But will Don yell at me for being late, or tell me I don't belong there?

The Director recently promoted me to lead the Maintenance Department, a position of some stature, certainly not up there with the Director, but I managed about twenty residents. I trembled at the thought of walking up front uninvited.

I sat down a few rows from the front, holding my head high while my heart pounded, certain DJ Don would invite me forward.

DJ Don looked me in the eye. "Wipe that smirk off your face, Janet!" My sunburned face prickled. I shrank into myself, trying to become invisible while feeling naked, on display, with the entire community staring at me. I bit my lip to keep it from trembling.

DJ Don took his eyes off me and surveyed the room. "There's a lot of bullshit going on around here, and we're going to clean things up right now." His voice rose. "We're sick and tired of you lazy bums fucking up our community. Who's sneaking drugs? Who's breaking containment? No one does this alone; it's time to break that contract with your friend."

Silence. Some squirming.

Containment? We're having a general meeting about containment?

I already knew about holding contracts. It was different from being "put on a contract," where a member had to earn his way back into the community's good graces. Holding a contract meant keeping someone's secret—a private pact, like knowing they were using drugs on the sly. I'd had it drilled into me that keeping such secrets could drive a person back to drugs.

But containment?

Containment was Synanon's latest experiment. The gist of it was that our community could provide everything we needed, so we had to contain our time and energy within Synanon. If we wanted something, we'd figure out how to make it, or a Lifestyler would bring it in, or the Hustlers would hustle it up. Our friendships and activities must be contained within Synanon.

I tried to disregard the tirade. DJ Don, ceaselessly screaming, reminded me of my father. I wanted to cover my ears, to hide, but there was nowhere to go. I sat and let the words wash over me. Intellectually, I knew DJ Don wasn't speaking to me, but it felt like he was. Each word stabbed me in the gut. My stomach was in knots.

One by one, residents spoke up and copped out to breaking a rule. Or they copped out on a friend.

"My roommate has so many clothes she can barely close her closet door."

A Tribe Leader bellowed, "What the fuck do you need all those clothes for? Bring them back to the general store where you got them! We have newcomers with nothing to wear. You're another taker. Take, take, take. I'm sick of you people."

"I've been breaking containment by going out to movies and spending my WAM on hot dogs," a man said glumly.

DJ Don snarled. "You don't get it. Breaking containment breaks our community. I gave up everything to live here. Synanon provides me with a great life. And I'm not gonna let you ruin it for me." He glared at the admittee, then spoke sternly. "Our community provides everything you need. There's nothing out there for you!"

He looked around the room, glaring at anyone who made eye contact. "Who else? Who else? There are more of you motherfuckers breaking containment!" I knew the pressure wouldn't dissipate until enough people copped out.

DJ Don's blue eyes flicked toward me; I wished I could make myself invisible. I looked down to avoid his eyes.

Surely this doesn't apply to me. I'm a square. Dopefiends should stay away from their old life, so they don't go back to using drugs, obviously. I'm just here for the social movement.

A few residents copped out to hanging out with Splittees. Splittee. That's what you were when you left, a quitter who didn't know how good you had it. When someone split, it was like they dropped off the face of the earth. We continually had to prove our commitment and gratitude to Synanon or split. Hanging out with Splittees meant you had one foot out the door; you weren't one hundred percent committed to Synanon. We were always reminded—and I believed it by then—there was no other place you fit in or belonged.

"Who else?" DJ Don demanded. "Who else is hanging out with Splittees?" He looked me in the eye when I dared to look up. "We're cleaning house!"

I broke into a sweat, a pit in my stomach. *There is one more.* I looked up at Don.

"Bobby goes out and plays cards with Andy and Rodney every Thursday night." There, I said it. I'm one of the good guys willing to break a contract with my husband.

"What the fuck, Bobby! You're hanging out with Splittees?" Don screamed, spittle flying.

I stole a glance at Bobby across the room, his face crestfallen.

DJ Don glared at Bobby. "We took you in as a kid, fed you, taught you how to live, and this is how you repay us?"

DJ Don disgraced Bobby before his community—his extended family—merely for seeing his old friends. And I'm the one who informed. Copping out on my husband was supposed to make me feel better. It didn't. The knot in my stomach turned to nausea.

What have I done? Mom always told me not to tattle. She was right. Why didn't I keep my mouth shut? Oh, Bobby, I'm sorry.

I put Synanon ahead of my husband. My chest tightened. It still tightens today.

Finally, the meeting ended, and I sought out Bobby. He gave me a bitter smile. "You're right, Beest," he sighed. "I won't see them anymore." That didn't make me feel any better.

Elizabeth tried to console me by touting the party line. "You were saving his life. We break contracts to save lives." It didn't feel like that; it felt like a betrayal, like I crossed my moral boundary. Bobby's crime was staying in touch with his Splittee friends. My crime was getting him in trouble. I'm certain he would have stopped going out to see his friends after the General Meeting—I didn't need to bring it up to the entire community.

I told myself I was honorable, yet I still get a knot in my stomach when I think about it all these years later.

We put the General Meeting behind us. By that, I mean we never spoke of it. Which is crazy, because in Games we talked about the minutia of life—work, anger, hurt feelings, sex—however Bobby and I never talked about that elephant in the room. Never.

Some years ago, our son Robert, who was born in Synanon one year after the General Meeting, started asking about Synanon. His dad and I never spoke to him of the place we met and fell in love. Bobby told Robert if it weren't for Synanon, we would still be together, and that our downfall started with him playing cards with his friends. Robert asked me, "Do you think he slept around on you?"

"No, that would have come out. There's no way he could have kept that secret."

But I know what Bobby meant. It wasn't the card playing; it was the General Meeting.

Bobby must have felt what I did: humiliation was something to endure. I learned that as a child, suffering my father's spankings and his mood swings—shifting from ignoring me to yelling at me. I'm sure Bobby had a similar response to being hit with a belt by his father, and then watching him hit his mother. We endured, then forged ahead. You can't let these mishaps ruin your life.

What was more important? Facing reprimands or embracing the life I cherished—living in community with friends and family and the man I was in love with?

DJ Don humiliated me, and then I opened the door for him to humiliate Bobby. Humiliation was one of Synanon's key manipulative tools. Bobby's and my childhood survival techniques followed us into Synanon.

Now I wonder if this was a test for DJ Don to prove to Chuck that he could stand up to the old-timers and kick butt. Or perhaps it was proof to himself that he was part of the power structure and had to lord that power over all of us.

All I know is that he made it clear he was in control, and Bobby and I were mere flunkies.

Chapter 15: The Breeders

1974 – Walker Creek, Marshall, California

The dining room was bright from the early evening sunlight flooding the windows when Bobby and I had dinner. The aroma of chicken made my stomach grumble.

We loaded our plates and sat near a window, watching the sun reflect on the buildings across the street. Before Bobby took a bite, I asked, "Did you hear about the Breeders?"

"What are you talking about? Breeders? Something at the Ranch?"

Grinning, I grabbed his hands and peered into his deep brown eyes. "I heard some talk on the Wire about a new group starting up. Anyone who wants to have a baby can move to Tomales Bay and join this new group called the Breeders."

His eyes lit up, and he opened his mouth to speak, but I was chattering too fast to stop. "It's kind of a play on words. Someone in the Agriculture Department named Cynthia thought it was a funny name. And Chuck liked it, so it stuck."

"A baby!" he said when I took a breath. "We can have a baby?"

"Well, we have to apply and get accepted first. But yes! Do you want to?"

"Of course." He stammered. "I mean, oh my God. We're going to have a baby!" He jumped up and then pulled me to my feet, laughing.

"Not yet." I placed my hands on his broad shoulders. "We still have to apply." Then I leaped into his arms. "But yes! Plus, we'd get to move to Tomales!"

We sat back down. "Mmm, dinner's delish tonight," he murmured, taking a few bites. He had calmed down, but was still grinning. "So, tell me again, how does this Breeders thing work?"

"The idea is that all the couples who get pregnant live in the same area in Tomales. Something about making friends while we're pregnant so we can support each other when we have babies." I grinned. "A baby!!"

"Let's do it, Beest! I want to have a baby with you!" His eyes twinkled. "We can start practicing tonight!"

We had to apply. Not to have a baby—lots of women in Synanon had babies. This was a chance to have a baby <u>and</u> take part in a new experiment. An experiment in Tomales, the heart of Synanon. We sent a letter via interoffice mail to Cynthia, saying we'd like to join the Breeders. Cynthia and her husband, Jay, were putting the group together. They had come up with the idea together, and then Chuck gave it his blessing. Cynthia told me later that Jay wanted to run the group to show his organizational skills so he could move up the ladder to management.

We received a welcome-to-the-Breeders note a few days later.

I threw my arms around Bobby, teasingly tracing my tongue along his ear. "Let's burn the diaphragm!"

I laughed, remembering the day our Lifestyler doctor fit me for it. I had switched from birth control pills to an IUD because of health scares over blood clots, but then the IUD made me bleed every time I had sex. Talk about spoiling a night of passion. Enter the diaphragm.

Lifestyler Doc had studied to be a pediatrician, but once he moved into Synanon, he practiced wherever needed, and Synanon needed an OBGYN. His father, a retired obstetrician, was also living in Synanon and was teaching Doc the OBGYN ropes. I must have been Doc's first victim.

With Father Doc advising from the background, Doc showed me a pliable silicone ring with a flexible cup that I was supposed to fit around my cervix. I knew this man, and here he was looking up my vagina!

It's okay, he's a doctor. Pretend you don't know him.

"First, squeeze the gel around the rim," he demonstrated, "like putting toothpaste on a toothbrush." The spermicide gel smelled medicinal and tasted worse, I would find out. "Then squeeze the diaphragm so that you can push it into your vagina." He squeezed it, and it shot across the room, landing next to Father Doc. I burst out laughing. Doc's face turned red. "Okay, let's try that again."

I used the diaphragm religiously, running to the bathroom before sex to smear smelly, slimy gel on its rim, then inserting it up my vagina. Did I put in before or after Bobby ran his tongue along my privates? Must have been after. But no, we wouldn't have stopped for that.

Bobby was looking at me funny. What was I laughing about?

"Just remembering getting fitted for the diaphragm."

I wasn't completely cut off from the outside world. Yet. We sent in our application to the Breeders about the same time that the Symbionese Liberation Army kidnapped Patty Hearst.

One dinner conversation began with someone saying, "No way she would join the SLA! She was rich. No heir would give all that up to run around with a bunch of terrorists. She was just acting as if so they wouldn't hurt her."

I argued, unknowingly echoing my own Synanon experience. "I disagree. While she was locked in that closet, they were preaching to her about feminism and anti-racism. They railed against the capitalists—her family. She's only twenty. She probably agrees with everything they said." I took a drink of water. "Look at the heiress."

Only Patty Hearst knows whether she became a true believer, if only briefly. And if she did, would she admit it? For forty years, I didn't admit I was a true believer. Or that I lived in a cult.

Change came fast in Synanon. I heard about the Breeders on a Monday, sent off a request to join on Tuesday, and received an acceptance letter within a week. Two months later, I was pregnant and had a job working for the facility manager at Walker Creek, one of the ranch properties in Tomales where the Breeders lived. ADGAP would transfer Bobby to phone sales at the Bay. There was no two-week notice to a boss, no termination of an apartment lease, no looking for a new apartment big enough for a baby, and no worry about childcare. It was blazingly fast.

While it felt thrilling at the time, I now believe the constant change was by design—meant to keep us moving too quickly to question, to consider consequences, or to notice that the higher-ups were making every decision for us.

*
**

Bobby and I rode the jitney north to Walker Creek—our new home. A tingling spread from my head to my toes as we took the Novato offramp onto the winding road to Synanon City. I leaned forward, wriggled in my seat, squeezed Bobby's hand. "Can't you sit still?" he implored.

As houses gave way to green rolling hills dotted with live oaks, I sighed deeply and leaned on Bobby's shoulder. We turned off the Marshall-Petaluma Road and drove down a gravel lane through an open, sun-bleached wooden ranch gate. I was breathless. We're here! Horses grazed near a freshly painted barn on the far side of a corral. Sprinkled throughout were prefab beige steel Butler Buildings similar to self-storage units seen along freeways—one the size of a sports arena; most the size of World War II army barracks—blemishes on the otherwise pristine ranch land. Concrete sidewalks connected the Butler Buildings combating the gooey winter mud that sucked your boots off like quicksand.

The jitney driver dropped us off at the largest Butler Building, which housed the kitchen, dining room, and all-purpose community room. Artist easels lined a mezzanine like a painter's attic. Compared to the Oakland Athletic Club, the Walker Creek buildings were sterile and utilitarian.

I breathed in the familiar scent of dried grasses and dirt, reminding me of our wedding.

"Well, here we are!" Bobby exclaimed, gently touching my stomach. "Can you believe we get to live here?" He could hardly stand still. "I'll get you settled, and then I'll move in a few weeks."

Bobby's transfer hadn't yet come through.

He strode over to the jitney driver. "Hey, can you drop our stuff over at our place? It's the Breeders' building, right over there." He pointed to one of the smaller Butler Buildings.

"Sure, no problem, Bobby," the driver said as we climbed back in. "I'll help you carry your things in." I was already pregnant, but not showing—barely pregnant enough to have lost my twenty-three-inch waist.

A tall, skinny woman about my age greeted us at my new home. She looked like a hippy with long, straight, mousy hair. "Hi, I'm Cynthia. Let me show you around." She ushered us into a small room, barely large enough for a featureless queen-sized bed and a bland dresser, a far cry from our one-bedroom Oakland apartment. It didn't matter. I would spend most of my time out in the community.

Our belongings included a Sony Trinitron television, our meager Synanon Store hand-me-down clothes, and, of course, overalls. I had long since traded my great-grandfather's oak dresser for a cheap, modern dresser to shed everything related to my family. Both dressers stayed in Oakland.

"Look at the view!" Through the tiny window, I could see cattle grazing on the hills.

Cynthia resumed the brief tour, pointing out whose room was whose as we walked down a narrow hall with bedrooms on either side. The room next to ours was empty. Cynthia said, "I think a couple just got pregnant—Lynda and Tyler. Tyler's a plumber, and Lynda works in accounting. They should move in soon."

The hallway ended in a small communal living room.

It was so different from the Oakland apartments. It reminded me of my dorm at U.C. Davis. I laughed to myself. Couples sharing the dorm rooms instead of students.

"The bathhouse is over there," Cynthia said, pointing to a building fifty feet away. "We share it with everyone who lives in this area of the ranch." The co-ed bathhouse had sinks, showers, and toilet stalls.

Yep, just like our dorms, only co-ed. And we have to walk outside to use the bathroom.

Surrounded by the golden hills dotted with cattle and feeling the warm sun shining through the cloudless sky, my heart swelled. Everything I needed and wanted was right here. I could walk to work without riding a bus through the city. I squeezed Bobby's hand. Paradise.

Cynthia ended our tour. "Okay, I'll let you get settled and then we can all meet for dinner."

Bobby went back to our room to set up the TV.

Hearing music blaring across the hall, I wandered over and peeked in the open door. "Knock knock," I called out.

A Black man looked up. "Hey, are you a Breeder? I'm Jerome."

"Yep. I'm Janet. Bobby and I just moved in." A basketball game was playing on his television, the ever-present Wire was running over the radio, and he was listening to jazz on a turntable.

"Why do you have the stereo and TV and the Wire on all at the same time? Doesn't it drive you bonkers?" I asked.

"Probably 'cuz I'm from the streets of Harlem. I'm used to lights and noise all day and all night," he laughed, with a hint of a New York accent. "Where you from?"

This was so different from my family, where Dad demanded quiet unless he was watching TV.

"I'm a square from the Bay Area."

"Well, welcome, Square," he laughed. "Tina's around somewhere. This will be fun, huh? Are you pregnant yet?"

"Yes! Are you guys?"

"Not yet, but we're working on it," he chuckled.

"Okay, see you around."

Jerome, I would learn, was a self-described Black street junkie from the streets of Harlem. At the urging of his parents, he flew out to Synanon in 1972, straight from Rikers Island, landing in the Santa Monica facility, where he kicked his heroin habit on the couch.

In the evening, Bobby and I wandered into the Breeders' living room, where Cynthia was laughing with Jerome and a petite woman with wispy blonde hair and skin untouched by the sun.

"Hi ya, Breeders!" Bobby was always comfortable around new people. He extended a hand to Ms. Petite. "Bobby and Janet," he said.

"Hi, I'm Tina. I'm married to Jerome." Her feathery voice matched her delicate features. "This is going to be so great. It's the reason I moved into Synanon. For community."

"Me, too," I said.

Bobby asked, "When are you due?"

"We're not pregnant yet." Her pale blue eyes locked with Jerome's dark brown eyes.

"As far as we know," Jerome laughed. "I'm about to have a baby. Does life get any better than this?"

I wanted to pinch myself.

A tall, lanky plank of a man with sparkling blue eyes walked in next to a woman half his height. "So these are the Breeders? I'm Rick." He pointed at the short, mousy-haired woman. "And this is Myra." He looked at me. "You look familiar."

"Really? Were you in Oakland?"

"No," he said. "I moved in in Santa Monica. Maybe it was the wedding. Myra and I were in the big wedding."

"Us, too." Bobby laughed. "I knew you looked familiar. Tall guy, short wife."

Rick continued. "Well, I just love Synanon. I moved in because I love what Synanon is doing. Myra and I met in the Game Club, and we both moved in. I work in automotive, so I'm happy we're all living at Walker Creek." He chuckled. "It makes my commute short."

I had noticed a large building with cars and motorcycles parked around it. Like me, Rick could walk to work.

Myra leaned on Rick. They reminded me of my six-foot-four brother and his five-foot-two wife. "I'm a teacher, and I work in the School. Our education is so much better than the outside. That's why I like it here. I can't wait to have my baby and put it in the School."

My face creased into a smile. I'm going to get wrinkles if I don't stop smiling so much.

The rest of our introductions came in our first Breeders Game a few days later. It was a getting-to-know-you Game, not the usual rough-and-tumble Game.

Cynthia started.

"Let's start by telling each other about ourselves." Nodding to a burly man, she began, "This is Jay. I'm sure you've all met him." Jay nodded.

"Okay, I'll start," Cynthia said. "I'm from Michigan and moved here after fooling around with drugs. I was going downhill and needed to get my life together. Now I work in the School and help out in the Ag Department. And I'm the beekeeper." So, that explained those white boxes sprinkled around the property. I stifled a giggle, imagining her in a white, head-to-toe beekeeper suit with a dorky netted hat.

"Jay?" Cynthia nodded toward the tall, stocky, blondish man.

"Well, this was my idea," he began arrogantly. "Unlike my hippie wife, I used the hard drugs and came here to get clean. I work in the accounting department." Maybe that's why he seemed restless. Sitting at a desk crunching numbers for ten hours a day would make me want to move around, too.

Jerome repeated his story of coming straight from Rikers, then continued. "I gotta' tell ya', when I landed in Santa Monica, it blew my mind. That was 1972, and I was twenty-five. I had just left Rikers, and here I was, living on a beach. That's crazy!" He grinned. "I came here for the program. But you know what? I like it. I'm married to a beautiful woman," he beamed, looking at Tina.

I gently placed my hand on my stomach, knowing my baby was growing inside.

Tina must have moved in about the time I joined the Game Club. I wasn't the only twenty-something square who moved in to live in a commune.

My face turned red as the next guy spoke. He and his wife had moved into the room next to ours. Bobby and I could hear them through the wall. First muffled words, then creaking bed, then moans. Then cries of release.

"I'm Tyler, and I came here to get off heroin. Synanon trained me to be a plumber, and I have one word of advice. Don't put anything in the toilet besides toilet paper!" His wife rolled her eyes while the rest of us laughed.

"I'm his wife, Lynda. We didn't plan to get pregnant, but here we are. We were told we had to move in with the Breeders." I didn't blink. Of course, she would have to join us—we were the vanguard, after all. Lynda had a professional air about her and didn't look all that excited to be with us. "I was living in Venice and addicted to prescription drugs, so I came in to get off them." She looked around and paused. "I work in the accounting department."

"I guess it's my turn," Lorena grumbled in a thick New York accent. She was short and thin with thick, golden hair down to her waist, a round face, and sparkling blue eyes. "I'm here to stay off drugs. I work in the Infant Program. Adrian and I met here and got married."

Adrian oozed Italian machismo with his thick, black, almost wavy hair. "Adrian, married to Lorena." His accent matched his wife's. "I'm in Food Service."

Bobby and I introduced ourselves last. Bobby said, "I work at ADGAP and am waiting to be transferred. I'm supposed to start doing phone sales at the Bay. I can't wait to get up here full time."

I grinned at him. "I'm Janet. Moved in as a Lifestyler a couple of years ago. This is my dream come true!"

A week after our introductory Game, I caught a jitney to the Bay property—Home Place, where Chuck and Betty lived—five miles west on the Marshall Petaluma Road, then south a couple of miles on Highway One, hugging Tomales Bay. I wanted to explore the property I had heard so much about. I had been there once for a Perpetual Stew, but had never walked around. The fog had burned off, and Tomales Bay was a calm, bright blue reflecting the brilliant sky. Lorena was in the seat behind me; I twisted back to say hello.

"Hi, Lorena. It's me, Janet. We're both in the Breeders."

"Oh, yeah, hi," she responded in a husky voice, daggers shooting from her eyes.

With heat rising in my face, I turned back around and swallowed hard. *What did I do wrong? Maybe it's because I'm a square?* I had heard that many ex-addicts resented us squares.

I was healthy and energetic during my pregnancy, with no morning sickness. When alone, I spoke to the tiny life within me. I felt like the entire community watched out for me. No horseback or motorcycle riding. Protect the baby. Each weekend, Bobby and I read a book about our baby's first nine months, depicting what our baby was doing in my uterus. Bobby spoke to the baby every week, caressing it and me.

In August, Bobby and I went to the Bay for the second-anniversary celebration of the Big Wedding, where we took over the ground floor of the Inn. Almost half the couples were divorced by then. We traded relationships like baseball cards. There was a table full of salads, cold cuts and bread. Tubs of Tab on ice. A large sheet cake.

I left to use the restroom.

"I'll be right back," I whispered to Bobby, not telling him my underwear was damp.

I sat on the toilet. My underwear was wet and red. Blood oozed out of my vagina. I squeezed my eyes shut.

This can't be happening! I'm three months pregnant!

Not wanting to get up from the toilet, I covered my eyes with my hands, willing it to be a mistake.

It doesn't mean I lost our baby. Maybe it's just minor bleeding.

But I knew. I felt numb all over. Taking a shaky breath, I stood and flushed the toilet, whispered goodbye to my baby, and wandered back to the party.

I found Bobby, who abruptly turned from his conversation when he saw my face. He gently guided me outside. "What's wrong, Beest?"

"I think we lost the baby. I'm bleeding."

Bobby held me. "Let's check with the doctor."

"I can't stay here." He walked me outside without saying goodbye. "Let's walk home."

We hiked across the hills from the Bay to the Ranch. The ocean breeze soothed me. When we reached the top, he took me in his arms and gently kissed me, licking the tears that streamed from my eyes. As always, his touch melted me; it turned into a caress, and we made love on the dry grass under the afternoon sun.

A few days later, I went to a Synanon doctor.

"I'm so sorry," the doctor said. "You definitely had a miscarriage. Did you see any large tissues?"

"Not really. Nothing bigger than a dime." I could still see that pool of blood in the toilet. But I had stopped bleeding right away, so I had held hope that my baby was alive. I was crushed.

"Well, we'll wait a few weeks and then might have to schedule you for a D&C. Don't have any sex until then." Oops.

Not only had I lost my baby, but I also thought I would have to leave the Breeders like the other couples who didn't conceive. Instead, I received a handwritten note from Chuck: "If at first you don't succeed, blah, blah, blah." Apparently, he was keeping an eye on his latest experiment.

Lorena approached me. We hadn't made fast friends, but we had at least been cordial. Bobby helped; he had a knack for making people feel comfortable. He and Adrian were friends, so Lorena and I tagged along, and the ice between us had thawed. "I'm so sorry about your miscarriage. That's so sad. I'm sure you'll get pregnant again. I just found out I'm pregnant." She was so short I felt like an Amazon beside her.

"Thanks, Lorena. That means a lot," thinking, *Act as if. Everything will be okay.*

I still felt pregnant. "It's just phantom feelings," the doctor said after telling me I didn't need a D&C. "Don't worry. You're young. You'll get pregnant again."

Within two months, the doctor confirmed I was indeed pregnant again. That's how I knew the exact day I conceived—up on that hilltop overlooking Tomales Bay. And that's when I knew my baby, Robert, wanted to come into our lives. It was as if he forced out the other soul, pronouncing, "This is my family."

Pregnant again, I joined the other moms-to-be in prenatal activities. An obstetrician in Petaluma, about twenty miles away, donated her services. We went two at a time for our checkups. Lorena and I went together, as our babies were due two weeks apart. The best way I can explain our growing friendship is we were both Leos, and, as the saying goes, Leos either love each other or hate each other. Our initial growls had turned to purrs as we spent time together. As our bellies grew, I sympathized with her about her morning sickness, and she comforted me about Bobby still living in Oakland.

After one pelvic exam, the doctor exclaimed, "Oh, look, there's sperm! Do you want to see it?"

No.

"Oh, sure." I bent over the microscope, face red, and watched Bobby's sperm swimming around. "Oh, interesting," I muttered. *I'll never have sex again the night before a GYN appointment!*

* *
*

On the weekends, we all took natural childbirth classes together. Dr. B, the father of the doctor who fitted me for a diaphragm, and who had been a proselytizer of natural childbirth in the 1950s when most women were being anesthetized during delivery, taught us the Bradly Method of childbirth. Different from Lamaze, Bradly uses deep relaxation.

We gathered in a dim, carpeted room and lay on the floor as Dr. B talked us through relaxation.

"Breathe in, breathe out. Relax your toes. Relax your calves. Relax your arms. All the way up your body," like the ending of a yoga class. Then Dr. B went around and lifted our limp arms to confirm we were relaxed.

"Relax between your contractions and relax during your contractions. Let your body do its work." It sounded so easy. "Husbands, your job is to remind your wife to relax. To push on her back if she has back labor."

I vowed to have natural childbirth.

Bobby was still living in Oakland, over an hour away. He must have stopped asking to transfer, probably tired of being accused of whining in Games. I missed him terribly, especially at night as I lay in bed alone, trying not to listen to Lynda and Tyler make love. Our weeks of separation in Detroit had prepared me for this—I worked my ass off during the day, played Games in the evening, and hung out with my new Breeder friends. I volunteered to videotape Directors' Games one or two evenings a week, so my life was full. I learned to ignore the hole in my heart.

Not everything we did as a group was centered on childbirth. Jerome announced one day, "Teddy needs help gathering stones for a fireplace at the Inn. I said we'd help."

Teddy was an artist known for his wooden sculptures. Chuck had commissioned him to upgrade the fireplace at the Inn, and now he needed stones. Large, heavy stones. I had already had a miscarriage, yet I jumped at the idea of being part of Teddy's project. The community gave us pregnant women so much—special housing, donated obstetric services, childbirth classes—I was happy to give back.

We weren't allowed to ride horses while pregnant, but hauling heavy rocks from the creek bed was somehow fine? What was I thinking? I wasn't.

Some of the Breeders

Photo courtesy of Synanon.com

Chapter 16: Bald and Pregnant

February 1975, Walker Creek, Marshall, California

Five months into my pregnancy, I was looking forward to scheduling my artistic maternity photo session.

Lorena, Adrian, and I were hanging out in the dining room after dinner, half listening to the Stew being broadcast over the Wire. It had been a warm winter day, but as dark descended, so did the temperature; we were cozy inside. Lorena had finally stopped throwing up after every meal—her morning sickness hadn't confined itself to breakfast. Now that she could finally enjoy dinner, we savored relaxing on non-Game nights.

One table over, a woman shrieked. "Rebecca just shaved her head!"

The chatter in the room diminished. *Did I hear her correctly?* I turned to her. "What are you talking about?"

"Weren't you paying attention?" the shrieker asked incredulously. I had learned to tune out the constant noise of the Wire. "Rebecca copped out to selling a camera that belonged to Synanon, and she kept the money."

Rebecca was a Lifestyler I had known in Oakland and was now in the in-crowd, her circle of friends being the directors. She worked in the graphics department, but why would she steal a camera? She was a square getting fifty dollars a month WAM, double my five dollars a week.

A guy chimed in. "Yeah, Chuck called into the Stew and told her, if you were a man, we would shave your head for stealing!"

My jaw dropped. *Chuck wants a woman to shave her head? What the hell?*

The guy sputtered as he spoke. "I heard him say, well, Rebecca, you're always talking about women's equality; why don't you shave your head? Now that's equality!" The guy paused, wrinkling his nose. "And she did!"

My body stilled as I began listening intently to the Wire. The Stew sounded chaotic, not the usual back-and-forth of accusations and defenses mixed in with navel-gazing.

Laurie, Rebecca's best friend, proclaimed, "I'll support you! I'll shave mine, too!" Followed by choruses of "me too."

A woman burst into our dining room, her long dark hair frizzy from the evening dew. "Women are shaving their heads here, too!" She ran back outside.

An invisible current swept through the room. Lorena, Adrian, and I—and soon everyone—ran across the property to the community room to watch.

Women's eyes were wide and glowing as they jostled each other to the front of the line to shave their heads. "Let's support Rebecca!" "Shave mine!" "Here! I'll do yours!"

And in the background, the buzz of clippers.

Massive piles of hair—blonde, brunette, curly, straight, long, short—spread across the floor as, one by one, women swarmed in a wild frenzy, clippers buzzing as they shaved their heads.

Recoiling as I watched women crowding in, begging for the clippers to shear their locks, I turned to Lorena. "What the fuck?" I wanted to look away but couldn't, like watching a car roll over on the freeway and burst into flames. Yet, these women-now-men wore grins from ear to ear. Hugging and laughing, rubbing each other's fuzzy heads, and jumping with glee, they passed the clippers from hand to hand as they buzz-cut each other's heads.

Backing away from the chaos, I searched for Lorena. She and Adrian had retreated to the mezzanine, their eyes flat, arms crossed, observing the melee.

I turned toward the buzzing clippers, drawn to the exuberance and energy. My friends. My community. It felt like the peace marches I had marched in at U.C. Berkeley, when we were all of one intent, chanting "Peace! Now!" Tonight, we were shouting, "Equality! Now!"

I enveloped myself in the fervor, the communal joy—the same zeal I felt when I moved into Synanon four years earlier. Passion and friendship were my addiction.

Excitement surged through me, and I shouted, "Shave mine!" I can still feel the vibration of the clippers across my scalp and hear the buzz as I watched my long curls fall to the floor, adding to the heap. I leaped to my feet and embraced the first shorn woman I saw; we jumped up and down in circles. I ran my hands across my buzz-cut, feeling a profound sense of freedom.

Then I looked up at Lorena. Her exquisite blonde hair was still down to her waist, shining like sunlight as she stood deadpan, with her arms crossed over her protruding belly. I felt a momentary pang of remorse. *What have I just done? Why aren't I standing there with my best friend?*

Banishing that thought, I turned back to the whooping crowd.

I don't know if my euphoria was a feeling of equality or the desire to fit in, but I suspect the latter. Did I want to belong, or didn't I? It wasn't a conscious choice but a gut-level feeling that something important was happening, and I wanted to be part of it.

I rubbed my hands through my hair, feeling only soft fuzz.

Bobby was in Oakland and wouldn't see my new hairdo—or lack thereof—for a few days. I'm sure he would have joined in. He would have held the clippers that shaved my head while lamenting, "Beest, your beautiful hair."

The next day, I looked in the mirror, an alien staring back at me. *What did I do?* Then, the joy, camaraderie, and sense of power washed over me.

If men can shave their heads, so can I.

I grinned at my reflection. Holding my bald head high, I walked to the dining room to join my shorn sisters.

The grins and hugs from the night before hadn't stopped. Laughing. Giggling. I could hardly recognize anyone. By now, most of us—men and women alike—wore overalls as our daily attire, and I couldn't tell the men from the women. Then I realized the women had shorter hair—maybe a quarter of an inch. I looked past the buzz cuts and recognized my friends.

Some women still looked beautiful, some looked worse, but we were all beaming in our stance of equality, rubbing each other's heads, and laughing at our audacity.

That's all we talked about during breakfast. "Ron called into the Stew and told Laurie, 'You're not doing this, are you? Well, I'd like to get into the Game and talk to you before you turn yourself into an ugly pig.'"

Laughter.

"That's why I shaved mine," a woman sniggered. "We have as much right to look like an ugly pig as the men do!"

Two days later, I watched Adrian shave Lorena's head. Her blue eyes were dead.

"Adrian said I'd have to shave my head if we want to stay here." Lorena spoke in a monotone. "And he's right. Who's left with any hair?" She ran her fingers through her hair that wasn't there. "I have to stay. We're having a baby. I don't know if we can make it outside."

I wasn't sure if they could either. Core indoctrination echoed in Games and over the Wire: Once a junkie, always a junkie. You can only be clean if you stay.

"It's only hair," I said, hugging her. "You look beautiful." And she did. She cut it to an inch, short enough to be acceptable, her thick golden hair glowing like a halo. But her blue eyes no longer sparkled.

Within days, nearly every woman in Synanon had shorn her hair. Betty D. issued a "Bald Statement of Purpose."

> On February 26, 1975, Synanon women shaved their heads, thus making a momentous decision to join with the organization's 800 men in a demonstration of commitment to its continuing work.
>
> Since 1959, Synanon's purpose has been to reeducate and rehabilitate drug addicts, alcoholics, and juvenile delinquents.
>
> The bald head in Synanon has always symbolized responsibility for the Synanon community, either in penitence for mistakes or in celebration of commitment. However, up to this time, women did not take part in these demonstrations.
>
> Determined to become full partners in accomplishing Synanon's work, many women will remain shorn as a constant reminder of their dedication to their common cause.

Did I hear that? If I did, it didn't sink in that I would have to keep shaving my head. I thought it was a one-time phenomenon, that our hair would grow back, and we would look back proudly at our moment of solidarity. Betty D.'s statement that many women would remain shorn was tantamount to a rule. A fifth cardinal rule, and now a symbol of Synanon.

Months—or maybe only weeks—after bald-head night, someone at the School shaved the kids' heads. Two-year-olds to teens.

One friend left. "I came here to get off heroin," she told me. "Not to look like an idiot."

Most women, however, went along. The peer pressure to conform was overpowering.

Some months later, Betty D. suggested Chuck let us grow our hair back. Interesting, since it was her idea to make bald heads a badge of honor. Maybe she saw our capitulation as a loss of power; I don't know. But Chuck embraced our baldness. "If you put long hair on a dog, you get a long-haired dog," he said.

What the hell? That remark wasn't broadcast over the Wire with the rest of his vitriol; I didn't hear about it until long after I left. Whoever heard it at the time should have reamed Chuck in a Game, but I don't think any of us stood up to him by then. He was king.

I recently heard another gem: Chuck asked the women at Home Place to grow their hair out a couple of inches, as he didn't enjoy looking at their bald heads. I always suspected he surrounded himself with the most beautiful women. I guess the rest of us were dogs to him. What a pig!

Why didn't I stand up and say we had made our point? Women are equals. If we did something wrong, we could shave our heads just like the men. I had a moment of power, and I didn't even notice that I let it slip away.

Looking back, I crossed a red line when I continued to shave my head; I caved into peer pressure instead of following my conscience. I did it to fit in, to belong. Then, I embraced it. Once I crossed that first red line, the next ones were easy.

What I got used to scares me now.

The Friday night after I shaved my head, I waited for Bobby's arrival for his usual weekend with me. I was restless, wondering what his reaction would be. A friend had told me her husband wouldn't make love to her because he felt like he was looking at a man.

"You look beautiful, Beest," Bobby cooed, putting his head against my belly, listening for movement from our baby, then rubbing my head. Grinning.

"Mom's family reunion is Sunday, remember?" I asked nervously. "Grandma's seventy-fifth birthday?" Now that the euphoria had worn off, I was embarrassed to show up with no hair. Being bald surrounded by my friends was one thing; explaining it to my family was something else.

Bobby laughed nonchalantly. "Ah, what do we care what they think?"

Bobby and I checked out a car and drove fifty miles to my parents' house. I hadn't left the cocoon of Synanon for a year and felt like I was driving back in time to an unenlightened world.

At least the idea of containment had blown over, and I didn't have to hear about seeing people on the outside. Synanon was now more of a lifestyle movement than a drug rehab center; there was little concern if we spent time with non-Synanon people. Or perhaps by now, fanaticism had taken over, and the non-believers had left.

Mom opened the door, her eyes wide. "Oh my God! Now what have you done? Come in." She began pacing. "At least put a scarf on your head. It's Grandma's birthday. All the relatives will be here any minute."

She ran upstairs to her bedroom and I heard her rummaging around in her dresser. The house no longer smelled of cigarette smoke as she had quit, and she made my dad smoke in the basement. Instead, I smelled eggs. Plates of deviled eggs, a big fruit salad, and a potato salad filled her dining room table. Mom's crystal dishes were out for the occasion, filled with cream cheese stuffed celery, cucumber spears, and olives—hors d'oeuvres I had only seen at Thanksgiving.

Mom came downstairs with a scarf. "Here, put this on," she pleaded.

"She doesn't need that—she looks beautiful," Bobby said.

Mom rolled her eyes. "Maybe to you."

I tied the scarf around my head. "The house looks wonderful,

Mom. Where are Dad and Jack?" My older brother and sister had both married and lived in their own homes.

"They're in the garage, tinkering with cars as long as possible before Grandma arrives."

Soon, my grandmother arrived, giving me a big hug and a quizzical look at my scarfed head. Relatives trickled in: my siblings, thirteen cousins, two aunts, two uncles, and various spouses.

"What's with the scarf?" Ben, my older brother, asked.

Fuck it. This is who I am. Deal with it.

I tore the scarf from my head, revealing my quarter inch of hair, and stated, "We all shaved our heads last week."

He laughed. My cousins studiously averted their eyes. Nobody asked.

My grandmother merely shook her head, a half-smile on her face, looking like she wouldn't let her willful granddaughter ruin her day. Grandma was too strong to let anything get to her.

Grandma and Grandpa moved to Berkeley in 1927 when their bank foreclosed on their Colorado ranch before the Great Depression. They had sold everything and driven to California with five children, the youngest—my mother—sitting on Grandma's lap. The top of the car came loose partway through the trip, and Grandma held onto my two-year-old mother with one hand and the roof with her other. "It was the first time I saw a paved road; the first time I had an ice cream cone," she had told me. "And then we got to Berkeley to stay with a cousin, and it was cold and foggy. We froze. We had sold our jackets, thinking we were moving to sunny California."

So, no, my bald head didn't faze her.

After the party, we drove back to Walker Creek. I had one more day with Bobby before he had to go back to Oakland for his sales job.

"That didn't go so bad," Bobby chuckled. "It could have been worse."

"The look on my mother's face when I took off the scarf!" I laughed.

*
**

On Monday, Rebecca, who sparked the shaved head movement, approached me. "A bunch of us are going down to Sproul Hall tomorrow to talk about shaving heads. It's such a feeling of freedom. We need to tell the world! Why don't you come with us?"

I looked down, not wanting to go, but oh my God, Rebecca was the crème de la crème, and she was inviting me to part of her group—the elite. Deep breath. "Sure! What time are we leaving?"

"Great! We're meeting at the jitney stop at nine."

Tuesday morning, my stomach roiled at the thought of spreading the word, having already experienced the raised eyebrows from my family. *Act as if. You're finally part of the in-crowd.*

As we drove over the Richmond–San Rafael Bridge, watching the fog recede into the distance, Rebecca gave us the game plan.

Rebecca had corralled a half-dozen women. We walked through Sather Gate, the bronze green from oxidation, just as I remembered. The Campanile bell tower peeked through the trees. As we headed toward the steps of Sproul Hall, there were only a few students out, not the crowds I remembered. I hadn't been there since the peace marches when I was a student.

Sproul Plaza was sacred to me, and I was reluctant to talk about bald heads at the birthplace of the Free Speech Movement. In October 1964, Mario Savio spoke from atop a police car in Sproul Plaza during the Free Speech Movement's early protests. Two months later, he delivered his famous "Bodies Upon the Gears" speech from the steps of Sproul Hall, after which students staged a sit-in that led to the arrest of more than 700 participants.

Sit-ins were part of my life. My best friend Jacqui and I organized one for our senior French class when we asked the teacher to hold class outside on a rare warm day. He refused, so we led our classmates outdoors and taught the lesson ourselves under a sprawling oak tree. I suppose that was actually a sit-out.

In eleventh grade, Jacqui and I often took the bus to Berkeley after school to watch the anti-war marches. We watched men burn their draft cards on the steps of Sproul Hall. We listened to women speak about equality. There had been excitement in the air, a hope of changing the world.

I felt the same excitement and hope in Synanon.

Here I was six years later, standing on the steps of Sproul Hall, but this time, I was trying to convince the young college women that shaving their heads would bring equality and a sense of freedom.

"Come hear our story!" we proclaimed. I felt ridiculous, but we kept it up for a couple of hours. I furtively watched for old high school friends, hoping I didn't see anyone I knew, not even realizing they wouldn't recognize me with my bald head. Besides, everyone I knew would have graduated by then.

No one stopped by.

We returned to Synanon, defeated but not deflated. I knew we were right. We needed to convince the world.

Mom visited me every month, seeming to relish my community experience. She laughed the first time she came up after we shaved our heads. "Oh, you guys all look the same!" We were all dressed in overalls. "How do you tell the men from the women?"

"You just do. You look at the person instead of the hair."

Then, she needed to use the restroom. "Oh, my God! Am I in the men's room?" she exclaimed. "Oh, right. Weird."

At first, I couldn't recognize the women with their shaved heads. I hadn't realized how much one's hair was one's identity. Yet, we didn't all look the same once I looked past the hair, at the faces, the eyes, the lips, the ears, and the facial expressions. For a while, some of us carved designs into our hair for decoration, but dangling earrings worked better—feather earrings for me.

We often drove twenty miles to Petaluma to spend our WAM. Men taunted me with catcalls: "I've never seen a pregnant man!" My chest would close in on itself, and every part of me wanted to run back to the safety of our compound. Instead, I held my head high and looked straight ahead.

Only in San Francisco, where I went for obstetrician appointments, was I ignored—one more weirdo.

My sister Julia and I were pregnant with our first babies, both due in June. Our grandmother took us to lunch in Napa when we were about seven months pregnant. Julia and I would have looked like twins except for Julia's beautiful long hair and my quarter-inch buzz cut. Julia and Grandma studiously ignored the stares I had learned to dismiss. At least no one derided me, like when I walked through Petaluma. Sadly, that is all I remember about being pregnant with my sister, which should have been a wonderful experience to share with her.

That's about the time I met my father-in-law. On one of Bobby's weekend visits to the Ranch, he seemed restless. Finally, he said, "I'd like you to meet my dad."

"Of course," I replied. "Definitely." I knew his father lived in Oakland and that he was an alcoholic. I knew he used to beat his live-in girlfriend. That's all I knew.

I spent the following weekend in Oakland with Bobby, relieving him of his weekly commute to the Ranch. We ate a leisurely breakfast and then checked out a car. The low fog dampened our jackets as we walked to the parking lot. I sat quietly in the car, hands clasped below my belly as I tried to keep them from shaking.

Oh, great. I get to meet my father-in-law for the first time with a bald head.

We drove a couple of miles to West Oakland, passing Victorian houses with peeling paint and weedy yards. Bobby pulled up to a one-story home. Three cement steps led to a door whose outer skin was flaking off.

"Here we are." He looked as nervous as I felt. "I haven't seen him since I moved in."

I grabbed his hand. "Let's do this."

An older version of Bobby opened the door. "Hey, hey!" he laughed, his smile lighting up his face like Bobby's. "I finally get to meet you. Come in, come in."

His house was small, with painted wood floors and the odor of stale cigarettes. Along one wall was a cabinet with bourbon and whiskey and faux cut glassware.

Bobby and I sat on a loveseat while his father—my father-in-law—sat on an easy chair, staring at my baldness. Averting my eyes,

128

I gazed instead at a dinette in the kitchen with yellow vinyl seats.

"I love your house."

"Interesting hairdo," he replied, breaking the ice, shaking his head and rolling his eyes. "Welcome to the family."

Did we have iced tea? I don't remember. I know he didn't offer us a drink.

*
**

My bald head became normal. Looking in the mirror, it was still me. Bobby still loved me. I was still going to have a baby. I still lived in the community I loved. It was simplicity itself, not having to deal with my hair in the morning, trying to take a three-minute shower to save water while washing my thick, long hair. And best of all, the shower's water massaging my scalp was soothing, a calm reprieve from the constant whirl of my life.

I wouldn't have the glamor picture I had imagined when my hair was halfway down my back. Kenny, the jazz cellist from my Stew, who was reluctant to play music without his drugs, had taken up photography and was our go-to person for pregnant glamor shots. Bobby took pictures of me pregnant and bald. I looked like an alien. I discarded those pictures many years ago, not wanting my children to see them.

I'm not troubled that I shaved my head. That felt organic, a groundswell of women supporting another woman who took responsibility for stealing, like women who shave their heads to support a friend going through chemo. What disturbs me is that we were forced to continue shaving our heads if we wanted to live in our community. Our bald heads became another loyalty test, a fifth rule: no drugs, no violence, no smoking, daily aerobics, and now, shaved heads.

I didn't even blink.

Me with some of my fellow Breeders
at Walker Creek.
Photo courtesy of Synanon.com

Chapter 17: The Hatchery

Summer 1975, The Bay Property, Marshall, California

Bobby and I sank into one of Bayview's large, comfy sofas. The house had a suitable name—Bayview—because it offered a view of Tomales Bay. It had three bedrooms, a small kitchen, and a living room with oversized couches and chairs surrounding a fireplace. The creamy white walls displayed art instead of the ubiquitous black-and-white photos of Chuck and Betty.

To us, it was the Hatchery.

I moved in about a month before my due date, and Bobby, still working for ADGAP in Oakland, stayed with me every weekend.

I put my feet up on the coffee table and leaned back, sinking deeper into the sofa. "Can you believe where we live?" I smiled, looking out the picture window at the brilliant blue bay, not realizing how it must have hurt him to have to leave every Sunday. A fisherman sat in a small boat, crumpled hat on his head, watching his line in the water.

"At least you can't hear everything through the walls!" Bobby laughed. "What do you think, little man?" he asked, caressing my belly, convinced we were having a boy.

"We're treated like royalty here," I purred, rubbing his head as we felt our baby move inside. "Someone from the horticulture department brings us fresh milk every day. It's still warm, like it just came out of the cow, and has cream floating on top! And we get the best food straight from the Beam."

"The Beam," he laughed. "That's what started you guys shaving your heads!"

Someone in the higher ranks of Synanon had consolidated the food service operations. Our contractors had built a large kitchen at Walker Creek to prepare food for all facilities, like franchise companies do today. The carpenters mounted a doorway beam less than six feet above the floor. Many people, including Chuck, had to duck to walk into the kitchen.

Bobby snickered. "It was hysterical. I heard Chuck screaming on the Wire." Bobby gruffly mimicked Chuck. "What idiot was in charge of that? Every goddam person who walks into the kitchen has to duck under that beam. What kind of way is that to run a nut house? Whoever was in charge should have his head shaved!" Shaking his head, Bobby went back to his own voice. "And it was Chuck Junior! And everyone shaved their heads."

I chuckled, thinking how shocked Chuck's son must have been when his father demanded he shave his head.

"But Rebecca's cop-out was a week later," I explained. "Not really related. Except that maybe the idea of shaving heads was in the air. If Chuck Junior could do it, so could Rebecca."

Bobby rubbed the fuzz which was now my hair. "I wish I could have been there," he lamented.

Bobby had to return to Oakland at the end of the weekend, and I had to fill the hole he left behind.

I wonder how he coped when he was living away from me five days a week, knowing his child was growing inside me, missing obstetrician appointments and childbirth classes. He probably did what I did: dove into work and found joy in friendships. We never talked about it. I practiced Act-as-If to suppress my feelings.

Synanon kept Bobby and me separated during my entire pregnancy. The humiliation of the General Meeting—when I threw Bobby under the bus—loomed over our entire marriage, causing us to unconsciously steer clear of anything that might bring the wrath of the community.

When I moved into the Hatchery, two mothers were transitioning themselves back to work and their babies into the School. Their husbands were at work all day, and the couples mostly stayed in their bedrooms in the evening. Lynda, one of the Breeders, had already moved in with her infant, now two months old. "Thank God you're here," she said. "Can you watch Dana while I take a shower?" Dana never made a peep. She was happy to sit cooing in her tilt-up baby carrier. Lynda jumped out of the shower, dressed, grabbed Dana, and waved goodbye. "I've got to get over to accounting. They're swamped." I stood with my mouth open. Wasn't she supposed to have this time with her baby?

The other Hatchery mother was Shari, who seemed relieved to be moving her colicky baby into the School. She and I walked every afternoon on a gravel path that wound through the property, breathing in the sea's scent and feasting our eyes on the sparkling bay.

I waddled beside Shari as she pushed an old-fashioned buggy with four small gray wheels and room for two babies and a diaper bag. A hinged cover swung in two directions to keep the sun from glaring on the baby. "This is the only thing that keeps her from crying," Shari told me, "so as soon as she starts, into the carriage we go." We walked underneath treetops swaying in the wind, watching shorebirds take flight, bouncing the buggy, calming her daughter and ourselves. Shari had been a heroin addict, such a commonplace story that I did not even raise my eyebrows.

"How did the Hatchery start?" I asked her one overcast day. As the wind blew off the bay, we bundled ourselves in jackets. Shari had swaddled her baby and covered her in a hand-knit blanket.

"I think it was when Kerry got pregnant a couple of years ago," she began. Kerry, Chuck's daughter. "She and a couple of friends had babies within a week of each other, so the three of them and their husbands decided to live close to each other at the Bay."

"That makes sense," I mused. "Everyone wants to live close to Chuck and Betty. And it's so much prettier here than the Ranch. Of course, she'd live here."

"Well, Kerry and one of them and their husbands all moved into the Bayview, where we are." She adjusted the folding top of the buggy to ensure the wind was still off her daughter, who was now sleeping. "The other couple moved into the Inn. They helped each other with their babies. Then, when the kids were all about six months old, Kerry and the moms and dads and babies all moved into the Bayview to get them ready for the School." She shrugged her shoulders. "I don't know who named it the Hatchery."

I laughed at our tongue-in-cheek name. Hatchery: a place to "hatch" our babies and raise them in a nest until they moved into the School. It wasn't as funny as The Breeders, but a catchy name to encapsulate our living arrangement.

In theory, besides helping each other with their infants, the Hatchery helped mothers avoid the isolation of being alone in their apartments while their husbands were at work. Before the Hatchery, new mothers went from immersion in the community to isolation with their baby, followed by the sudden flipping back into the community. Like in the real world back then, there was no paternity leave. But our mothers had six months off instead of six weeks.

It all sounded so benign, so kind to us mothers.

Except for the babies moving into the School—sleeping in the School. Mothers who had bonded with their babies twenty-four/seven were suddenly childless.

Chuck had began blustering about new mothers splitting. "The hardest part of raising a child is until they're two. We put time and money and resources into these kids, and then the mothers split, just when it gets easy."

I guess he never heard about the terrible twos. Of course, he didn't raise his children—both his wives divorced him when their kids were young.

Was keeping the mothers living communally in the Hatchery one more way to encourage dopefiends to stay in Synanon? To keep us all in Synanon? Keeping the mothers together reinforced the non-stop propaganda: You can't make it in the outside world. Why would you want to? We are an enlightened community. You're all character disorders; why else would you live here?

I doubt that Kerry and her friends saw the Hatchery as a way to keep mothers in Synanon—they were joyfully helping each other out. But, like shaving our heads, the Hatchery became mandatory, another rule. It was a rule I liked, along with no smoking and aerobics, but a rule nonetheless. The leaders were telling me how to live, and I went along.

When Shari moved out of the Hatchery, Lorena and Adrian moved in.

"You're here!" I gushed when they arrived. "It's been so weird without the Breeders."

We were too pregnant to hug. Lorena never gained weight while pregnant, maybe because she spent the first three months throwing up every meal. She didn't even look pregnant from the back, but she was huge from the front. I, on the other hand, gained thirty pounds and looked pregnant from every angle.

"It's so beautiful here," she sighed, plopping onto a couch and looking at the brilliant bay. "Finally, no work. I couldn't even pick up the babies anymore." She kicked off her shoes and stretched out her legs on the couch. "And we're out of that tin can we lived in." No one had complained about the Butler building when we lived there, but we were all glad for the larger surroundings. She grumbled, "Bobby should be here. I still can't believe they made him stay in Oakland all this time."

"He gets to live here a while after our baby is born."

"Too bad we're not staying," Lorena added. "But at least you tried."

I guess she's not looking forward to moving to Santa Monica either, I thought. But I would not be negative around my ex-addict friend.

I don't remember an announcement about our move. Word simply spread. We were moving to Santa Monica. I used my Breeders Game.

"I don't want to move to Santa Monica!" I hollered. "Whose idea was this?" I flailed my arms, wanting to stomp my feet in a tantrum. "The Hatchery has always been in Tomales!"

"It'll be fine," Jerome said. "Synanon's always done right by us." As usual, he took Synanon's side as if saving his life had given Chuck the right to move us around arbitrarily.

"You don't get it! I hate Southern California. My mom is up here. My sister's here. I want them to be a part of my baby's life. I just moved into the Hatchery. At the Bay! I can't believe this! Doesn't anyone else care?"

"Hey, we'll all be together," Tina rationalized. "That's what's important. The Infant Program moved there, so what choice do we have? We want to live by our babies."

"And what's the matter with the Infant Program here?" I demanded.

Myra knew the ins and outs of the Infant Program, since that's where she worked. "There are a few infants up here and a few in Santa Monica," she explained. "We need to get them all in one place. There's lots of room in Santa Monica, and it's crowded up here. And it's on the beach. It'll be great."

I sighed, somewhat mollified. "I get that. But still...."

Cynthia chimed in. "I agree with Janet. I've got all my beehives up here. And I work in the School. The entire School isn't moving. And besides, Kerry started the whole Hatchery thing. But we're not royalty like her, so we're just being pushed aside."

At least I had an ally.

Rick, rational as always, had another explanation. "You know, there's a water shortage up here. Everyone's taking three-minute showers, and there's still not enough water. We're the easiest group to move."

Lorena, usually the angry one, took it in stride. "We're the Breeders. We'll be a force. We'll be okay."

I sighed, feeling like a pawn.

Chuck now lived at the Bay, so everyone wanted to live there—near our leader and the power center. Why waste this beautiful property, close to Chuck, on a bunch of infants? And on a bunch of worker-bees?

Being bald and pregnant, working my ass off wasn't enough. Someone was making all my decisions for me, and I was along for the ride. But I didn't see that yet. I had lived in Synanon for four years and had moved from Oakland to Detroit, back to Oakland, then to Walker Creek, and now to the Bay. Santa Monica would make the fifth move, meaning new jobs and friends. Were we purposely kept off balance?

I should have been celebrating. It was 1975. The Vietnam War, the impetus for my dropping out of society and joining this commune, had ended. The war was over after all my peace marches. I remember vaguely thinking, *finally*. But I didn't pay attention. The move to Santa Monica was looming.

Act as if.

For the first time, I understood the phrase I had heard for years. Act as if you are responsible, and you will become responsible. Act as if you're happy, and you will become happy. So, I acted as if the move to Santa Monica was the best idea in the world.

It didn't work.

I fumed inwardly for days. Then, Lorena mentioned Chuck was

in the Stew. I strode over to the Stew Room, which was housed in a nearby building, and sat in the gallery awaiting an empty seat. It looked exactly like I remembered: a circle of about twenty comfortable chairs, snacks off to the side, and several seats where people could watch. This time, Chuck sat in his overstuffed recliner, concentrating on his whittling. Next to him was the heiress. I recognized several Academy folks—the twenty-somethings who were under Chuck's tutelage. Everyone wore overalls.

My heart jumped to my throat—was I actually going to do this? Yes! This was my only chance to stay in Tomales.

I didn't hear a word of the Stew. Finally, an old-timer hefted himself out of his chair and waved goodbye.

"My time's up," he said. People nodded at him as the Stew's conversation continued.

Ignoring my racing pulse, I grabbed his chair before I lost my nerve. Seeing Chuck across the room, I quivered and sat on my hands, trying to keep them from shaking.

During a rare lull in the Game's banter, I took a deep breath, looked directly at Chuck, set my jaw, and willed myself to speak. "I'm in the Breeders, and we've been told we have to move to Santa Monica. I don't see why we have to move." I was losing my nerve. Chuck was larger than life, ten feet away. He was leaning back in his easy chair, still concentrating on his whittling. He cocked an eye toward me. I withered on the inside, but held his gaze. Barely above a whisper, I said, "I'd like to stay here in Tomales."

Before Chuck could respond, the heiress cut in, her voice both soothing and cold. "You're just in the nesting phase of your pregnancy. It's perfectly natural. Everything will be fine once you have your baby and settle in." It was almost like she was putting her arm around me, but no—she was shutting me up.

My mouth opened, but no words came forth. My body felt heavy as I tried to shrink into my chair, tears stinging my eyes. I would not let them see me cry. I gave a half-hearted shrug.

What choice do I have? This is my community. My family.

I stayed in the Stew for a while to be polite, then slunk out. At least Bobby would move to Santa Monica with me. And my best friends would move with me, and I'd raise my baby in the Hatchery in this new society we were building.

Back at Bayview after the Stew, Bobby's absence left a deep void. I filled my days with Lorena, preparing our hospital go-bags and exploring the property.

We walked along the same paths Shari and I had followed, as if walking might hasten our deliveries. The Bay, whether glistening in the sun or gray in the overcast, kept me calm, kept me from thinking about Santa Monica, and kept me from missing my husband and my Breeder friends. After a year of bonding, we were scattered.

View of Bay property from Tomales Bay.
Photo courtesy of Synanon.com

Chapter 18: Our Baby is Born

June 1975, San Francisco, California

I woke up Monday morning at two a.m. with a jolt, groaning and clutching my protruding belly. Bobby was instantly wide awake. I had gone to sleep in his arms, stifling tears, knowing he was commuting back to Oakland in the morning for his ADGAP job.

"Oh my God, are you in labor?" He turned on a light. "I'm about to be a dad! Are you okay?"

"It stopped." I took a deep breath, trying to relax. "I think this is it! Our baby wanted you to be here! Do we call Juliette now?"

Juliette was one of several doctors who had moved into Synanon. She had instructed us to call her when the contractions were close.

"Let's see when your next contraction comes. She said to call when they're ten minutes apart." Bobby moved the clock and stared at it. "Time to breathe and relax your body." He tested my arms to make sure they were limp.

We waited twenty minutes.

I felt the next one coming and took a long, deep breath. Concentrating on breathing, I squeezed Bobby's hand as the contraction swept over me. "Ugh. I thought these were supposed to be light at first. Gradual." I relaxed as the pain subsided—deep breaths.

"Okay, Beest. That was twenty minutes. I'll keep checking."

"Thank God you're still here. I can't imagine having these contractions by myself."

"Me, too." His dark eyes sparkled with tears as he bent over and kissed me. "C'mon little guy. Out you come!" I loved that he always talked to our baby before he was born.

Bobby rubbed my lower back, which already ached, and then double-checked my hospital bag. By five o'clock, the contractions were ten minutes apart.

Bobby called Juliette, then said, "Get ready! She's calling the ambulance."

Synanon owned an ambulance along with three fire engines. Our men, trained as EMTs, served as the volunteer fire and rescue department for rural West Marin County.

We heard a knock on the door in a few minutes, and it opened before we answered. Juliette was there with Jeff, tall and muscled, an ex-addict and now a licensed EMT, who announced, "I'm taking you to the hospital. Let me help you in the ambulance. Maybe I'll get to deliver your baby!"

"No offense, but I hope not." That early in labor, I still had a sense of humor.

Jeff helped me into the back, directing me to lie on the rock-hard gurney. Bobby sat beside me while Juliette jumped in the front next to Jeff.

The hospital was in San Francisco, a ninety-minute drive through commute traffic. About two months before I was due, a Director told me I could no longer use donated services—something about being a Lifestyler and Bobby working for ADGAP. Something about the tax consequences of providing donated services to squares. Thus, I transferred to a U.C. San Francisco Medical Center, a public hospital, three times the distance to Petaluma.

So much for putting pregnant mothers first; I ignored that minor hiccup and went along as usual. Sometimes, I want to go back and shake myself. *Stand up for yourself!*

Riding in the ambulance over the roads I knew so well, I caught only fleeting glimpses of the sky as night transitioned into dawn. My world consisted of breathing through back pain and feeling Bobby countering by pushing on my back. Breathe. Relax. Breathe. I suspected we were getting close when the ambulance slowed to a stop. Jeff turned around and proclaimed, "Now would be a good time to have the baby. I would love to deliver it on the Golden Gate Bridge!"

It would be another ten hours before Robert made his appearance.

Meanwhile, my sister had also gone into labor at the same time. Her delivery was so quick that when Mom called to tell me I was now an aunt, whoever answered the phone told her I was in the hospital in labor. Mom's first grandchildren were born on the same day, nine hours apart.

Finally, we made it to the hospital, where a nurse helped me into a wheelchair; I felt like I was in a science fiction movie as she wheeled me past gurney after gurney, lining the hallways. "You're lucky you waited until today," she explained. "The nurses' strike just ended. We were the only hospital open, so we were packed. We had to put all the labor patients in the hallways and haven't had time to move the gurneys out of the halls."

I scored a labor room all to myself.

I lay on the bed, taking deep breaths to relax my body through the unbearable back pain. Bobby pushed on my back with all his weight for what seemed like forever. It had been hours! I hadn't expected childbirth to be so painful. I had vowed to have natural childbirth; a little pain wasn't going to stop me.

At about noon, a nurse checked my baby's heartbeat. The look on her face scared me. Gently, she said, "I think the umbilical cord is wrapped around your baby's neck."

An eerie calm enveloped me. I've always been calm in the face of danger. I fall apart later.

"Let's get you on your hands and knees. We'll try turning you to see if it unwraps itself."

Just do what she says. Don't think about it.

Feeling like an elephant doing circus tricks, I pulled myself onto my hands and knees. The contractions were still coming every two minutes. The nurse helped me turn on my back again. Back to hands and knees, then back to my back.

The nurse retook my baby's pulse. "Normal pulse. I think it worked."

As she spoke, several doctors hustled in, asking me to sign a consent for surgery. "We want to be ready in case we need to do an emergency C-section." I signed. I would sign anything to have a healthy baby. Never once did I consider something might go wrong.

I lost all sense of time, wondering what was happening, panic creeping in. My contractions still hurt, but they were bearable by comparison.

A doctor inserted a wire into my cervix, attaching something to my baby's head. He inserted the other end of the wire into a monitor, which displayed my baby's heartbeat. I spent the next four hours glued to the monitor, expecting an abnormal blip.

The nurse spread my legs and checked my dilation. I hardly noticed.

"You're at eight centimeters. Transition. Don't push, even if you feel like it."

I felt no urge to push, but the pain was excruciating. At least it's almost over. Transition is supposed to be quick.

A doctor came in and examined me. "Your baby is sunny side up. It's pushing with the forehead instead of the crown. That's why your back hurts so much. Let's see how fast you get to ten centimeters. How's the pain?"

"Awful," I admitted. I could no longer bear it. *Fuck natural childbirth.*

"We can give you something for that. You've been at this for twelve hours. The medicine will only affect your uterus; it won't affect your baby."

I raised my eyebrows and looked questioningly at Bobby, not wanting to want drugs, but wanting them.

He leaned over and gently kissed me, then placed a cool cloth on my forehead. "I think you should take the pain meds, Beest. You look exhausted."

"Okay." I looked at the doctor. "Please give it to me."

Instant relief. I still watched the monitor but glanced out the window for the first time as the sun lowered into the fog creeping over the Golden Gate Bridge.

The doctor came in again at about 5:00 p.m. "You're dilated, but your baby just isn't dropping. We're going to try forceps." They wheeled me into an operating room, bright lights blinding me.

I was a forceps baby, but I was breach. Mom remembered nothing, saying they knocked her out as they pulled me out by my bottom. I imagined an enormous set of barbecue tongs, wondering how they would fit up my vagina. I steeled myself. At least I was no longer in pain.

The wire protruding from me twirled.

"He's turning!" the doctor exclaimed. "You'll be able to push him out! Don't push until we tell you."

I had no urge to push. The drugs had dulled all sensations, so I followed the doctor's lead.

My doctor leaned over as I spread my legs and bent my knees in the pushing stance.

"I'm sorry, but I have to turn you over to Dr. So and So. I've been on shift for thirty-five hours and really have to sleep. You'll be fine."

And like that, he was gone, replaced by someone I had never seen. They all looked the same in their scrubs. Then Juliette, my Synanon doctor, appeared, and I grinned. I didn't realize she had been in the waiting room all this time. Was Jeff, the ambulance driver, still there, waiting to hear if the baby was a boy or girl like in a scene from the 1950s? The only important people in the room were Bobby and Juliette.

The new doctor introduced himself and looked questioningly at Juliette.

"I'm Dr. S., her personal physician," Juliette said.

"New Jersey?" Bobby asked New Doctor, recognizing his accent. Bobby, Juliette, and New Doctor leaned over me, shaking gloved hands, exchanging stories about New Jersey. I didn't know Bobby had been to Jersey, but I guess it's close enough to Virginia.

Hey! I'm the star of this show, I wanted to shout. I felt like they had been gabbing for an hour, but it probably wasn't even a minute. New Doctor finally turned his attention back to me.

"Okay, time to push," he said. Turning to Juliette, he asked, "Do you want to do the delivery?"

"Sure!" she beamed, her serious doctor demeanor replaced with exuberance. Then, after sixteen hours of labor, Robert dropped into her arms after a few pushes.

"It's a boy," New Doctor exclaimed, "and he has more hair on his head than you!"

The nurses cleaned my baby up and took measurements, and then Juliette placed Robert on my breast. "Try to nurse him."

He wasn't interested. He simply gazed into my eyes as if to say, "So that's who you are!" As I held this little life I had known for nine months, I thought my heart might explode. *I didn't know I could love someone this much.* My love encompassed Bobby and this baby we created.

I knew Robert came into my womb right after my miscarriage

because he wanted to be in our family. Then he timed his birth so his dad could be there.

If DJ Don hadn't spoken up for me in my first Game, I wouldn't have joined Synanon. If I had refused to sell my Alfa Romeo, I wouldn't have moved into Synanon. If I had said no when Bobby proposed, I wouldn't be lying here gazing into Robert's eyes.

A nurse wheeled me into a semi-private room shared with a woman who tried her best to ignore me. Within a few hours, her parents moved her into a private room.

She must be rich to afford a private room, I thought. It never dawned on me until years later that her parents probably didn't want their daughter and new grandchild sharing a room with a bald lady. Or with a Black baby.

I was restless, pacing the halls and walking back and forth to the nursery to see Robert. My body wanted to move. I had been doing aerobics for three years and couldn't bear to lie around in a hospital bed. The doctors wanted me to stay at least one more day so they could perform his circumcision. They were falling behind because of the recent strike. I wanted to go home and assured them one of our doctors at Synanon could do the surgery. I only stayed in the hospital for two nights instead of three.

Bobby drove us back to the Hatchery via Lucas Valley Road, the curvy part of the route winding through the coastal hills past what is now Skywalker Ranch. Since car seats weren't required by law back then—they didn't even pass crash safety tests—six-pound Robert lay balanced on my lap, his dark brown eyes gazing into mine, his tiny fingers clasping mine. We drove in and out of shadows under the coastal oaks, the hurt-your-eyes blue sky contrasting with the still green hills, the fences changing from barbed wire to weathered wood to freshly painted white.

I knew Robert came into my life for a reason. Maybe that's why I had to move into Synanon, to birth him. It took me another two years to learn what he came to teach me.

Chapter 19: Rotated

1975, Santa Monica, California

I recall little about Robert's first month. I remember my milk coming in, and the nurse—a friend—bursting out laughing at my change from A cup to double D. My last Synanon journal entry was, *Having a baby was miraculous, spiritual. I'm so busy… I'll write later.* Bobby had to go back to work in Oakland, so I spent my evenings with Lorena and Adrian. At bedtime, I was alone with Robert. I had no time to stress over the coming move to Santa Monica.

That first week, Robert's sleep schedule was backward. He took a four-hour nap during the day, then was wide awake for four hours, beginning at midnight. He cooed and wriggled his hands and feet while my body ached and my eyelids tried to close.

Can I pretend I never had a baby and go back to work tomorrow? Working was so much easier.

I shuddered. Where did that thought come from? I stared out the window at blackness; there were no outside lights, not even moonlight. Tears trickled down my cheeks.

Mom and Dad came to see Robert when he was six days old. It was a Saturday, so Bobby was with us. Mom sat in the Hatchery living room and cradled Robert in her arms, touching each finger, a softness in her face I had never seen. Seeing my resolute mother show her emotions left me feeling all mixed up inside.

"Here, honey, you hold him," she said, handing him to Dad. He held those six little pounds in his large railman's hands and looked tenderly at Robert. Did he ever hold me as a child? I don't remember him holding my baby brother, either. My heart softened, and for the first time, I felt love from my parents—love for my parents. That dreadful night flashed through my mind like a stray hair in my eyes. I swept it away. *How can I both love and hate this man?*

Mom knew I was taking her first grandson five hundred miles south, but never said a word. She had always been a hands-off mother, encouraging independence and trusting my decisions. In retrospect, it seems she was reliving her life through me—carefree with someone else to cook, clean, and raise the children. She had three babies by the age of twenty-four and a fourth at thirty-two. I never confided to her how my move to Southern California was against my will; I presented my life to her—and to myself—as one big adventure.

My new adventure was suddenly upon me. When Robert was four weeks old and Lorena's son, Nathanial, was two weeks old, we had to move. My stomach roiled. At least someone in management recognized the babies shouldn't fly until they were two weeks old. But isn't that still a little soon?

Somehow, we got our sons ready at the crack of dawn, waiting to nurse them on the way to the airport. We left as the sun rose, casting long shadows from the redwoods. The calm bay was bluish-gray, reflecting the dawn; a small fishing boat floated in the distance. I felt like time slowed as I took that last ride through the coastal hills, the same route I had taken to the hospital. My heart ached when we drove across the Golden Gate Bridge with the sun sparkling on the bay. U.C. San Francisco, where Robert was born, was easily discernable by the antennae on the hillside behind the campus. Then one last glance toward the East Bay, where I had spent most of my life. I sighed.

The Hustlers had come up with standby tickets at San Francisco Airport for Lorena and me, but none for our husbands. Bobby and Adrian had to take the Synacruiser south a few days before us, leaving Lorena and me to fend for ourselves. I didn't even stop to think how crazy it was to send us on our own. Couldn't the Hustlers come up with two more standby tickets? Or couldn't we have taken the Synacruiser with our husbands? Synanon kept pushing Bobby out of my life.

The jitney dropped us off at the airport. We carried our gear and babies to the gate, weaving through crowds of people—we had no money for a porter or a cart. At least this was pre-TSA check-ins. We finally reached our departure area, found two chairs, and spread everything on the floor. We were so used to our shaved heads that we thought the sideways glances were directed at our pile of stuff, not at us.

I wanted to sit and enjoy the time with Robert and Nathanial, but within minutes of settling into our chairs, babes on our breasts, our names echoed across the waiting area.

There was room on the next plane.

"Already?" Lorena asked. "We just got here. I guess we didn't need to bring so many diapers."

Time sped up as adrenaline rushed through my body. "Where can I make a call?" I asked the desk attendant. She directed me to a bank of pay phones, where I made a collect call to the Connect in Santa Monica to arrange a pickup at the airport.

"Bill will meet you at the Gate," the clerk told me. "Just look for the Synanon sign." As if we wouldn't recognize the bald head and overalls. Men hadn't yet begun shaving their heads at the first sign of hair loss. It was the day of the comb-over.

Gathering babies and bags and purses, we boarded the plane, grateful for not having to spend the entire day at the airport. Exhausted, and it wasn't yet noon.

"What were they thinking," Lorena grumbled, "sending us on a plane with these babies?"

Constantly aware that she was a dopefiend (and could fall down a manhole if she left), I put on a cheerful smile. "We can do this."

When we deplaned at LAX, a tall, thin, light-skinned Black man holding a cardboard "Synanon" sign walked right up to us. Lorena and I were easy to spot. "I'm Bill, and I'll take you to the Santa Monica house."

Grateful to have someone carry our bags, we followed Bill to a four-door off-white sedan, typical of the nondescript Synanon fleet. Sitting in the front seat holding Robert on my lap, I first noticed palm trees, then the deep blue ocean, gentle waves breaking on the sand, so different from Stinson Beach and Santa Cruz, where I grew up. I could smell the ocean and taste the salty air. I thought of my mother ridiculing palm trees. "What a stupid tree! It doesn't provide shade and it drops crap all over the sidewalk. What is the point?"

Glancing in the rearview mirror, I watched Lorena, stone-faced, with Nathanial on her lap, while I made small talk. "Where's downtown?" I asked, expecting familiar San Francisco high-rises.

"We're not close to downtown," Bill explained. "This is the beach!"

Bill drove down Ocean Boulevard and then turned left onto Pico.

The street ended at a massive U-shaped brick building with articulated rooflines, creating the illusion of a compound. Paned windows covered each wall. The top windows were arched, making the building look taller than its five stories.

"Here we are," Bill announced. My jaw dropped as I realized this exquisite building would now be my home. I turned toward Lorena, who was finally smiling.

Bill pulled the car alongside a porte-cochere in front of thick, double-glass doors. He carried our gear up a dozen stairs to the lobby, with the Connect on the left and the Bench on the right, like the Oakland house. Past the lobby was a large living room with floor-to-ceiling windows overlooking the Pacific and miles of sand.

Maybe this isn't so bad.

It was the old Casa Del Mar Club, which had initially opened in 1926. Synanon purchased it in 1967. Today, it is an upscale hotel on the beach where a cup of black coffee costs eight dollars.

Bill leaned on the counter of the Connect. "Here's Janet and Lorena from Tomales. Where should I take their stuff?"

"They're on the second floor across the street. Go up the stairs, turn left, and you'll see the Hatchery at the end of the hall."

While I waited, I held Robert against my chest, his head nestled in my neck, and wandered over to the bank of windows. A few surfers rode two-foot waves.

Bill came to get me. "That's our private beach," he smiled, pointing to a fenced area below us. Swaying Robert in my arms, my body relaxed as I gazed at the turquoise expanse.

Lorena and I followed Bill across the street. Word had spread that we had arrived, and our Breeders friends—now Hatchery moms—flooded the hallway. Tina, the soft-spoken waif, was in the lead, getting her first glimpse of Robert and Nathanial.

"You must be exhausted," she said sympathetically. "Come on in. We've set up your rooms for you." She outstretched her arms. "Do you want me to hold Robert for a while?"

Tina took Robert to a rocking chair, resting him on her shoulder while another mom held Nathanial. That was the beginning of my becoming a mother to nine babies.

Bobby and Adrian came over as soon as they got off work. Bobby wrapped his arms around Robert and me, encircling our family. Then he held Robert in one arm, cradling his curly head. "How's my little man?" he cooed. "God, how I missed you, Beest." We sat on my bed with Robert on Bobby's lap, gazing into his father's eyes. I wanted to stay like that forever.

"Me too," I sighed, leaning on his shoulder, loving that our family was together.

My friends expanded from our original Breeders group as couples who could not transfer to Tomales joined us.

In the evening, a very pregnant Nora waddled in. She and her husband were Lifestylers who both worked outside of Synanon— Nora as a secretary and he as a dentist. Shaved head like the rest of us, Nora brazenly wore a wig to work. "After all, I have to make money to live here; I can't do my job with a bald head."

I had a private room with Robert, but Bobby, like the rest of the fathers, lived in his own apartment, so we still lived apart. Why didn't the fathers get to stay with us in the Hatchery? In the original Hatchery with Kerry and her friends, the couples shared the Bayview home at Tomales, with each couple having their own bedroom. Somewhere in those two years between Kerry's Hatchery and mine, the men were banished. Only sweet, tall Rick spent the night. He still lived at Walker Creek as he ran the automotive department, but took the Synacruiser south every weekend, and stayed with Myra at the Hatchery. What fun it would have been with all of us together— chaotic, but fun. Bobby and I could have lived together with our son.

Tears well as I grasp how cruel it was to keep the fathers from being a part of their babies' lives. My heart aches to remember how Bobby came by every day after work and often in the morning before work. That's all he got. How our lives would have changed if we stood up and said, *This isn't right*. We could have been a family. We could have raised our baby together instead of letting Synanon come between us. But back then, Synanon was still our family.

Photo by Laurie Pepper

Chapter 20: Co-Mothering

1975-1976, Santa Monica, California

The smell of coffee and eggs greeted me on my first morning in the Santa Monica Hatchery. Robert had lain in a bassinet beside me, waking up hungry every couple of hours, an improvement over his first week. With Robert nestled in one arm, I followed the scent into the kitchen. A tall, muscular Black man was making coffee and a stocky, mousy blonde woman was cooking eggs.

"Oh, you're up. Hi, I'm Mary. I just nursed Aubrey and she's quiet, so I thought I'd throw together some egg burritos for everyone."

"Oh, hi. I'm Janet, and this is Robert." What was I supposed to say? I wasn't expecting a man standing in the kitchen. "Mmm, you're making my stomach growl. I'm famished. I hear you're a cook?"

"In real life, yeah. Grab some coffee." She nodded toward the counter. "Sam just made a fresh pot."

Sam smiled as if it were normal to be in this apartment full of women and babies. "Good to meet you. I'm off to work. We start early in the warehouse." He kissed Mary, went into the living room and kissed a baby, and then went out the door.

I poured coffee and walked to the living room. The west-facing windows let in enough Southern California sun to light the room. A young brunette woman rocked her baby in one of the three rocking chairs. Another baby lay on a twin-size mattress on the floor—a makeshift play area with mobiles and stuffed animals.

"You must be Janet." The woman smiled. Her baby cooed in her arms. I would learn that she was a single mother, having become pregnant despite a Dalkon Shield IUD. Her husband had split; I thought how lucky she was to live in the Hatchery instead of alone in the outside world.

Against one wall was a changing table with stacks of cloth diapers, diaper pins, and A&D ointment, with a musical mobile hanging above it: a tiny umbrella with dangling miniature, bright-colored stuffed animals. Something white, vaguely resembling a folded diaper, but thinner, was stacked on the shelves below.

"What are those?" I asked.

"Disposable diapers!" the IUD Mom exclaimed. "It's a donation, so we're trying them out. They don't really work very well."

"Why not?" I wondered out loud.

"They're just rectangles with thin tabs that don't stick for long," she explained. "And the boys pee right out of them."

"And the trash!" Tina had just walked in, placing her baby, Jabari, on the changing table and winding up the mobile. "I like the cloth ones better. I don't like the plastic next to their skin." She struggled to keep Jabari still while she changed his diaper.

Lorena wandered in, looking well rested. "Morning everyone." She grabbed a rocking chair. "Sorry I crashed so early last night. Thank God Nathanial didn't wake up once." I glowered. Nathanial had slept through the night since birth.

"Once everyone has breakfast," Tina announced, "we can go over the schedule. You'll like it—we all get time off. I have a break this afternoon."

I had heard of this schedule from a Hatchery mom in Tomales, the one with the colicky baby. Each mother would get a night off for a sleepover with her husband or boyfriend. And we would each get a three-hour afternoon break at least once a week.

After washing the breakfast dishes, I sat with Robert in a wooden rocking chair, its surface worn smooth by years of use. He latched onto my breast, his eyes locking with mine, and like the moment he was born, I felt that profound connection, as if we were one. Background noises dimmed, and I listened only to the creak of the rocker and the soft suckling of my son. Then his eyes drooped, and he fell into a drunken stupor, milk dribbling down his chin. I softly inserted my finger in his mouth to break the seal and gently rocked.

After lunch, Tina left for her three-hour break, leaving one extra baby to feed and change. "Okay, I'm off," she announced, kissing Jabari and laying him in his bassinet. "I just nursed him, so he should be fine until I get back. If not, I pumped some breast milk."

Jabari didn't sleep. We let him cry for about five minutes, and then Mary placed him on her shoulder and stood, swaying and bouncing until he settled down.

An hour later, Jabari started crying again.

"He must be hungry," Mary guessed. "He usually nurses every two hours. I don't want to waste the pumped milk—we need it for Game night." We had no formula as we all breastfed. Mary felt her chest. "I have milk." She unbuttoned her blouse, placed Jabari on her breast, and his screams turned to suckling.

My stomach flipped, and I tried not to stare.

Jabari's mom returned an hour later. "Who's hungry? My boobs are so full they hurt!"

"I just fed Jabari, so I'm empty," Mary remarked. "You can nurse Aubrey—she should be hungry soon."

My eyes widened as I watched them swap babies. It kind of looked natural, Tina and Mary breastfeeding each other's babies—but no, it was weird. I looked away.

A few days later, Lorena took her three-hour break. Two hours in, Nathanial wound himself up for a cry like cranking a toy siren that gets increasingly louder. His mouth opened wide and his face turned red before released his wail. His bawling pierced my ears. My breasts leaked milk. I looked in the fridge and there was no Nathanial milk. Should I nurse him? I couldn't let him cry. I picked him up and rocked him. Like a kitten, his mouth searched for my breast. "Okay Nathanial, it'll be alright." I unbuttoned my blouse and offered him my breast. Like Robert, he quieted and looked into my eyes, and I felt that same connection. It must be primal, this giving of your milk to a tiny human. The tiny human became one with me.

And that's how I fell in love with all the babies: Grant, with hair that stood straight up; Aubrey with skin the color of Robert's; Melissa, chubby face with dark curls; dainty Madeleine, with delicate features like her mom; Jabari, who seemed to want to walk from the day he was born; Matthew, mellow; and Nathanial, who felt like my son.

Beekeeper Cynthia and Teacher Myra moved from Tomales a month or two after me. Finally, our Breeders-now-Hatchery group was back together.

The last mother to join us was Georgina, whose son was born three months after Robert. She was a square who had been coming around Synanon since she was a teen. Her husband was a Director—royalty to me. He didn't come around the Hatchery much, but having a Director's wife living with us made me feel like we mattered. I had felt like an imposter, like I didn't belong, ever since Synanon shuffled me off to Santa Monica.

With no job and no one looking over my shoulder, I felt a lightness in my step, maybe for the first time in my life. I savored the pure ocean air, wiggled my toes in the sand, gabbed with my friends, and played with our babies.

One day, several of us piled in a jitney and took the children to the zoo, pushing them in umbrella strollers and joyously pointing out the animals, oblivious to people's stares. Another day, I laughed all the way home from an afternoon trip to Beverly Hills Park—a small strip of grass along Santa Monica Boulevard—where we let our children crawl around naked while we giggled at the gaping passersby.

We drove to the Getty Villa on Pacific Coast Highway and pushed our strollers past the Roman statues. We found seats to nurse our restless babies. Afterward, we strolled to the car, soaking in the cloudless cerulean sky merging on the horizon with the azure Pacific.

Lorena and I took leisurely walks as we had at the Bay. Sometimes, we only took Robert and Nathanial, but usually, we had three babies, two in umbrella strollers and one in a backpack. We walked half a mile to the quirky Santa Monica Pier, back when it had only a few shops selling popcorn and ice cream, long before the iconic Ferris Wheel graced the skyline. Or we ambled several blocks to the rundown Third Street Promenade, now a tourist destination filled with high-end restaurants, an Apple Store, and an REI. In 1975, half the stores were closed. We didn't shop; there wasn't much to buy with five dollars a week.

We finally had something to buy in August when our babies were almost three months old. My grandmother mailed me a ten-dollar bill for my birthday with a note, "This is for you. Don't give it to Synanon. Buy something for yourself." That's fifty dollars in today's money. Tears streamed down my cheeks. I knew Grandma was disappointed when I didn't apply to Chapman College in Republican Orange County, but she never mentioned it. How did she know I would give the ten dollars to Synanon? Mom must have told her. And I probably would have, but somehow she knew she had to give me permission to spend it on myself. My heart swelled.

Lorena helped me choose a blue and white wraparound muslin skirt I cherished for decades. I smiled every time I wore it, thinking of Lorena and the love of my grandmother.

One day, Georgina, married to the Director, returned from a walk, laughing, with Aubrey and Grant in tow. Aubrey was dark-skinned with black curly hair; Grant was pale white with straight blond hair.

Georgina grinned. "Guess what someone said to me?"

Expecting the usual derogatory "Are you a man with boobs" I looked up questioningly.

"There I am, walking toward the mall with Aubrey and Grant in strollers. A woman leans over and says, 'Oh, they're so cute. Are they twins?'" Georgina rolled her eyes. "Twins! Talk about unobservant!"

Aubrey extended her arms toward me, and I tenderly scooped her up from her stroller, giggling along with Georgina's contagious laughter. "And she didn't notice your bald head? That's a first!"

One morning, Georgina slept late. She was usually one of the first to make coffee. Leaning my ear against her door, I heard her baby squirming, but no noise from his mom. I gently knocked and poked my head into the room.

"Are you okay?" I asked.

"My whole body aches. I'll get up in a minute."

"Don't worry," I whispered, picking up her baby. "We'll take care of Grant. You sleep."

Georgina slept past lunch while we cared for Grant.

Then it was my turn. One morning, I woke up fevered and sweating, struggling to get Robert out of his bassinet. Lorena must have heard me stirring, or maybe Robert was crying, and I didn't hear him. She poked her head in, then tiptoed in and took Robert out.

"Sleep," she murmured.

Finally waking up with the late afternoon sun streaming in the window, I found Robert fed, diapered, and clothed, as happy as could be with his co-moms.

Bobby came by every day after work. He couldn't get enough of Robert and loved to help put him to bed, kissing him, then kissing me. On his days off, we took Robert out in a stroller and walked along the Promenade, the salt breeze chilling my scalp. Bobby sauntered, singing to Robert as if he wanted the afternoon to stretch out forever.

Adrian and Jerome often came by in the mornings before work, putting on a pot of coffee. They added cocoa, cinnamon, and vanilla to the coffee grounds, brewing up flavors that could compete with any high-end coffee bistro today.

We pumped milk and froze it, and sterilized baby bottle nipples by boiling them.

One morning, a smell of burned rubber wafted through the Hatchery. "What is that stench?" Mary, the cook, asked. We all looked at each other. Should I call the Connect to report the Hatchery is on fire?

"Oh, my God!" Tina exclaimed. "I forgot about the nipples!" She had placed them in boiling water and then a crying baby distracted her. The water had boiled down, leaving the rubber nipples stuck to the pan, melting and stinking, black smoke filling the room. We opened all the windows to air it out.

At least once a week, I made chocolate chip cookies, leaving extra cookie dough in the fridge, which I ate by the spoonful after Robert was asleep.

Robert developed colic when he was about two months old. At four o'clock every afternoon, he started wailing. Remembering the mom back at Tomales, I swaddled and rocked him alone in my room, my stomach in knots. My Hatchery friends began giving me breaks, but no one could bear hearing Robert cry for so long. Finally, I took him to our in-house pediatrician who gave him some medicine, which only worked for a week or two.

The dentist father was into holistic medicine. One evening he suggested garlic. "This will sound weird, but garlic soothes stomach aches." Ready to try anything, I bought garlic oil capsules from a local health food store, squeezed them into Robert's mouth, and then nursed. Miraculously quiet! The room smelled like an Italian restaurant, but who cared? Was it the garlic, or had he finally outgrown colic? I believed it was the garlic.

We still did our aerobics, running in place while the babies were sleeping. I noticed Nora wasn't doing her aerobics and, like a goodie-two-shoes, confronted her in a Game.

"Why aren't you doing your aerobics? Just because you had a baby doesn't mean you don't have to follow the rules!"

Nora replied in a voice riddled with ridicule. "I just had major surgery, you idiot. I can't run in place." She'd had a caesarian birth. I grimaced and tried to avoid her for a few days.

One night, all of us moms went to a Hatchery Game. A few women who had put their babies in the School a year or two earlier offered to babysit. Our Game went longer than expected, and the babysitters ran out of pumped milk.

One of them poked her head in our Game. "The babies are hungry and we're out of breast milk!" I ran back to the Hatchery, milk staining my shirt, and nursed Robert. A calm settled over me. The mom told me she had offered her breast to a hungry baby, hoping her milk would come back in. It didn't, and the baby simply screamed louder. I laughed, imagining Nathanial winding up for a wail.

Maybe that's why I don't remember any of our Games—my heart was with Robert.

Was this any easier than taking care of my baby by myself? Of spending evenings with my husband and sleeping with him every night? I think it was more complicated, but we had each other. I wouldn't trade it for the world.

These were my best days in Synanon. If I could take a time machine back, I would travel to have all my sisters, Bobby, the fathers, and the babies back together before change came at blinding speed.

Hatchery mothers and babies.
Photo courtesy of Synanon.com

Chapter 21: The Synanon School

January 1976, Santa Monica, California

We had nine babies—and ourselves—to prepare for the School. Nine squirming babies, five and six months old.

My tears came unbidden. Robert wasn't crawling yet. He was barely sitting up. How would he feel being cared for by new adults—strangers—instead of his nine moms? I shook myself. Get a grip. I was providing the best life for him.

My feelings aren't important.

Robert would grow up with all his friends, loving teachers, and multiple parents. Whenever my stomach quivered, I re-ran the pluses of the School in my head, including the studies highlighting how Synanon's children excelled intellectually and in their interpersonal relationships. Sure, I had to make sacrifices, like not being able to nurse Robert or be with him all day and all night, but what an amazing life he would have.

I never uttered a doubt. Not even in my Games. Nor even to myself.

First up, no more breastfeeding. When Robert grew a couple of teeth, he bit my nipple. God, that hurt! Maybe I was ready to wean him after all. I told myself I was weaning him because he bit me. My mother didn't breastfeed any of her children—formula was de rigueur in the fifties. Five months seemed plenty. As my milk dried up and my boobs deflated, I refused to surrender to my sorrow of giving up motherhood. There was too much to do.

"We have to get them on solid food." Mary was the first to speak as we gathered in our living room after breakfast. She bounced Annie on her knees. "I got a table and chairs from the School, so we can start tonight with dinner."

"I think they have to feed themselves," I added.

Outside, the clouds looked like rain, yet surfers carried their boards toward the waves—another world.

"Okay, let's do this," Teacher Myra chimed in. "We'll have to tie them to their chairs, so they don't fall out. I'll gather receiving blankets. Mary—will you bring the rice cereal? I think we should mix it with breast milk."

We had no highchairs, so we set up a few two-foot-high round tables surrounded by miniature chairs, making the room look like a dollhouse, a dollhouse with the bland smell of rice cereal. For once, all nine of us were together. I sat Robert on a chair, bending him at the hips when all he wanted to do was stand, and wrapped a receiving blanket around him and the chair. Keeping him balanced with one hand, I spooned a glob of rice cereal pre-mixed with breast milk and plopped it onto the table. Robert waved his arms and babbled as he looked around the room at his nine mothers kneeling on the floor, holding their babies upright. We should have played music. Instead, our accompaniment was tiny hands slapping the tables punctuated with, "Put the food in your mouth." "You can do it." "Yes, you did it!"

I scooped up some cereal with my fingers and squished it into his mouth. Most of the food ended up on his face. He slapped his teeny hands on the pile of cereal, smearing it around like fingerpaint. Bringing his goopy hands to his mouth, he managed to eat.

"Oh, that went well," Lorena sniped as we wiped the cereal off their hands and faces and threw their clothes in the washing machine.

"I'm sure they'll figure it out," I quipped, waving her off. "We have a month."

"You know, we have to have them sleeping through the night before they move into the School," Lorena admonished. "And they go to bed at 7:00 in the Infant Program." We had been getting bits and pieces of information from the Demonstrators as if our babies were going to preschool. I knew she wasn't worried about Nathanial, but most of our babies woke up at least once.

I tried to keep Robert awake all day so that he would go to sleep at 7:00 p.m. The babies in the Infant Program didn't take naps. Instead of questioning that, I practiced mind over body—or mind over emotion. What were my emotions compared to the grand life I was providing for Robert?

Jabari, who had slept through the night for months, started waking up as if on cue. At first, he woke up once, and Tina nursed him back to sleep. Then he started waking up every couple of hours. Convinced he was waking up for attention as he had been sleeping through the night since birth, I volunteered to sleep with him to deter him from crying in the middle of the night.

I moved Jabari's coffin bed into the living room so he wouldn't wake up Tina when he cried.

Yes, their beds were called coffin beds. At least they didn't have lids! I don't know who coined the phrase; it was another example of our irreverence. We twisted words to make them our own, like Breeders, Hatchery, Hustlers, dopefiends, squares, and coffin beds. In the spirit of having the children's house child-sized, Synanon infants slept on handmade beds on the floor so they could crawl in and out instead of being trapped behind bars. The beds were one-by-eight boards connected into a rectangle the size of a crib mattress.

Jabari slept in his coffin bed, and I slept on a couch in the living room, covering my head under the blankets whenever Jabari squirmed, letting him cry himself back to sleep. Each time he cried, my heart ached, but I refused to give in. By the third night, Jabari slept until morning.

"Thank you," Tina hugged me, tears welling. "I couldn't have done that."

Nora-the-Lifestyler refused to put her baby to bed that early. "I'm not letting Jessie go to bed without seeing her father." Steve still came by every night after work and rocked their baby to sleep. Nora had not lost herself to Synanon as I had.

In the midst of this, Chuck demanded we stop eating sugar. A sixth cardinal rule. Healthy, right? Chuck's wife, Betty D., had diabetes. If she couldn't have sugar, none of us could have sugar.

A sixth cardinal rule. I had stopped counting. I had stopped noticing.

I sucked in my breath. No more chocolate chip cookie dough after Robert was asleep. I had helped Mom make chocolate chip cookies before I could walk, fighting with my siblings over scraping the bowl. But my favorite dessert was her apple pie. The scent of baking apples, cinnamon, and pie crust would fill our entire house, and to this day, the smell of baking crust makes my mouth water.

It was my comfort food.

But sugar was the least of my worries.

Bobby and I had to apply to the School—how strange, because

if we wanted to stay in Synanon, Robert *had* to be in the School. The application process must have been a holdover from the early 1970s when Lifestylers put their children on a waiting list to get into Synanon's innovative school.

I took a deep breath, calming the ache in the back of my throat, and hunched over our Hatchery dining table while Robert happily played on the floor.

"How about this?" I asked Bobby, wiping my sweaty hands on my jeans. "Dear School, we always wanted to put our baby in the School and are so happy that this moment has arrived. We will be involved parents. Something like that."

"I guess that works." Bobby nodded. "What are they going to do? Say no?" He bent over and picked up Robert, bouncing him on his lap.

"At least we'll finally get to live together again." I grinned as butterflies flitted in my stomach. Then I looked at Robert. The butterflies couldn't compete with the large knot in my gut. "But it's going to be awful not to be with him."

"We'll see him every day, just like I've done since we moved down here." He sounded so confident, but he had been forced to live by himself instead of with Robert and me, so he was used to being a visitor. Or maybe it was only his act as if.

"Yep, and we're all doing this together." The propaganda rattled around my head. Nuclear families are evil. There is no place for me in society. I live in an enlightened community.

I had such idyllic visions. When I had visited the School in Tomales, toddlers played quietly and shared toys in a child-sized room. The Demonstrators who cared for the children kept to the sidelines, allowing the toddlers to resolve their own spats.

I thought the School would be inspiring and transformative for the children, certainly better than my family life and public-school education. I expected the School to be one large extended family where the parents played a huge role. I was wrong. It was transformative, but not in the way I expected.

Then the day came. Nathanial and Robert moved into the School together.

Lorena and I had spent two weeks leaving them at the School for a few hours at a time. One afternoon, I came to get Robert and found him sitting in a room by himself, wailing. I picked him up, and he immediately stopped crying. A Demonstrator came out.

"We're trying to get him used to being alone."

"He doesn't like large spaces," I scolded, rocking him in my arms, refusing to admit he might be crying because he was deserted or missed me. For six months, mommies and babies had surrounded him.

I should have grabbed him and run away. I should have grabbed Bobby and kept running. Our love was still strong then. We could have raised our mixed-race baby together. But no, I still believed in Synanon. I think Bobby did, too.

The first night Robert slept at the School, I was okay. I had spent one night a week with Bobby while I was in the Hatchery, so it was a comfort to make love and fall asleep in his arms. But I woke up with a jolt of adrenaline. I wasn't going back to the Hatchery.

We had breakfast, then visited Robert at the School. The Demonstrators welcomed us, and Robert seemed like his happy self. I knew everything would be okay. It was another set of mommies for Robert. Bobby and I could come and go as we pleased. Or so I thought.

The second night was worse. I was with Bobby, but I felt alone. After seven months of shared motherhood, of shared babies, it was only Bobby and me. My heart was across the street in the School. I woke up in the middle of the night to phantom crying. *Robert is hungry.* I jolted awake. *No, he's with someone else.* My chest squeezed tight with a pang that has never left me.

Is he waking up? Will someone hold him? Does he know I'm gone? He's used to waking up with another mom, so he'll be fine. But these aren't his moms. He's ready. He's such a big boy.

More worries. I would start my temporary job that night—graveyard shift at the School. It was supposed to be my transition back into the community—a month of working at the School—although I didn't know how a graveyard shift watching over sleeping babies would ease me back into real life. I'm a morning person. I dreaded staying up all night.

Finally, I drifted back to sleep.

My shift began after the babies and toddlers were asleep. I tiptoed into the sleeping room and watched Robert. The air was filled with the gentle breaths of slumber and the sweet scent that only babies have. He slept with his blankie, the satin edge clutched in one hand, thumb in his mouth. A stuffed lion as big as him—a gift from my brother and his wife—lay at the foot of his coffin bed.

Sighing, I started my chores. I did loads of laundry comprising miniature clothes from size nine months to size eight and arranged outfits for the next day. Each child had a cubby bearing their name. Then, I cleaned the tables and bathrooms.

By 3:00 a.m., I could barely keep my eyes open, so this was when I mopped the floors. The movement kept me awake. I played quiet music in the background, which probably didn't help keep my eyes open, but it kept me company. I listened for kids stirring in their sleep, but none woke up. Every night, I hoped Robert would wake up so I could hold him, but he never did. He was finally sleeping through the night.

The morning shift came in at 6:00 a.m. with a bustle of energy. I could only stay long enough to tell them none of the kids had woken up during the night. I watched a few toddlers get out of bed, rub their eyes, and hug the Demonstrators, but the babies were still asleep. My ghost shift was over.

It helped to be back with Bobby, but as I shut off my emotions toward Robert, I also shut out my husband. Instead of talking about how hard it was to put Robert in the School, I picked fights with Bobby, griping about everything. He wasn't paying attention to me. He wasn't making the bed right. He was late. Anything and everything. Neither of us uttered a negative word about Synanon. We had interwoven our entire relationship around the community and planned to spend the rest of our lives there.

With all my idealism about the School, I never considered the feeling of waking up without Robert.

I woke up empty; part of me was missing. Was it my arm? A leg? No, it was my heart. I had a big hole in my heart.

So caught up in my own feelings, I didn't wonder what it would be like for Robert to wake up to a Demonstrator instead of his mother, to wake up to a stranger, to someone whose job it was to watch over him, to Demonstrators who changed every week so they could enjoy their week off on the Cubic Day.

Sure, Bobby and I could visit Robert, but someone else fed him, comforted him (I hoped), bathed him, and put him to sleep. I wonder what the separation did to Robert. Cynthia told me that when she visited her seven-month-old at the School, her daughter didn't want to be held; she only wanted to play with her toys. Had she already learned to substitute toys for hugs?

Separation at six months old! Why did this make sense to me? Who decided we had to give up our babies before they became too attached to their mothers? Like that is a bad thing. I don't know where the idea originated, but I stupidly accepted it as gospel.

Many parents left with their kids when it was time to put their babies in the School. I always assumed they split because of the abrupt transition from isolation with their babies to being flung back into the community. I thought they were selfish, not enlightened like me. Didn't they know the School was the best way to raise kids? But now I know they split because they were expected to *give* their babies to Synanon. The propaganda was that parents would be involved with the School—a community/parent partnership. That was a lie. I will never understand why Synanon separated children from their parents. Maybe so we would be more productive. Wasn't it enough that we worked for free? Did they destroy all primary attachments to keep us off balance and bound to Synanon above all else?

I will never understand why I went along with it.

The children of Synanon are now talking and writing about missing their parents, about feeling like their mothers abandoned them in an orphanage. About the abuse they suffered. Did I place my son—my six-month-old baby—in an orphanage? An abusive orphanage? How did that make sense to me?

It's been a long road for me to forgive myself for handing my baby over to the School. Robert has forgiven me, but he doesn't remember. But I do. I will never forget.

Chapter 22: Bat-Shit Crazy

1976, Santa Monica, California

Some might say Synanon tipped into madness when we all shaved our heads, but in hindsight, that felt almost benign. For me, the true bat-shit crazy began with the vow of childlessness.

It was more a declaration than a vow. Chuck announced we would no longer have babies, and the members vowed to follow. Not me—I kept silent, grateful I already had my baby while shuddering at the new edict. I thought childlessness simply meant women would stop having babies. I never envisioned how soon it would cost me my child.

I missed the official announcement. I was juggling my new job in the manager's office, reuniting with my husband, and convincing myself that placing Robert in twenty-four-hour care was the right decision—constantly trying to reconcile my churning gut and broken heart with my belief in Synanon.

I heard about childlessness when Brad and Nadia announced their pledge in a Stew in Santa Monica. Brad and Nadia, our Brangelina, had spent nearly their entire Synanon lives in the Academy under the tutelage of Chuck and Betty. Now, they were making the rounds of the facilities, hosting public Games to discuss—compel—childlessness. Chuck didn't travel like he had when he kicked off aerobics; instead, he sent his minions—his true believers.

My body froze as I watched Brad and Nadia in the Stew Room. Nadia's eyes glittered, and she sounded well-rehearsed. "We have chosen not to have children. If you have a child, your first instinct when something goes wrong, like perhaps a fire, is to save your child instead of the community."

And what's wrong with that?

My mouth fell open, but I closed it before anyone could notice. My chest felt like there was a vise around it. I had to remember to breathe.

Brad was talking. "We are committing ourselves to Synanon, not to children."

And just like that, no more children.

Where does that leave me?

Almost overnight, we Breeder moms went from being treated as princesses who had birthed the next Synanon generation to being called headsuckers—people who wanted to be with their babies so much they may as well be sucking on their heads. No helicopter parents in Synanon! If we even mentioned our babies, we were accused of not being committed to the community.

As a parent, I had become obsolete. If I wanted to remain in the community I called family, I had to love my baby in silence. I lived in two worlds—one secret, where I was a mother, and the larger one I also loved. I felt like I was being torn in two.

Like a seagull soaring on the wind currents, I watched myself from above: my head was in my job where it was terrific yet awful to think about something other than babies. But my heart was with Robert, and I wanted to fly back to our nest to protect him and nourish him.

It never occurred to me to leave. I thought childlessness was a crazy idea that would soon blow over. How can you have a community without children? Synanon was filled with kids; the School was one reason Lifestylers—including me—moved in.

All this will pass, and we'll go back to our tender loving community.

Why I didn't run will haunt me forever. Maybe it was my unhappy childhood that allowed me to believe in Synanon more than myself. Maybe it was peer pressure. Maybe it was brainwashing. Whatever it was, I pushed my feelings aside and stayed. Silent.

I focused on work and blocked out everything else. And there was Bobby, acting like we could simply pick up the pieces of our marriage after being separated for over a year. My only joy was visiting Robert at the School, as short as those moments were. Everyone wanted a piece of me.

Chuck, removed from the day-to-day curing of drug addicts, removed from the children, surrounded by his sycophants, ranted over the Wire from his Home Place perch.

David Gerstel, in his book *Paradise Incorporated: Synanon* (1982),[7] quoted the speech I missed: *Childbirth Unmasked*. I can almost hear Chuck's gravelly voice telling us what was coming next.

> "The only reason we would permit anyone to have children is to indulge the woman. This movement doesn't need children. We don't need it. We have millions of starving children, children who won't get an education out on the streets. We have all the goddamn children we want... And one day we'll stop it...
>
> "The problem is, it's too expensive. All the motorcycles in Synanon, all together, don't cost as much as to raise two children to the age of sixteen....
>
> "I think the nuts had better realize we are going to move ahead now on this issue... We're going to control births, like the wealthy people in the world have always done. The people who rule the world always control their births.
>
> "Now, I want to move ahead. Do you?... You have to come to terms with some of these things. You do. I don't. I am way ahead of you. I have already come to terms with it five years before. You must come to terms with it. Because you're not going to change the direction by all these resistance deals.... I have to know when to say GO. And then everybody's got to come along or out. OUT!"

Children are too expensive? What kind of rationale is that? The Demonstrators—unpaid labor—cared for the children. Wealthy people controlling their births? Who was wealthy in Synanon? Only Chuck and his sycophants. I now suspect he never liked children. All that our Breeders/Hatchery group did was take nine women out of his unpaid workforce for six months.

Chuck ranted and raved, telling us to go along with him or leave. Quit. Split. That was always the choice. I followed, not realizing how it would tear my family apart.

I wasn't going to be a quitter—a Splittee. Surely this would blow

---

7. Gerstel, *Paradise Incorporated: Synanon*, 209–210

over. Do you leave your husband because you aren't as happy as you once were, but you are still in love, and have kids and a house? Do you leave your job because your boss is having a bad day and rants at the employees? What about your paycheck, the friendships you have developed, and the pride in your work? That's what kept me there: Bobby, our son, my friends, and my faith in communal life felt like a counterweight to Chuck's more extreme ideas.

Chuck's speech triggered a groundswell that reverberated through me, as if the ground beneath me was shaking like an earthquake. Not only did Chuck's speech kick off childlessness, it kicked off a Big Squeeze, a squeezing out of negative people; a hint of negativity was not tolerated. Not even in a Game.

I would hear: "If you are not 100 percent with us, you're a drag on the community." Was this in a Game? A Stew? Or was someone talking over the Wire? I could no longer differentiate one from the other.

One day, Chuck was shouting over the Wire. "Get Cynthia in here! I want to hear from this negative ingrate!" Cynthia, my friend, my co-mother, founder of the Breeders.

"What's going on?" I asked Jerome, my fellow Breeder, the father who had come to Synanon straight from Rikers Island. He always had a pulse on the Wire.

"Chuck was yelling for names of people who aren't one hundred percent." Jerome brought me up to speed as if he were announcing a baseball game. "Then Lisa said how Cynthia had written her a letter about not being sure about the School." He sounded nervous. "Chuck went ballistic." Lisa was a Lifestyler who had studied behavior among mothers and children and was high up in the Synanon echelon.

Chuck was still fuming about Cynthia as I squeezed my eyes shut, trying to breathe. "After all we did for her."

I knew Cynthia couldn't pop in the Stew. She was in Santa Monica with us, and the Stew was in Badger, two hundred miles away in the Sierra foothills compound.

We put together a Game of our Hatchery-now-School mothers. Cynthia was shaking. "It's so hard putting Madeleine in the School," she sobbed. "I had no idea how difficult it would be. I don't know if

I can give her up." She took a deep, shaky breath. "I wrote to Lisa about it, thinking she could help me." Her breath hitched. "I don't know why she gave Chuck my name. I was only asking her for help dealing with my feelings."

I imagined Lisa in that Stew suffering Chuck's wrath. She probably felt the same pressure I felt in that General Meeting when DJ Don demanded names. Only worse—this was Chuck. Anything to take off the pressure.

Myra spoke calmly. "It's hard for all of us. But putting our kids in the School is the right thing to do. You worked in the School. You know how good it is for the children."

There we sat, spouting the party line, rationalizing our feelings, convincing ourselves we were doing the right thing.

Tears streamed down Cynthia's face. "I don't know if I can live here. And I don't know if I can make it outside." If a fearless beekeeper and a Demonstrator who was assured of a job in Tomales near her daughter felt the squeeze, where did that leave me?

My mind fragmented, half of it repeating, *if you're not one hundred percent, you should split.* But she was my friend, my sister. I wanted her to stay. I joined Myra. "Give it some time, Cynthia. We can do this together. This craziness will pass."

The next day, Cynthia split with her baby. I felt as if my arm had been severed. One day, I had a sister and a daughter; the next day, they were gone. I'm sure I said goodbye, but maybe not. I was afraid I might be ostracized if I stayed too close to her.

Anxiety churned in the pit of my stomach. If this could happen to her, it could happen to me. My loyalty to Synanon twisted me like a pretzel.

When Chuck announced there would be no more babies, the community took up the drumbeat, like warnings echoing from mountaintop to mountaintop.

Jasmine, a work-out Lifestyler living in Santa Monica, was pregnant, her baby due any week. I was in a Game with her when someone confronted her.

"How could you be so irresponsible to get pregnant when you have diabetes? Your baby could be born with disabilities." This was one of those Games that gave the Game a reputation for being attack therapy.[8]

"I didn't plan to get pregnant," Jasmine said. "But I want this baby. I've followed everything the doctor suggested for a healthy baby."

"You are so selfish. I suppose you think the community is going to take care of your baby if there are any problems. Why should we pay for this?"

As one voice, the tone of the community had changed from empathy for Jasmine to attacking her for being pregnant. No one in the Game told her it would be okay and that we—her family—would be there to take care of her. To my shame, I too stayed silent.

Jasmine's baby was born with severe medical problems and died three days later in the neonatal intensive care unit (NICU). In my heart, I knew the community murdered that baby. I don't remember if I said that out loud in a Game or if I kept it to myself. My memories swirl around like an oily puddle of rain.

No one had asked Jasmine to have an abortion—she was too far along in her pregnancy. After her baby died, I sat with her as she showed me her only baby pictures, photos of her daughter she barely got to hold, wrapped in IV tubes and heart monitors. I held Jasmine and let her cry.

Jasmine and her husband split right after that, finding no comfort in our community.

Another woman, five months pregnant, succumbed to the peer pressure. She, too, had been mercilessly gamed. "What makes you think you deserve a baby? Who do you think is going to take care of this baby?" She was an ex-dopefiend who had lived in Synanon for over five years and was well-respected in the community. She had planned her pregnancy.

She had an abortion.

I remained silent, remembering another baby, only a few months older than Robert, born prematurely at five months. That baby lived, but now here was a mother aborting her baby at five months. *This is*

---

8. Laura Wixon and Jordyn Krauss. "Playing the Game: The Origins and Impact of Synanon - Breaking Code Silence." https://www.breakingcodesilence.org/playing-the-game/, accessed May 2, 2025.

wrong! I was afraid to speak up, afraid I would be squeezed out like Cynthia. Never realizing that would have been better than enduring the next two years, destroying my family in the process.

More women had abortions, which I discovered decades later when watching the HBO documentary, *The Synanon Fix.*[9] My heart aches for these women.

Nadia had sounded so positive during that public Game about childlessness when she asserted, "It feels so good to give myself over to the community, so incredibly free." To me, it became a horror. I spoke the party line out loud, while I dared not let my feelings show, even privately. I became so bottled up I could no longer express my opinions about anything—a far cry from the honesty of the Game that first attracted me to Synanon.

I no longer stay silent. I watched my community destroyed by silence—by our going along. I will not be silent while children are torn from their parents at the border. While people are dragged off the street and locked in cells because of the color of their skin. I know exactly where silence leads. But I didn't know it then.

---

9. The Synanon Fix: Did the Cure Become a Cult?, directed by Rory Kennedy. (2024: HBO).

Chapter 23: Dissociation

I woke up in Bobby's apartment—Bobby's and my apartment—wondering where I was. Why is Robert so quiet? My chest caved in.

Oh, right, he's in the School. Will I ever get used to this?

It seemed like yesterday I had nine babies, but now I had none. I had to pull myself together. Remind myself Robert was better off. Stop being selfish. Give myself to the community like Nadia had said.

I lived in a nightmare I couldn't wake up from. My dream-state drifted from laughing with friends, running along the beach, making love to my husband, and eating lunch at the manager's table, to fleeting visits with Robert that left a quiet ache inside me. All the laughter, jogging, dining, and lovemaking couldn't fill my emptiness.

I closed my heart, so I didn't have to think about Robert being in the School. I closed my heart so I didn't have to think about Cynthia being gone. I closed my heart, so I didn't have to think about abortions or Jasmine's dead baby.

I closed my heart to Bobby. And that devastates me. He had only been on the fringes of my life since we joined the Breeders. For nine months, we only saw each other on weekends. Then, for six months in the Hatchery, he was a visitor. We only had one or two nights a week and a few afternoons. I no longer knew how to be a wife. I wasn't sure if I wanted to be a wife.

My heart still fluttered when I was near him. My body tingled at his touch, and I melted in his muscular arms. He was the gratifying part of my dream-state. But it wasn't enough to pull me out of my doldrums.

I had to shake myself out of the nightmare, and the only way I knew to do that was to seal off my feelings, put everyone behind me, and start over like I did the day I moved into Synanon. I would look forward, not inward. I would throw myself into my job.

My new job was in the Manager's office, and I dined with the managers and Tribe Leaders at lunch. I stood tall, shoulders back, feeling like I belonged. I thought they were pulling me into management.

Bobby was never invited to the manager's lunches. Neither of us were invited to their dinners. So, no, they weren't pulling me into management; I was filling an empty seat. My boss said as much. "Come eat at our table. We don't have enough people to fill it up."

My Games were again with the entire community, not the Hatchery. It was the same old back and forth, but I grew a shield around me, never speaking about deserting Robert in the School. What a far cry from way back when in the Game Club, when I used the Game to open up and be honest. Now, I was an impenetrable shell.

People ganged up on Bobby in Games, accusing him of not working hard enough, of not having the proper attitude. Did he fake his sales figures? He said no, but there was some distrust. He didn't measure up to Synanon's fanatical standards. It was as if the snarling wolves in Synanon never forgot his containment transgression from way back in that General Meeting. The community had a long memory and remembered that Bobby had slipped up. A pack of wolves followed his scent.

All I knew was I was unhappy. Refusing to admit I was no longer content living in Synanon, I concluded I must be unhappy with Bobby. It was his fault. Sure, he was the same Bobby I fell in love with, but he wasn't enthusiastic enough.

I couldn't be with someone who wasn't a pillar of the community. I needed to be surrounded by one hundred percent positivity to hold myself together.

Maybe Bobby had wrapped his heart in armor the same way I had. Maybe he hoped moving back in together would heal his wounds. He must have been living through the same nightmare I was.

God, if we only we had talked. If only we had admitted putting Robert in the School felt wrong. Admitted that it tore us apart inside. But we didn't.

Synanon sent me to a Stew at Tomales Bay, almost five hundred miles away. Back to where Bobby, Robert, and I lived together so briefly—our only time together as a family—back when I saw a bright future.

All of us Hatchery moms had been scheduled for Stews, but not together like we needed. We needed time to kick around our feelings—feelings only we could relate to. But no, Synanon scattered us. Now I think it was intentional to break our bonds. We had to be bonded to Synanon, not each other. And not to our husbands. That last bond—to spouses—would be broken a month after I left.

I rode the Synacruiser to Oakland, then transferred into a jitney to Tomales Bay, riding over the familiar roads. I should have felt a pang being back in Tomales, where I always wanted to live, but I felt nothing through my miasma.

Twenty-four hours in a Stew, twenty-four hours of sleep deprivation, was usually enough to break down my subconscious barriers. In the wee hours of the morning, we settled back and talked about our past, our loves, and our hurts.

"How are things with Bobby now that you're out of the Hatchery?" someone asked.

My stomach flipped. "Not so good. He's always in trouble. We're always arguing."

No one asked me, "How do you feel now that you've given your baby away?" I would have lied, anyway. I didn't admit, even to myself, that it was so much easier to pick a fight with my husband than confront the fact that I gave my baby to the School.

Another person asked, "Why do you stay with him? He's not going anywhere. You could be with anyone in the community."

Maybe my life would be simpler without him.

Out loud, I speculated, "I am thinking of leaving him. I'm just not happy anymore." I refused to admit to myself that my unhappiness was over the loss of my baby. I refused to talk about my heavy heart, my low energy, my losing track of time, my dream-state.

I spent the rest of the Stew thinking about leaving Bobby and starting fresh.

Maybe he will do better without me. I'm probably an anchor sinking him.

Bobby hugged me when I returned to Santa Monica. "I missed you!"

I returned a stiff hug, averting my eyes.

He must have heard the Stew over the Wire. Do I want to break up with him?

Over dinner, he acted like he hadn't heard a word. I pushed the food around my plate, unable to swallow.

A couple of days later, we were in a Game together. My stomach roiled as we filed into the windowless room with twelve other people. I sat on a faded director's chair, arms folded across my stomach, looking at the floor, trying to breathe. I felt like a stone was crushing my chest.

There was a lull in the Game. I took a deep breath.

"Bobby, I want to break up."

His face went slack, and his dark skin lost its warmth, replaced by an eerie, ashen tone. "I thought you were just blowing off steam in the Stew."

"I'm just unhappy. I need to move on."

I often describe the Synanon Game as group therapy without the therapist. But that's a lie I've told myself. In our divorce Game, we didn't explore why I might want to break up with him, why I was unhappy. The Game took my side, just like DJ Don had done in my very first Game when he lambasted my neighbor who owed me money.

After the Game, Bobby took my hand and gazed into my eyes. "Are you serious?"

"Yes," I told him. Stone cold. My heart was locked away in the same steel locker holding memories of my father. I could only stay in Synanon by detaching myself from my feelings.

I went to the Connect, our hub for housing and transportation, and asked for new housing. I moved into an apartment in the same building as the School.

I didn't realize that I had surrendered to the pressure, placing the community before all else, with my marriage trailing far behind. And my baby? I longed to be with him every day, yet I was expected to let him go.

I could not hold on to both my marriages—one to Bobby and one to the community. How little we had actually lived together. Our marriage never had a chance.

Oh, Bobby. His best friends had split, and he was forbidden to see them. And then I left him. And then Synanon left him. He was on the outs, like a Splittee. He never talked about how once he'd been the darling of Synanon, and then he was no longer, how once he was my darling, and then he was no longer.

The Game had changed. We only heard about what we did wrong or how we weren't doing enough. Maybe it was always that way, and I never noticed. Suddenly, the whole world—our entire world—didn't love Bobby. He was dancing to an audience that no longer cared.

*
**

I decided to file divorce papers. So many people in Synanon got divorced. Our marriages were like revolving doors. Without worries about jobs, housing, and childcare, we could easily walk away from a relationship.

Friends told me a do-it-yourself divorce was simple. We owned nothing; we had nothing to divide.

I walked to the Santa Monica courthouse, a few short blocks from Synanon, and asked for divorce papers. "We can't give legal advice," the clerk explained.

"Well, can you just give me the forms?" She gave me a stack of papers, anything related to divorce. I didn't talk to any of our in-house attorneys. Instead, I sat with my divorced friends and sorted through the paperwork. Bobby and I had nothing to divide—Synanon owned everything. I asked for joint legal custody and no child support, assuming Bobby and I would live in Synanon forever. By then, I had heard of husbands who had split and fought for custody of their children, but I didn't even think about it. Those were things that happened to other people.

By the time I went to the final court hearing six months later, friends had suggested I should ask for at least one dollar in child support as "your life might change in the future. It's easier to ask for a modification of your child support than to petition the court later."

The judge asked me if my papers were final. "I'd like to ask for child support," I nervously replied.

"To do that, you need to re-file your papers, re-serve your

176

husband, and then wait another six months for your divorce to be final." I didn't want to wait. I don't know what the hurry was; I certainly didn't have a new husband lined up. I needed to move forward. It was all I could control.

"Well, I'll just leave the papers as is then," I replied.

He struck the gavel, and I felt it plunge through my heart. I was officially divorced.

Chapter 24: Then They Stole My Baby

Spring 1976, Santa Monica, California

In early spring 1976, Lorena and I walked to the Santa Monica Mall. No babies or strollers, only us. Empty-handed. Empty-hearted. Our babies had been in the School for two months. The morning sun warmed our backs, but didn't warm my heart. I had filed for divorce, but the gavel hadn't yet struck.

"I heard the Infant Program is moving back to Tomales," Lorena said, raising her eyebrows as if I might know something about it.

I was a secretary in the Manager's office. Even if I had inside information, I would have kept it confidential. But I didn't know anything about this.

"That doesn't make sense," I answered. "The whole reason they moved us here was to beef up the Infant Program. I haven't heard a thing." I had a sinking feeling.

We walked silently for a couple of blocks as exhaust fumes and the hum of traffic replaced the salty air and the crash of the ocean. Lorena gave me a look like she didn't believe me.

"I'd love to move back to Tomales," I said, imagining once again living at Walker Creek, playing with our children, and visiting my family. "I'll let you know if I hear anything. And you tell me if you hear."

She nodded.

What had she heard?

Within days, or maybe hours, I found out. The infants were moving back to Tomales, but most of us parents would be left in Santa Monica.

No one called a meeting. No one called a Game. Word spread via the gossip mill. We parents weren't even important enough to tell in person. I wasn't important enough.

Synanon was moving all the babies to Tomales Bay, five hundred miles north.

This can't be real.

I had found an uneasy balance with Robert in the School. I had visited him daily until a Demonstrator asked me to come less often.

"You don't need to come by every day. Robert needs to learn to be without you," she told me.

Strangling a sob, I had refused to let her see my weakness. My heart pounded, my hands clammy. My words stuck in my throat. Backing away, I muttered, "Oh, okay. I'll see you in a couple of days." I felt like she had ripped my heart from my chest. But moving my baby five hundred miles north was worse; it was cruel.

Seeing Robert every two days was all the distance I could handle. Sometimes, Lorena and I took Robert and Nathanial for walks along the Santa Monica Promenade or merely watched them play and crawl. Robert seemed happy, and I had finally quieted my monkey chatter, my endless stream of wondering if I was on the right course.

And now they were moving him. I sought out Lorena, and we met for dinner as the sun set over the Pacific, turning the water golden.

Lorena soothed me in her thick New York accent. "Don't worry. I heard they're finding us all jobs up there." Her blue eyes were clouded. She grabbed my hand and looked me in the eye. "I'm moving with the babies. I'll watch out for Robert until you get up there." Lorena had worked with the infants in the Synanon School before becoming pregnant, so she was lucky to be rotated north along with the babies.

Time stopped.

The day of Robert's move came, and I stood frozen, weak-kneed, watching Robert in that white jitney. I already missed his chubby arms and fat thighs, his round cheeks, his laughter, and even his crying. It happened so fast that I had no time to filter my feelings. The shell of my body was in Santa Monica, but my heart and soul were in the jitney.

Suddenly, there they were, buckled into the jitney. Lorena sat nestled between Robert and her son, Nathanial. She glanced up at me, face emotionless, and gave a small wave. *Lorena is with him, so he'll be okay.* I stood tall and held back my tears. I thought they would move me there soon.

Not soon enough. I can't bear this.

I trusted Lorena. She would take care of Robert until I moved. My chest burned as panic settled in; the burn crept into my throat and stung my eyes. *They'll move me soon.*

I wanted to run downstairs and stand in front of the van like a tree hugger protecting a redwood, but I didn't. I wanted to yank open the jitney door, grab Robert, wrap him in my arms, and snuggle my nose in his neck to breathe in his scent, but I didn't. Mostly, I wanted to take him back to my apartment to watch him crawl and play and be his mom again, but I didn't. I stoically watched, my heart a stone. It was the only way I could cope.

And then they drove away.

How could I give them my baby? Why didn't I shout, What the fuck are you doing? This is my baby, not yours! What do you mean I can't see him every day?

I remember believing so strongly in the community, believing they were right. Everyone I knew had their babies in the School. Everyone seemed happy about it.

For seven years, I heard Synanon preach nuclear families were the root of all evil—I couldn't inflict that on Robert. For seven years, I heard Synanon preach I couldn't be happy in the outside world. What was out there for me? A dead-end job? A life with no purpose? Racial strife? I couldn't inflict racism on my Black baby. For seven years, Chuck preached I should be grateful for everything Synanon gave me. Whatever that was—I worked for room and board.

What bullshit I bought into. I believed it all. Is this what brainwashing is?

When they said, "We're moving your baby five hundred miles north," I swallowed and nodded. I froze, afraid of the repercussions of standing up for myself. With Cynthia's splitting fresh in my mind, I conformed, compartmentalizing my anguish, stuffing it in that locker in my mind. The locker was getting full.

I had moved Robert into the School with the stuffed lion my brother and sister-in-law brought when visiting us. Now he and his lion were gone. My limbs were heavy as I walked sluggishly across the street to the Del Mar Club. I died a little that day. I never considered that Bobby did, too.

Poof! Just like that, I was alone. My best friends, the mothers and fathers in the Breeders, and my co-mothers in the Hatchery were scattered back to work, some in different facilities. After spending almost two years bonding, loving each other, and loving each other's babies, it was as if our group never existed. Synanon had moved on to its next experiment: Childlessness. I hung on, still mindlessly believing in Synanon and loving the community.

My programming kicked in. I smiled. I acted as if.

But in the middle of the night, my heart ached. Who puts him to bed? Does he wake up at night? Will he remember me?

I consoled myself, knowing that my fellow Breeders had put their babies in the School and that our babies were still together. We could ride this out.

Cynthia was lucky that she left before watching her baby drive away.

I grasped at the straw of moving to Tomales, confident I would be transferred north, that I would be an involved parent, co-parenting with the Demonstrators. But Synanon needed me in the manager's office. I was afraid that if I spoke up, I would be squeezed out of Synanon, like Cynthia. I didn't know then that would have been the best outcome.

Frozen in my mind is a snapshot of Robert and all my babies strapped into a jitney and driving away. My throat constricts as I relive that day. I should be angry; I should scream at the Demonstrators who took my baby, at everyone who lived in Synanon and turned their heads while we sequestered the children, but I am guilty. I let them take him. I have not replaced my guilt with anger.

Suddenly, there were no children around. Not one. Even though I didn't work in the School, I had always seen children jumping, skipping, and laughing. When I was in Oakland, the kids lived in several apartments at the Clumps where I lived. Their joy filled the air. In Tomales, I watched them run, climb trees, and ride horses. In Santa Monica, children were in the apartments across the street from the Del Mar Club. Always children, often playing at the beach.

Then, Synanon squirreled the young children away at the Ranch in Tomales; the teens were moved to Badger. The children were no longer part of our community. The village was no longer there to help raise, care for, or protect them.

I never want to live where there are no children.

I threw myself into my work, keeping up my façade, while secretly thinking, I have to keep that pack of wolves off me. They're not going to drive me out.

I lived in a haze, like driving over Mt. Tamalpais in the fog. My brother's words from long ago echoed in my head: "In the fog, you can't tell if the road is going up or down. You know there's an ocean on one side, and when you reach the summit, you should have some visibility. Just follow the white stripe on the curvy road, and you won't go careening off into the ocean. Don't look up; the headlights will reflect the fog, blinding you. Don't look at the car approaching you; its headlights will blind you. Just follow the white line."

When I drove in the Berkeley Hills or over Mt. Tamalpais as a teen, when I reached the top, I could see San Francisco above the fog.

After Synanon took Robert, I lived in the fog, following the white line; I never reached the top. Sometimes, I didn't know if I was awake or dreaming.

> *I'm in a department store. Alone. But, no, can't be a store because there's no merchandise. Just a huge empty room with tall windows, but no view. I run to an exit, my footsteps echoing on the gray wooden floors. The exit disappears. I spot another and run across the room. It too is gone. I squeeze my eyes shut and take a calming breath, certain I'll see the exit when I open my eyes. I only see walls. How do I escape? I run in every direction, my heart pounding in my ears, my chest burning as short breaths escape through my raspy throat. Finally, an elevator. A freight elevator with yellow wire cage doors. I push the down button, but it flies upward. Then sideways, spinning and tilting. I cling to the cage door. And then it drops. Fast.*

I jolt awake, my heart still pounding, my body soaked in sweat. Just a dream. A dream that stayed with me for days.

I hid my feelings so far down I couldn't find them. Like a battered wife, I stayed in my Synanon marriage.

How could I give them my baby? Why didn't I shout, What the fuck are you doing? This is my baby, not yours! What do you mean I can't see him every day?

I remember believing so strongly in the community, believing they were right. Everyone I knew had their babies in the School. Everyone seemed happy about it.

Fuck childlessness. It didn't even make sense on an intellectual level. Chuck was going to control births like the wealthy people. Chuck was wealthy by then. He lived in a compound in the Sierras and had cars, motorcycles, a driver, cooks, housekeepers, and servants. Maybe he squirreled away money. He convinced us peons we were wealthy because we had access to all of Synanon's properties. Yet, I owned nothing.

I didn't even have control over my child.

What happened to The People Business?

Chapter 25: Only a Visitor

1976, Santa Monica, California

A few months after I broke up with Bobby, friends asked whom I wanted to date. Why did I have to be a couple? Even with our shaved-head stance of equality, we never dropped the idea that you had to be a couple to be complete. Staying single never crossed my mind.

DJ Don boomed my name over the Wire. "Janet Best! Call into the show and tell us who you're eyeing."

Wow, a bigshot is noticing me.

Noticing me in a good way. My whole body tingled, and my lips broke into a grin—a genuine grin, not the fake smile I had been wearing.

My heart raced as I called in. "I'll just say his initials are JG," hoping Jeff, the ambulance driver who wanted to deliver Robert on the Golden Gate Bridge, was listening.

If Jeff was listening, he didn't respond. Did he even remember me? Well, I wasn't going to put myself out there and go after him. Although I should have—he lived in Tomales. He could have been my ticket back to Robert. I wasn't that brazen.

God, Bobby probably heard the entire exchange. I shuddered, then pushed that thought aside.

Sam, the butcher, hit on me. He had recently celebrated his five-year Synanon anniversary, over eighteen hundred clean-man-days, and lived in a private room overlooking the Pacific. Sam was a little taller than Bobby and muscular with a light-brown bushy beard, unusual in clean-shaven Synanon. He claimed shaving gave him a rash.

As we sat on the beach, the sun warming our skin and sand drifting over our bare feet, Sam's voice rose above the sound of the crashing waves. "I started using in Vietnam. Heroin was passed around like candy over there. It's the only way I could face another day. Everyone shot up." I nodded. I had heard this story so many times.

Sam's brown eyes looked far off. "I came back, and people spit at us and called us baby killers. I'm not using that as an excuse; I'm just sayin'."

I knew about anti-war protestors yelling at the vets returning from Vietnam like it was their fault. It had been all over the news. Most of the soldiers were drafted, flown to the other side of the world, and ordered to kill. I never considered what it would be like to be that soldier returning home to hate. Certainly different from how the U.S. treated our men returning from World War II.

I squeezed Sam's hand, tears in my eyes.

"I just never stopped using. My mom tried to get me to stop, but I was hooked. She finally suggested Synanon."

"How did you get to be the butcher?" I sipped on my saccharin-sweetened Tab.

"I started in Food Service and helped cut the meat one day. I had a knack for it, so that's what I've done ever since." He laughed. "I have a blast. Give people some fresh meat, and they'll love you forever."

I closed my eyes and leaned back in the chair, smiled.

"Whatcha' smiling at?"

"Just life." Guys in wetsuits were out surfing. I watched the waves, enjoying the attention of a handsome man respected by the community. No drama.

I threw myself into a new group of friends—Sam's friends. They distracted me from my constant reminder of Bobby and the babies. I felt the fog that had settled over me lifting, giving me hope that the Synanon I loved was still there.

After a few months of dating, Sam and I were Love Matched. Chuck had come up with the idea of a Love Match to replace marriage. In 1976, the California Supreme Court deemed nonmarital cohabitation lawful, meaning that you could legally shack up without being married. Chuck and his cohorts decided that if a couple wanted to live together, they could apply to be Love Matched—no need to bother with getting marriage licenses from City Hall.

Sam and I sat in a circle with a Director and a few friends. Like the vows in Bobby's and my wedding, we committed to each other and to the community. *Do I take his last name?* We were married in the eyes of the community, so I changed my name, shaking off the last vestiges of my marriage to Bobby. I even changed my name on my driver's license.

Bobby and I would run into each other in the hallways, the dining room, and at Saturday night party. I had seen couples break up and stay friends, but I couldn't do it. Every time we ran into each other, my lips trembled and my insides bubbled. I took a deep breath, forcing cheer into my voice. "Hey, how's it going? You look good." Talk about act as if.

He still wore his radiant smile, but his eyes were clouded. "Hey, yeah. All's good. Take care." Something like that. Some stupid lines we said just to say something.

I hoped whatever was troubling him would be mended with me out of his life. I wanted him to be the dashing man loved by the community, the man I fell in love with. I wanted him to be smitten with someone else—surely that would ease my heavy heart. Whispers of his dating teenagers reached my ears. I had seen him flirting with younger women—were they teens? God, I hoped not. He would be gamed mercilessly for that, maybe even run out of Synanon.

Sam and I had no baggage, no memories of a General Meeting gone bad, no memories of child separation. We could simply have fun. Sam was part of the Motorcycle Club, which organized motorcycle rides along the Pacific Coast Highway. On one day trip, twenty of us rode eighty miles along the coast from Santa Monica to Santa Barbara. I rode on the back of Sam's motorcycle. Mostly men drove the motorcycles, but a few women rode their own. Rocky cliffs rose skyward on the right, the ocean sparkled on the left. Dolphins replaced surfers. I hugged Sam's waist, leaning into the curves, reveling in being part of the group, breathing in the ocean air, blocking out thoughts of Robert. Wearing helmets, long sleeves, and pants, we could only feel the wind on our faces. We devised a system for changing lanes: the lead cyclist would signal left, those behind him would all signal, and then the last in line would change lanes, clearing the way for the entire procession to change lanes en masse, like an elegant ballet.

Synanon had devised a way for members to own motorcycles; in reality, they were more like a lease. You had to be a resident for a certain number of years and pay money saved up from WAM. The motorcycle was yours to use as you pleased as long as you maintained it. Until you split. Then, the motorcycle stayed with Synanon.

Two of my new friends were Brody and Myra, one of the few couples who remained married after being rescued from heroin addiction. Brody was a tall, thin carpenter with sparkling, laughing eyes, always finding humor in any situation. Myra, with black shorn hair and dark skin like she had a hint of an Indigenous in her bloodline, was more serious and was a secretary to the Directors. Brody and Myra had a pre-teen daughter in the School, but we didn't discuss her. The kids had their own lives.

The four of us hosted burrito parties at least once a week. Sam brought fresh pork from the kitchen, cooked it up with sour cream and onions, and rolled the mix in tortillas, served with a side of raw jalapenos. We drove to Boys Market in Marina del Rey to buy sugar-free Shasta soda, pretending we were drinking sugary drinks.

One weekend, we all rode motorcycles to Badger. Expecting fog, we dressed in layers. No big deal. I grew up in fog, but this tule fog, this dense ground fog, was different. It was cold and wet; it seeped into my shoes, clothes, and skin. Riding through it on a motorcycle added wind, which hastened the misery. San Francisco fog floats through the Golden Gate Bridge, gently spreading and settling on the ground, but tule fog arises from the ground when the air reaches the dew point. It's as if icy fingers are reaching up and grabbing your ankles, creeping up your legs, over your torso, and seeping into your back and neck. We couldn't see anything through the fog, but Sam and Brody knew to follow the white line. We pulled into a cafe for hot chocolate, and the server laughed as we peeled off helmets, gloves, and layers of clothing, shrinking from hulking giants into waifs.

I never recognized that I was living two different lives: my I'm-a-Synanon-fanatic life, and my I'm-a-mother life.

In my Synanon fanatic life, I was promoted to the Director's office (at Myra's suggestion), dined with the Managers in the corner of the dining room overlooking the sparkling Pacific, and completed my aerobics by running along the beach, feeling the wet sand between my toes, sometimes blinded by the sun reflecting off the waves. I jogged along the palisades overlooking the ocean, watching surfers and sailors in the water below, and weightlifters on the sand. I lived in paradise, yet the moment I paused my busy life, a sadness crept in like tule fog eager to consume me.

My other life was visiting Robert at the School.

At the School, I was merely a visitor. I had to call ahead to say I was coming, like getting permission to visit my child at a boarding school. When I arrived after a seven-hour drive, I found a Demonstrator who led me to Robert. Then I spent the day soaking up his presence, watching him play, holding him. Sometimes I took Robert, Nathanial, and another toddler on a picnic. We all held hands as they walked on their wobbly legs. We didn't walk far, but on the way back, they fell asleep while walking. I held one for a while, then switched kids and held another. These kids needed naps!

Afterward, I had to say goodbye again, holding my breath, holding back tears. I buried my feelings, still telling myself this was the best way to raise a child. How did my feelings compare to this wonderful education he was getting, surrounded by his toddler friends and taught by the cream-of-the-crop Demonstrators?

One fall day, when Robert was about fifteen months old, I rode the Synacruiser to Tomales to visit him. It's a long, boring drive—three hours north on Highway 99 for a stop in Visalia to pick up passengers from Badger, then a cutover to Highway 5 through the Central Valley for another four hours. At least through the valley, I could watch fields of vegetables whiz by. Back then, there were no fallow fields, and the farmers erected signs announcing their crops: corn, broccoli, artichokes, and onions. The sealed windows of the Synacruiser blocked out all smells, but I could imagine the scent of onions.

Arriving at the School, I announced myself. "Hi, I'm here to see Robert."

"Oh, go on outside. Robert's playing in the sandbox."

I walked behind the building and saw him sitting alone in the sand. His chubby arms held a shovel, and he was concentrating on scooping sand into a bucket.

"Robert!" I called out. He didn't look up.

"Robert, it's Mommy!" He glanced at me but kept shoveling.

My chest caved in and I stopped breathing. Tears stung my eyes. I stood like a stone statue, blood drained from my body.

Oh my God. He doesn't know who I am.

Right when I thought my heart would break in two, he finished filling his bucket, stood up on his wobbly legs, and ran into my arms. I could breathe again.

Of course, he knows me. But...

Then my intellect kicked in. He was merely finishing what he was doing.

I stayed a while; I don't know how long. That's another image etched in my mind and heart: Robert ignoring me.

Why did I not scoop him up, call my mom, and run?

Being brainwashed, being a true believer, is a bitch.

Robert and Nathaniel at the School

Chapter 26: Fat-a-thon

1976, Santa Monica, California

In late 1976, when I was twenty-six and had lived in Synanon for five years, someone came up with the idea of Gracious Dining. Maybe it was Betty D's idea. She always spoke of graciousness, surrounding ourselves with beauty, and savoring life. Other than those at the Directors' table, few lingered over dinner. Sam and I usually grabbed a bite to eat and left, like running into Taco Bell and scarfing down the food in ten minutes.

Instead of figuring out why no one hung out over dinner, Chuck issued a new edict in the name of experimentation: Gracious Dining. A way to slow down, unwind, savor the meal, and converse.

Did no one think maybe we stopped lingering over dinner because our world was topsy-turvy? Who wanted to talk to anyone? I had accepted the vow of childlessness and heard about abortions; I had given my baby to Synanon. Gracious Dining was one more rule thrown at me.

Every Friday night—maybe more often—we dressed up for dinner, foregoing our overalls. The men wore long robes, a fashion statement that had started while I was pregnant. Chuck was still overweight and was no longer comfortable in overalls. While we all continued doing aerobics, I suspect he had long since stopped. He and his coterie dressed in long robes made from colorful fabrics. The Directors followed suit, so to speak. Robes for Saturday Night Party, and now robes for Gracious Dining.

Sam and I held hands as we stood in line with Brody, Myra, and a few dozen people, waiting to enter the dining room. Beyond the line, I could see the dimly lit room, which glowed pink from the sun setting over the Pacific. As we closed in on the dining room, the wait staff manning a soup table greeted us. The soup was a vat of broth into which we scooped bran—another push to be healthy: adding fiber to our diet.

We then proceeded to the dining room, where the tables were set up restaurant-style, with plates, silverware, and napkins, similar to the Director's table. While the Directors sat at their private table, we minions were supposed to sit with people we didn't know, breaking up the cliques of friends that naturally formed. Sam and I filled our plates cafeteria style.

The food hadn't changed; we just ate and talked until our two hours were up.

One evening, there was a bowl of dehydrated corn in the soup line. I was standing behind DJ Don and the other Director I worked for. Both wore their formal attire: floor-length robes, one dark blue with off-white sparkles, the other deep green. The men in robes reminded me of peacocks, with their vibrant, showy feathers.

DJ Don declared in his deep DJ voice, "The idea is to add a kernel of maize to your broth and then see how fast it goes through your intestines." The line quieted. We paid attention as if there would be a test. "The quicker it comes out the other end, the healthier you are." He laughed. "Just look at your poop tomorrow."

My stomach flipped as I imagined peeking into the toilet, searching for maize. Was I supposed to squish my poop through my fingers, searching for a kernel of corn? I had to take part; I worked in the Director's office where we had to be ramadoulah, our word for super positive.

DJ Don went on the Wire the next day to announce his score. People called in: Eight hours! Three hours! I wasn't going to scrutinize my poop. Besides, eating bran didn't change my poop schedule.

Over the weeks, when Sam was out of town, I screwed up my courage and sat with people I didn't know, especially if a newcomer was sitting alone. "Mind if I join you?" The newcomer was more nervous than I was; my heart lightened as I drew him into conversation, watching him relax, and then smile. Maybe laugh. "Where are you from? How long have you been here? Where do you work?" Another connection; another friend. I was once again in the People Business, helping an addict and being a big sister.

As we continued our two-hour gracious meals, our stomachs expanded.

Another drumroll.

"Everyone's getting fat," Chuck announced. So, we had to lose weight.

191

A Fat-a-thon. Mandatory weigh-ins.

I had always been thin; now, post-baby, I weighed about 135 pounds in my five-foot-eight frame. But that wasn't lean-normal. The lean-normal charts indicated I should shrink to 122 pounds.

In the HBO documentary, *The Synanon Fix,* the narrator said they all met with doctors to determine their health and ideal weight. But he worked at the Home Place for Chuck and his entourage. In Santa Monica, we didn't see doctors; we read a chart.

We held weekly Weigh-Ins like Weight Watchers on steroids.

At the first weigh-in, we wore everyday clothing. At the next weigh-in, we wore shorts and tank tops. We began wearing less and less clothing to the Weigh-Ins, anything to show a bit of a loss. Many women didn't eat the day before the weigh-in, unable to bear the shame of not dropping a pound.

We gathered before breakfast in the living room in front of the tall windows framing the Pacific Ocean, watching the surfers on their boards trying to catch a wave, and stood in a shame line waiting to step on the scale. A Director called out results like a basketball broadcaster announcing player statistics. So-and-so lost two pounds this week! Uh-oh, so-and-so gained a pound! There was nowhere to hide. Anyone who didn't lose weight heard about it in a Game.

One woman's boyfriend broke up with her because she couldn't lose her last five pounds. I now understand how a man during those bat-shit crazy days would end his marriage over weight gain. The community—and its peer pressure—came first, marriage second. Although I didn't admit it, on some level, I broke up with Bobby because he didn't measure up to the community's standards. It breaks my heart to think about it and how it affected our son's life. Forever.

Social pressure to conform seeped into my soul. I was unaware that I caved in to survive, brushing away any fleeting doubt like crumbs off my shirt. I went along, drifting in and out of a fog.

At one weigh-in, we heard that Betty D. had appeared in her underwear at the Home Place. Like lemmings, we all followed suit. I bought pretty lingerie to parade around in. One week, a bunch of us wore black bras and panties. Wilma, the ex-madam who had admonished Bobby and me not to get married, looked at us and proclaimed, "You all need a Madam." Laughing at our boldness, we took a group picture with her lying in front of us.

A few weeks later, as we gathered in the living room, the fog over the ocean now barely a mist, a whisper traveled through the room. Everyone at the Home Place had disrobed for a naked weigh-in. I looked around. I wasn't the only one sitting in stunned silence.

Are we now expected to be nude?

My gut flipped. I was so used to my flipping gut that I hardly noticed. I could swallow the panic effortlessly.

Sam leaned over. "I'm going to call the Home Place to see if this is true."

He left the room and returned a few minutes later, buck naked, his golden pubic hair there for everyone to see. His penis dangled. Raising his arms in a victory stance, he proclaimed, "It's true!"

Charlene, barely twenty years old—the Charlene who couldn't keep her eyes open at the Stew so many months ago—was sitting next to me and gasped. Her dark brown skin paled. She crossed her arms and looked at her feet. "I can't believe we're expected to do this," she mumbled.

But, mostly, everyone laughed, and nearly the entire room jumped up and stripped. Feeling the fog drifting in front of me again, I joined in, nervously giggling with everyone else. I took off my bra and looked around at perky boobs, saggy boobs, and deflated penises. Then I removed my underwear and leaned forward to cover myself. Charlene took off her bra, her voluptuous breasts for all to see, but left her underpants on. "I'm on my period," she grumbled, body rigid.

I shook the fog from in front of my eyes and consciously joined in the fun. These were my friends! We were breaking society's norms! I didn't feel the giddiness I felt when I first shaved my head, but joining the crowd swelled my heart, hiding the pangs of deserting my son.

I recall only stripping that one time, and that was enough. I'm sure we didn't do it again, but I could be wrong. What other memories have I suppressed?

Shortly after the nude weigh-in, I was in a twenty-four-hour Game with Jordan, the old-timer from my Stew who helped Belinda with her nightmares about the keyhole. He was one of those old-timers who could seemingly hug a hundred people at once.

"Later tonight, we'll have a nude soak," he said matter-of-factly, like announcing we would have cookies and milk after dinner. I inwardly groaned. We were in a twenty-four-hour Game, and no one questioned whether a nude soak was a good idea. By now, those left in Synanon had accepted every edict, from no smoking to shaved heads to no sugar to childlessness to nude weigh-ins. I had stopped questioning when I surrendered to the heiress in that Stew at the Bay when she told me my feelings about moving to Santa Monica didn't matter.

Our Game turned from emotional to rational as daylight turned to night and the moon reflected on the ocean. Instead of talking about what a stupid idea the imminent nude soak was, we talked about how boobs and penises float in the water, so to expect that. We intellectually discussed what-if-I-get-turned-on. About midnight, we changed into our bathing suits, met at the soaking tub, numbly took off our suits, and got in the water. I looked at the water, avoiding eye contact. My breasts floated in the water, but I didn't see any penises floating. I didn't notice any hard-ons. The hot water soothed my body but didn't relax me.

After about ten minutes, we got out of the steaming water, put on our bathing suits, and ran into the ocean to cool off from the heat of the soak. *There, we did it.* Returning to the Stew Room after dressing, none of us spoke of it. Relief washed across our faces as we silently acknowledged we had survived an ordeal. It may have been the only time I experienced such quiet during a Game.

I never did it again nor spoke of it. What was the point? Nude soaks, thank goodness, did not become fashionable, at least while I lived there.

The mandates were coming faster and faster. I didn't have time to adjust to one before another was piled on—childlessness, abortions, Gracious Dining, and Weigh-Ins. Now, nude soaks. Outwardly embracing every new edict, inwardly, I cringed, clinging to the community after losing Robert.

This is better than the outside world. This is where I belong.

Chapter 27: Snip

January 1977, Santa Monica, California

Almost nine months had passed since they moved Robert north—nine months of telling myself that my sorrow was worth it if it meant he could have the best life possible. I *had* get rotated too, but how could I do it without making waves? I listened for every whisper of job openings, every hint of a chance. Nothing. Just silence, frustration, and the quiet, constant terror of provoking the elites' wrath.

Nine months of building a life with Sam. Nine months of crossing paths with Bobby, both of us silently pretending it wasn't painfully awkward.

Nine months caught between the joy of communal life and the sharp, unrelenting ache of missing my son.

And then Chuck announced a new rule, and my chest tightened, my pulse spiking as the moment seized me, shoving all thoughts of Robert and Bobby to the edges of my mind.

All the men who had lived in Synanon for over three years had to get a vasectomy.

No one named it a loyalty test, but how else would you define this edict?

Where did I hear this? Over the Wire? Or snippets of conversations over a period of hours: "It can't be true... It's just a suggestion... If you don't want to have a kid, why not get a vasectomy?... What about the women? Can't they get their tubes tied instead?... A bigger procedure... Anesthesia, maybe a hospital stay... For men, it's just a simple snip... I'm signing up; I want to stay here... Not me..."

I hid my pounding heart and sweaty palms. Only listened. *What the fuck? Can this be happening?*

There were no suggestions at Synanon, only rules. What was good for one person was good for everyone.

I sat down with Sam at lunch. "Did you hear?"

"The vasectomies?" He shrugged. "Sure, why not? We're not having kids."

How can he be so blasé?

"But it means you can never have a baby!"

"No one's having babies here. It's great. No more birth control."

It was absurd logic that twisted my mind.

At least I have **my** baby. And I'm giving him the best life possible. I clung to that thought.

I ran into Bobby after lunch and grabbed his arm. "Are you going to get a vasectomy?" It felt so final. Even though we were divorced, tears still welled when I thought of no more little Roberts.

Bobby shrugged. "What choice do I have?"

I squeezed my eyes shut. This can't be happening. Why is everyone so happy about it?

But not everyone was happy about it. Dozens, maybe hundreds, split.

My mind ran in circles. I alternated between isn't-this-fun-we're-all-doing-this-together and this-can't-be-happening.

Sam and Brody made back-to-back appointments.

Sam trembled as I dropped him off in the nondescript room off one of our hallways in the Del Mar Club—not at a medical facility. He had sounded nonchalant, but now reality hit. A Lifestyler doctor performed his vasectomy with the help of our home-grown medical assistants. After forty-five minutes, Sam and Brody emerged, each holding ice packs against their groins. Patting each other on the back, they laughed. "That wasn't so bad."

I let out a long sigh and hugged Sam. If he was okay with it, I was okay with it. Or so I told myself.

Today, someone is paying eight hundred dollars a night to stay in the room where Sam and Brody got their vasectomies.

Maybe, after their vasectomies, the men felt the way I did after shaving my head—an overwhelming sense of belonging and being on the team. My team logo was a shaved head; theirs was an ice pack.

I laughed instead of recoiling in horror. Laughter hid that voice whispering, *What the fuck are they doing? What the fuck am **I** doing?*

We were still attending weigh-ins—in underwear, not nude, thank God. Everyone was slim by then. Flat stomachs and thin runners' legs below hairy chests. Boobs barely filling in the bras. We were the fanatics who survived the vasectomies and who lost the weight and our right to have children.

I had an idea and headed to the sewing machines. I drew tiny scissors, maybe three inches square, and cut them into appliques. Then I sewed them onto Sam's and my underwear, right above the crotch. We kept it secret. The next Sunday morning, we strode into the living room hand-in-hand and stood by the scale in front of the picture window overlooking the skateboarders below.

The room exploded with laughter, but the laughter echoed off the walls; so many men had split instead of getting snipped that our community room was no longer brimming with residents.

I had given my baby to the community—I *had* to believe in everything Synanon was doing. If I didn't believe in Synanon, how could I justify letting them take my baby? These were not conscious thoughts, only rationalizations I can now understand.

Weigh-in Santa Monica
Photo from author's collection

Chapter 28: Maybe We Need to Break Some Legs

Early Spring 1977, Santa Monica, California

"Knock 'em down if they won't listen," Chuck bellowed over the Wire. "Sometimes kids need to be hit. We're in charge. Not them."

What the hell? Cardinal Rule Number One: No Violence.

Maybe if I hadn't let Synanon take Robert, maybe if I hadn't turned a closed eye to abortions and sterilization, alarms might have gone off in my head. Maybe, maybe, maybe.

Chuck's rants over the Wire hit like punches to my stomach. I toughened my gut, like a boxer training for the next match. I could take a pounding without being knocked out.

I knew Chuck was talking about the Punk Squad—the delinquents Synanon took in. The unwanted children we were supposed to take care of, instead of having our own babies. But hitting them? What happened to no physical violence? It made no sense. I didn't say this out loud. I didn't even think of saying it out loud. I would not make waves.

I had to be a good citizen, so I could be reunited with Robert.

Besides, what did I know about taking care of troubled teens? That was someone else's job; someone who knew what they were doing, or so I thought. Honestly, I had stopped thinking. I had stopped feeling.

Then Chuck formed the Imperial Marines. Only men—men considered the best of the best. Imperial Marines was an ominous title, but surely it was another play on words to differentiate this group from the Boot Camp. I thought Chuck was taking a group of men under his wing, similar to the Academy years back. Who wouldn't want to apprentice directly under Chuck?

But I heard rumors: The Imperial Marines were security guards for Chuck. This made no sense. Why would we need our own marines? Who was he protecting himself from? Us—the minions?

I thought Chuck was getting paranoid and I didn't take it seriously.

Weeks later, Chuck ranted over the Wire. "Maybe we need to

break some legs. Tell the nuts out there, don't fuck with Synanon."

What the hell? He can't be serious.

My chest clenched in panic even though I told myself it was just rhetoric.

Chuck spoke, and we followers listened. And acted.

I watched my friends, my friends who had embraced non-violence, who had put their street life behind them, lobby to be part of a new group: the Hey Rubes. They would be our protectors. They met privately to learn defensive techniques. I don't know who taught them. Maybe they taught themselves. They strutted around with black berets.

They carried guns. In holsters.

They would get the word out: Don't fuck with Synanon.

Get the word out to whom? To the local surfers? That's why I didn't take them seriously. Who would attack us?

But the guns! Cold black steel meant only for death.

I kept coming back to our first cardinal rule: no violence or threat of physical violence. Wasn't carrying a weapon a threat of violence?

I flinched every time I saw a gun, averting my eyes and assuring myself the man carrying it was protecting me. *But only bad guys carry guns, and we're the good guys.* I felt like my mind was breaking in two, watching our good guys carrying the black, menacing weapons.

Once again, I stayed quiet. Didn't voice my opinion. Swallowed my fear and went along.

I was DJ Don's secretary. He, too, wore a gun on his hip, so I had to see the cold, black steel every day. I forced myself to look at his eyes, not the bulge on his hip. I forced the tremors out of my voice, feigning normalcy.

One night during Gracious Dining, as Sam and I lined up for the before-meal broth, Don and another Director approached me in their formal attire: long robes. I wondered if they were wearing their guns under their robes.

"Where's the letter to so-and-so I gave to you to type?" DJ Don asked.

"It's on your desk," I answered, thinking I would put it there right after dinner. We were at Gracious Dining, after all. I didn't realize that he wanted it right then, that his job was twenty-four-seven.

DJ Don came back in a few minutes, his blue eyes stormy. Sam and I had just filled our bowls with bran and broth. "The letter's not there. Where the hell is it?"

"It… it's still on my desk," I stammered. "I was going to put it on your desk after dinner." I wanted to crawl into a hole and skip Gracious Dining. The sight of the soup nauseated me.

DJ Don stomped off.

The next day, the facility manager approached me, all chipper. "You're getting a job change. You're going to work for me." I flushed, mortified. Job change? Bullshit! I had been fired.

Smile. Act as if.

A few days later, I experienced the Hey Rubes in action.

A commotion near the front door startled me. Shouting. Running. I hurried to the lobby to see what was going on. Men donned their black berets and ran outside, frantically shouting, "Hey Rubes! Come to the street!" Were we under attack? I hadn't taken all the talk of protecting our community seriously, but maybe I was wrong.

Several of our men dragged two shaggy-haired surfer-types up our stairs and into the Stew Room. I followed and sat in the gallery to watch, my stomach roiling. The Hey Rubes pushed the surfers into a couple of chairs. The Directors and Tribe Leaders joined them in the circle, shoving the surfers back in their seats when they tried to get up. I wanted to puke.

"You animals peed on our building!" a Director screamed. "Maybe we should shave your heads to teach you a lesson."

All this for peeing on our building?

The surfers sat silently, eyes wild. Everyone in the Stew circle joined in the berating. These two young men were experiencing their own General Meeting. Transfixed to my reality show, I sat in the gallery, arms clutched over my stomach, feeling helpless.

The Directors finally released them with the statement, "Get the word out to your friends! Don't fuck with Synanon!"

Chuck spoke. We listened. Pissing on our building was disrespectful.

As I blindly spouted the party line about what a wonderful community I lived in, I had more nightmares.

The dreams sometimes came to me as I walked along the palisades or the beach. I didn't know if I was remembering last night's dream or if I was dreaming while walking.

> *I'm floating on a blissful, azure lake, gazing at the clouds, totally at peace, when suddenly the lake turns into a tidal wave. I'm on the frothy top of the wave, desperately trying to swim back to the lake. I'm swallowing water, drowning, then I look up to see the wave is about to crash me into a stand of trees.*

I woke up shaking, adrenaline rushing through my veins. *Take a deep breath. Take a deep breath.*

The only way to escape was to wake up. Trembling. Did I scream in my sleep?

What is happening to me?

Officer Richard Grotsley of the LAPD holds the rattlesnake that bit Paul Morantz
https://lamag.com/religion/synanon-cult/

Dederich and two Synanon 'Imperial Marines' were charged with conspiring to murder lawyer Paul Morantz by placing a rattlesnake in the mailbox of his Pacific Palisades home in 1978. They pleaded no contest.

Chapter 29: Bobby Split

1977, Santa Monica, California

I walked into the dining room for breakfast. It must have been a Sunday because I smelled bacon. A couple of sailboats headed north along the coast.

Myra walked up to me before I reached the buffet and pulled me aside.

"So, I hear Bobby split?"

"What?" My heart skipped a beat. "He did? He didn't even tell me." But why would he? I left him a year ago. My entire chest hurt, a pain radiating from my sternum across my ribs, down to my stomach, up to my throat. I took a deep breath, shaking off the anguish and pushing it into my hidden locker. I didn't even have to tell myself to act as if. It was a reflex.

"Thanks for letting me know." I smiled, trying to sound adult. At least I wouldn't have to run into him in the halls anymore, seeing him with girlfriends. I didn't know how all these couples who had separated dealt with seeing each other every day. But he split? After getting a vasectomy? Why did he go?

I felt like he abandoned me, even though I'm the one who abandoned him.

I sat by myself at breakfast. Where would Bobby go? His mother and siblings were in Virginia; only his father was in California. I remembered meeting him that one time when I was pregnant. *Maybe that's where he went.* I didn't remember the address. Somewhere in rundown West Oakland.

I pushed my food around my plate, ignoring the dining room chatter.

It's tragic how people split. No goodbyes, just suddenly gone, like they no longer existed. How many people had dropped out of my life? It had started way back in the Game Club as squares decided Synanon wasn't for them. I thought of my neighbor Gary, who left after DJ Don pounced on him for not paying back my fifty dollars. I thought of Kathy with the Datsun who didn't want people controlling her life. And the artist who was whisked away to the elites and then left shortly after. What spooked her? I thought of Cynthia, who couldn't bear to put her baby in the School. And all my Breeders friends who were in Synanon but weren't here with me.

And now Bobby.

Bobby couldn't even say goodbye to our son. He was the one who was strong enough to hug our baby at the jitney when they drove Robert away, but now he had to leave without a goodbye. He had been one of the most involved fathers in the Hatchery—he must have been as heartbroken over the School move as I. Tears stung my eyes as I remembered him kissing us goodnight, and singing to Robert on our walks.

How stupid that we didn't talk about it. Were we both scared to utter a word of negativity? Scared of what? Scared of not living up to expectations? Scared of being ostracized?

He could not hang on as long as I did. How could he stay when he wasn't wanted?

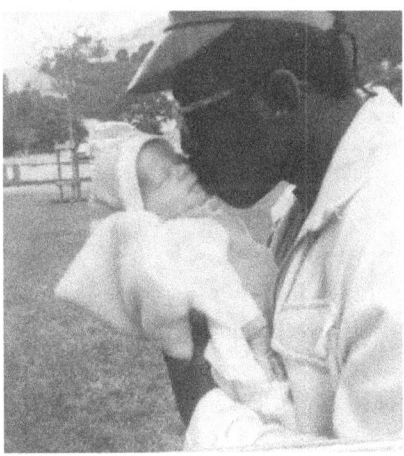

Bobby and baby Robert 1975

Chapter 30: A Sleepless Trip

1977, Santa Monica, California

Maybe I should go on a Trip. Not a vacation like an unhappy couple takes to save their failing marriage, but a Synanon Trip to revive my community passion. To remember why I was living there. To quell the rumbling in my stomach, the whispers in mind. *Something is wrong.*

Everyone waxed poetic about their Trips. "Trips. I loved them. It was such a rush when all the garbage was out of the way and a great joy would fill us up. We experienced pure love at the end. A most amazing journey."

That's what I needed. Pure love.

Somehow, I went eight years without going on a Trip. Most people were tripped during their first year of residency. I think I had stayed in the Game Club for so long that by the time I moved in, everyone assumed I had been on a Trip. No one invited me and I never asked.

What about me? The thought of asking left my stomach roiling. *They should notice me. They should ask me.* No one asked; no one noticed. I was lost in the shuffle, forgotten. When people compared Trip stories, my stomach clenched, knowing I wasn't truly part of the community; I hadn't taken communion.

Maxwell, the Director-father in the Hatchery, stopped me on my way to lunch. "Janet, got a minute?" Maxwell seldom spoke to me. Even as a co-parent, he wore a smirk the few times he was around.

Masking the sudden tightness in my gut, I squared my shoulders and smiled. "Sure."

"We're planning a Trip and we'd like you to be a Shepherd."

I let out a breath I didn't know I was holding. A Trip leader—a high honor. I shifted my weight. Should I just go along and pretend I knew what I was doing? I opted for honesty. "I've never even been on a Trip."

"You haven't? Well, let's get you on this Trip."

That's how I found myself wearing a white muslin robe in a room with mostly newcomers. My peers were wearing colored scarves.

My stomach fluttered as I met my fellow Trippers in the living room. Outside, it was dusk; the ocean was midnight blue. Inside, the dimmed lights suggested preparation for sleep, but sleep would have to wait. There were probably fifty of us, all wearing heavy long white muslin robes, robes reserved for Trips. When I swapped my overalls for my Trip robe, I felt like I stepped into a sacred garment passed on from earlier Trippers. It was the same feeling I would have twenty years later stepping onto the John Muir Trail, following the same steps as John Muir. On this day in 1977, at age twenty-six, I walked in an unknown old-timer's footsteps, wearing an unknown old-timer's robe.

I once heard Chuck say, "I love Catholics. They are so used to rituals that all I have to do is set up a ritual—like a Trip—and they are putty in my hands." Somehow, he knew that giving his followers a spiritual awakening—even if induced by sleep deprivation—would leave them wanting more. Waiting for their next high.

He also said there were exceptions—the Trip didn't work for everyone.

I knew the theory: dressing the same was the first step in breaking down our egos—our psychic barriers that separated us from our true natures and from each other. Knowing this, the robes had no effect on me. We already had bald heads, after all. But my robe was soft and comfortable.

Being a participant instead of a leader was weird. I wasn't a newcomer; I should be leading the Trip, but how could I do that when I hadn't been on a Trip? I felt like I was watching a movie, maybe a contestant in a reality show. Maxwell, the Trip Conductor, wore the same white Trip robe but had a long purple scarf draped around his neck. Other old-timers wore yellow scarves, identifying them as Shepherds. They would run the Games. They knew how to push people's buttons, how to break them into tears.

Mostly, I remember being tired and disoriented. The forty-eight hours were broken into four-hour sessions. Even knowing this, I lost all sense of time, like a prisoner deprived of sleep and fed at odd hours. Was it day or night? My entire world was reduced to the white robes and the colored scarves who led us around, who decided when we could eat and sleep.

Early in the Trip, maybe the first four-hour bit, we were all in one room, the men on one side and the women on the other. One Shepherd asked if anyone had had a homosexual experience. The room was silent. Then, a couple of people stepped forward, heads down.

"Who has thought about having a homosexual experience?"

A few more stepped forward.

"Who has been attracted to the same sex?"

A few women giggled and stepped forward.

The questions became more and more specific. I finally stepped forward when the Shepherd asked, "Have you ever looked at a picture of a naked woman and thought she was beautiful?" How stupid. Was this to show we were all the same, or was it simply one more exercise in humiliation—to call out the gay people?

We didn't acknowledge same-gender attraction, so what was the point? Several members were gay; we just didn't talk about it. One gay friend told me, "I know I can't have sex while I'm here, and that's okay. I'm here to get off drugs."

We broke into Game groups and followed our Shepherds into windowless rooms. Unlike most free-for-all Games, the Shepherd of my group directed the Game, sometimes keeping the Game on one person for hours. He had done his homework on each participant—his past and his Synanon past—like a Google search we would do today.

More Games.

"I missed Ray's funeral," I said, hanging my head. "I drove to U.C. San Francisco for my OBGYN appointment, and when I got back, you all had had his celebration of life and were back at work like nothing happened." Tears threatened my eyes, but I still couldn't cry. "He was just suddenly gone." I felt hollow as I imagined Ray sitting across the room. A big man with shocking black hair back in the day, chef's hat, smudged white apron wrapped around his expansive chest and belly, wide grin, laughing. He had ridden his motorcycle on the curvy road between the Ranch and the Bay, something he did every day. An oncoming car crossed the line—and maybe Ray hugged the corner too closely—and poof! Ray was dead.

I wanted one of his hugs.

More Games.

"I felt so horrible when I was demoted out of the Director's office. Sure, I get to work for Kathy" (the facility manager) "and I get to manage the apartments, but still, I was basically fired." Heat rose into my face; I felt my ears turn red. They hadn't outright fired me after DJ Don humiliated me in line for Gracious Dining that night. No, it was only a job change.

"We get job changes all the time," someone responded. "What's the big deal?"

I tensed. "No, it was because I lied. I told Don a letter was on his desk and it wasn't. It was still on mine. The next day I got a job change."

"Good lord, get a grip. You're making way too much out of it."

The Game moved on, but I knew my little white lie was the cause. I would never do that again. And I haven't in my entire life.

Ray's memorial service and my firing were easy to talk about. I didn't talk about my father. I didn't talk about my baby. I kept those feelings locked up in that cupboard of my mind. I still didn't feel safe.

An Ouija session at midnight. Two Shepherds, their yellow scarves barely visible in the dim light, sat at the Ouija Board in the middle of a large room, their fingers touching a planchette, moving from letter to letter, sometimes fast, sometimes lingering, then whipping across the board to another. One called out the letters; someone else transcribed. We white-robed Trippers surrounded them, heads snapping up after nodding off to sleep. I had played this game as a kid and I still didn't believe the spirits were speaking. But I sensed a shift in the room, a feeling of awe.

An art session. Beyond tired, my body ached, craving sleep. Bleary-eyed, I sat with my fellow Trippers at a long white table, squinting as the sunlight reflected off its surface, glaring straight into my eyes. So it was daytime. Artist Michelle must have talked about art, about expressing ourselves, about putting our feelings down in pictures. I don't remember. She handed me a posterboard-sized piece of paper. My mind blank, my eyes wanting to close, I doodled. Then we were shepherded somewhere else. Maybe a walk outside along the beach. That must have been a sight for all the Santa Monica tourists to see. Bald, robed cultists following a leader. A cult? Nah!

The artist told me afterward, "Your drawing was so haunting that I cried. It was so obviously a uterus tied in knots." So, I had drawn my feelings after all. Feelings I didn't even acknowledge. I never saw my drawing again, but I remember it. A large oval of twisting squiggles.

At last, the forty-eight hours were up, and we all gathered in one room for a wrap-up. I had heard this is when the Trippers hug and cry, their emotions raw from forty-eight hours of sleep deprivation and Games. But for reasons unknown to me, our Trip Shepherds made us watch a silent clip from the Vietnam War: that famous clip of a little girl running down the road, burned from napalm, with the caption, "We have met the enemy, and it is us."

A shudder swept through my entire body. Why did they bring in the war? That skinny little girl, running naked, screaming. My heart should have broken, but it was already broken. I simply stared. I like to think I saw myself in her, running from the enemy, running from my community, and maybe I did. I just didn't know it.

I didn't know then how true that phrase was: We have met the enemy, and it is us. Synanon destroyed itself from within.

That was the climax? We were supposed to run downstairs dancing and hugging after that clip? My limbs were too heavy.

But run I did. I ran down the stairs with my fellow Trippers, and smiled and hugged as expected. I was numb.

I was one of the exceptions Chuck spoke about. The Trip didn't work for me.

I had to shake my ennui. The Trip hadn't done it. Getting love matched hadn't done it. Sure, we had fun, but I couldn't shake the feeling of pointlessness.

Maybe if I moved away from Santa Monica, away from the memories of Bobby and the Hatchery, my joy would reignite. I was afraid to ask for a transfer to Tomales, afraid of being called a headsucker, of caring about my son more than I cared about Synanon.

I never considered leaving. Synanon was my home and my son's home. I still believed the School was best for my baby and that I just had to suck up my feelings.

All that remained was to sketch a uterus tied in knots.

Chapter 31: Betty D. Died

April 1977, Santa Monica, California

We knew she was dying. Betty D. shared her dying life publicly, the same way she shared her entire Synanon life. She was always teaching. Unafraid.

Diagnosed with lung cancer in December 1976, gone by April.

Almost prescient, in her dying months, Betty urged, "Be sure to keep your journals; things are going to change." Betty had been Chuck's ballast. When she was gone, only his yes-men were left.

Synanon held a day-long celebration of Betty's life. In Santa Monica, we gathered in the living room overlooking the Pacific, and people who had known her told stories and cried. The stories gave me goosebumps. She touched so many people. Saved so many people. But I didn't know her.

Betty D. was a champion for women, encouraging us to break the male power structure. During my tenure, there were only one or two Directors. About the time we shaved our heads, Betty began a Mudslide Academy, under her tutelage, to empower women. Mudslide, according to Betty D., describes women's power: women tend to garner a movement that is slow, gathers energy, and spreads widely, like a mudslide. It is imperceptible at first, but by the next day, you realize a house has been moved across the street.

How were we supposed to gain power when we still submitted to shaving our heads?

I only met Betty once when she came to see our three-month-old babies in Santa Monica. The afternoon sun streamed through the windows as we moms gathered around a ten-foot spool table in the dining room, excited for her attention. Our babies sat in plastic baby carriers tilted into seats, and we hoped they would smile for Betty.

Betty waltzed in, a broad smile lighting up her dark skin. She wasn't imposing like Chuck, but there was a magnetism about her. I don't remember her words, but she seemed kind and thrilled to see the newest Synanon babies. She cooed at each of them, eliciting smiles.

Other than that, I only heard stories.

Chuck spoke over the Wire. He must have been heartbroken, but he sounded philosophical, almost detached. I know that feeling.

"A great life is possible in Synanon. Betty reached a peak. She became as good as you can get. We are not gods; we are human beings. She did leave us better than she found us, and she'll make us better than she left us. It seems to me that summarizes a great life."

He immediately sought a new wife. He didn't wait for her body to get cold, as they say. He asked married women to marry him. He took applications. Finally, he settled on Ginny, a woman I had known in the Game Club. She couldn't fill Betty's shoes.

Ironic how Chuck said, "We are not gods," because he certainly acted like one. His word was the law. I look back and see how I deferred to his every whim. At first, I believed in all his ideas for our experimental community. Then, as time passed, I acquiesced even when it was against my moral code. Shaved heads, childlessness, vasectomies, abortions, guns. It became easier and easier, especially since everyone was following along.

Sometime during these batshit crazy days, Chuck, an ex-alcoholic, fell off the wagon, and his so-called friends secretly bought him booze. Was it before his decree of childlessness, while Betty D. was still alive, or after she died? I don't know, and those who know—his enablers—will not say. They hid his drinking and spearheaded his crazy ideas. I didn't know about his drinking until decades after I left.

Did Betty D. know Chuck was drinking? Was she part of the group who kept his drinking secret? Someone knew Chuck had fallen off the wagon. I've heard names, but until that person speaks, it's only a rumor. The rumor is that when Chuck heard Betty was diagnosed, he asked one of his staff to buy him liquor, and they did. And they never spoke a word. The people who knew he was drinking kept quiet. It sounds almost romantic: he started drinking when his wife was diagnosed with cancer. I'm not the only person to believe Chuck started drinking before Synanon went bat-shit crazy—before childlessness, vasectomies, and abortions. By then, his sycophants, who followed his every whim, surrounded him, and the rest of us

211

followed a drunk down his path of destruction. That makes his entire entourage, including Betty D., complicit in hiding his secret.

One of the bedrocks of Synanon was breaking contracts—exposing secrets—to keep addicts from going back to drugs and alcoholics from going back to booze. To me, keeping the secret that Chuck was drinking felt like the ultimate contract. Back then, I believed the glue that held our community together was the Game, and if Chuck wasn't called out in a Game like anyone else who broke the rules, it was all over. For years, I blamed his enablers, the ones who covered for him, for bringing Synanon down. But I see it differently now. It was always Chuck's house, his family business. He was CEO and Chairman of the Board, untouchable. He built Synanon—and he was the one who brought it down.

Why did I stay? I ask myself this question over and over and still have no answer. Maybe it was brainwashing—persuasion by propaganda or salesmanship, as Merriam-Webster defines it.[10] Cult expert Steven A. Hasson, Ph.D. says, "Brainwashing doesn't always look dramatic; it often employs subtle tactics to bypass critical thinking and reshape beliefs and identities."[11]

Chuck was a salesman in his prior career, but he was more than a salesman. He was a master manipulator.

I heard the same phrases over and over, day in and day out: Nuclear families are the root of all evil. You are all character disorders who don't fit in with larger society. Stay here to avoid living a life of quiet desperation—Henry David Thoreau's quiet desperation that I tried to avoid when I left home.

Still, I lived in quiet desperation—trying to fit in, clinging to my belief in the communal life, even as my moral core whispered, *something is wrong. Abortions? Vasectomies? Violence? And who was raising my son?*

---

10. Frederick C. Mish, Ed., Merriam-Webster's Collegiate Dictionary, 150.
11. Steven A. Hassan PhD. "How People Get Brainwashed Without Realizing It." https://www.psychologytoday.com/us/blog/freedom-of-mind/202412/so-youve-been-brainwashed-without-realizing-it-what-now, accessed May 2, 2025.

Chapter 32: The Strip

Spring 1977, Badger, California

Shortly after Betty D. died, I heard about a job opening at the Strip, a property Synanon had purchased in the Sierra foothills a year earlier. The Strip, named because there was an old landing strip like those sprinkled on farmland throughout the United States, was about five miles down the road from the new Home Place.

In the fall of 1975, while I was juggling babies, Chuck and Betty moved to a three-hundred-fifty-acre property near the small town of Badger, California, where they built luxurious headquarters. No more living simply for Chuck and Betty. Our live-in architects designed the buildings; the unpaid carpenters and apprentices built them. The entire power structure relocated: Chuck's kids and their spouses, the regents, several Directors, the lawyers, and all of their staff.

The following year, 1976, while men were getting vasectomies and we were starving ourselves into lean normal weight, Synanon bought an eighteen-hundred-acre property five miles down the road from the new Home Place. Tradespeople and their apprentices built a lodge and a common area. Everyone wanted to live there, close to Chuck, close to the power center. So, they needed a Clerk—a facilities coordinator.

I jumped at the chance to move. The thought of leaving Santa Monica left me lighthearted. Away from the ghost of Bobby. Away from the recurring vision that left me trembling—the vision of Robert being loaded into that white jitney. Surely, I would fall back in love with Synanon if I could escape Santa Monica.

I didn't have the nerve to demand—even ask—to move to Tomales. No, that might let loose the raging wolves—the fanatics. They weren't going to drive me out of my utopia.

My utopia? Yes—I still idealized our community lifestyle. Somehow, I could ignore the horrors of the vasectomies and abortions; somehow, I could deny that Synanon stole my baby. I moved all that into my hidden cache in the back of my mind while I embraced the camaraderie.

The Strip was two hours closer to Robert. Even closer by

motorcycle. And I would be back on the Cubic Day—seven days on and seven days off—I could visit Robert every two weeks. A new job in the beautiful Sierras, closer to my son—it was a win-win.

Visit my son. A skewed concept of parenting. I had to visit my son like a criminal with visitation rights.

By that point, my thinking was so distorted, being five and a half hours away from my child seemed reasonable—it was better than seven and a half. Robert was almost two years old, and I hadn't lived near him for a year. I felt sly, as if I were outmaneuvering the Synanon wolves, inching up the coast toward my son.

I landed the job ("of course—you're perfect") and Sam and I moved within a week. My insides fluttered while I gleefully packed. It was the first time in six years that I chose where I wanted to live.

We rode the Synacruiser to the Visalia Airport, where we would transfer into a jitney for the drive up the mountain. When the fourteen-passenger van pulled up, my breath caught in my throat. The van was identical to the one that had driven away with Robert a year earlier.

Don't think about that. You're starting over.

The jitney was driven by Corrine, whom I'd known since the Game Club. She was still married to the architect she had moved in with—though that would change a month after I left, with the arrival of the Changing Partners decree.

Sam and I stepped down from the air-conditioned Synacruiser onto the asphalt parking lot. Sweat beaded under my armpits as the sun reflected the heat, adding ten degrees to the ninety-degree day. In the distance, private airplanes shimmered through the heatwaves. The smell of the Synacruiser's diesel exhaust assaulted my nostrils.

Taking a deep breath, I grabbed Sam's hand and pulled him over to Corinne. She hugged me. "Look at us," she beamed. "From the Game Club so many years ago, here we are! I'm so glad you'll be my counterpart. I'm swamped." Corinne and I would share the job, each working ten or twelve hours a day for seven days, then having seven days off while the other worked.

"Hey." I hugged her back. "This is Sam. He'll be working in Food Service."

"Welcome, welcome," she said, embracing Sam. "Let's get out of this heat."

Sam and I were the only passengers. The tension drained from my body as Corinne drove us along Highway 198.

Goodbye, Santa Monica, and your bad memories.

City buildings gave way to agricultural fields, and the faint smell of manure filled the van. As we drove northeast out of Lemon Cove, the fields gave way to oak trees, and the road began winding its way up the mountain.

Shortly after turning onto Highway 245, we passed Badger, population 140, with an elevation of about three thousand feet. Quaint. Only a few miles to go.

Corinne turned onto the property and gave us a quick tour. Wooden buildings and cottages dotted the landscape, trails wound through the trees, and some teens splashed each other in a small pond.

"The airstrip is over there." She pointed east. "Don is always giving rides on one of the airplanes. You'll probably get to go." DJ Don had moved to the Home Place and was a part of Chuck's inner circle, one of his yes-men, enjoying fine dining, airplanes, and servants, and doing Chuck's bidding.

I smiled. This is where I belong.

Corinne dropped us off at a two-story wooden building resembling a mountain lodge. Stepping out of the van, I breathed in the crisp mountain air, ten times cooler than the Central Valley. The ground, still damp from the snowmelt, emitted the sweet, woody fragrance of the forest, decaying wood giving way to new life. Birds chirped in the trees.

"Here's the Shed." Corinne smiled and pointed at the lodge. "Come in and have some lunch before I show you your cabin. Janet, our office is upstairs, but you can see that tomorrow."

The familiar smell of buffet food permeated the Shed, which was sectioned into a kitchen, dining room, and community room. The Food Service staff bustled in the kitchen. Mismatched couches and chairs dotted the living room, and along one wall were tables with piles of leather, suede, and whittling and woodworking tools. Even sewing machines. My eyes widened. It reminded me of the Oakland Hut—our women's retreat—but on steroids.

"Hobby Lobby," Corinne explained, following my eyes to the woodworking area. "We usually hang out here in the evening when we're not in Games." She turned toward the door. "I've got to catch up on some work. I'll be back in a bit."

Chuck had taken up whittling. As always, what was good for Chuck was good for the community, so we all started whittling. We didn't have a Hobby Lobby in Santa Monica, but this close to Chuck, the zealots mimicked him.

Sam and I grabbed food, cafeteria style, and spotted Brody. He and Myra had rotated a couple of weeks earlier. Myra was a highly regarded secretary, and she moved when the Directors she worked for moved—the same Directors who had fired me. She commuted to the second property, Home Place, while Brody worked in construction, helping to build out the Strip property.

"Hey, you guys," Brody called to us. "Come sit over here. Have you seen your cabin yet?"

We shook our heads and joined him at a spool table sized for six people. I shaded my eyes from the sun streaming through the windows reflecting off the varnished table.

"It's right next to ours. You can walk from here." He lifted his chin to point across the property. Tall pines, massive oaks, and red-barked manzanita covered the land.

As we finished eating, Corinne popped over. "Let's get you settled. I'll take the jitney to take your stuff over."

We drove over a dirt road to a one-room cabin nestled under a twenty-foot oak tree and unloaded our few possessions. I tipped my head back and looked toward the top of the tree like I used to when camping under the stars.

"Sam, we have this place all to ourselves!" I grinned. It wasn't a dorm, an apartment, or a butler barn with paper-thin walls.

Sam put his hands in his pockets and warily looked around.

"It's not New York, I'll give you that."

In the evening, the stars enveloped me, the Big Dipper, my compass growing up, welcoming me home.

The Clerk job was more complex than its title. Corinne and I oversaw resident housing, guest housing, transportation, the Pop Sheet (keeping track of the Strip population, which changed daily as

216

residents transferred in and out), and mail services. We distributed WAM and picked up visitors at the Visalia airport. As the cool spring turned into hot summer days, I lived in cutoff overalls and tube tops and rode around on a Honda 50 motorcycle.

Most evenings, Sam and I hung out in Hobby Lobby, talking and laughing with our friends. We were only five miles down the road from Home Place—the power center—so the unspoken social pressure was intense. It felt like a beehive where we followed the queen bee, not because we were forced to, but because we wanted to. The buzz was addictive. The fanatics, the true believers, surrounded me, the one hundred ten percent committed, those who embraced every experiment with "Right On!" It wasn't mandatory to hang out at Hobby Lobby, but why wouldn't we?

We sat at tables under bright lights, breathing in leather, wood shavings, and glue scents. I gathered fallen manzanita branches and sanded them to a silky finish. In one, I carved the Synanon logo, creating a paperweight. I made a fur-lined hat from donated leather. The smell of freshly baked, sugar-free apple pie often drew us back to the dining room for a sweet indulgence.

I should have been happy: love-matched, living in the mountains, working in a challenging job. On my days off, when not visiting Robert in Tomales, I rode dirt bikes, jogged along the trails, sunbathed on giant boulders at a nearby river, and visited Sequoia National Forest.

But as spring turned to summer and the summer wore on, I still lived a fragmented life.

My heart was with Robert in Tomales. Why didn't the separation bother anyone else? Was there something the matter with me? I knew Corinne had an older child in the School, but I don't remember her talking about her daughter. We only talked about our jobs as if our children didn't exist.

I kept busy working, motorcycle riding, hiking, and acting as if life was grand. My thoughts of Robert would come unbidden in the middle of the night, the now familiar ache in my chest keeping me awake. *Is he sleeping? Does he miss me? Who's taking care of him? Am I doing the right thing?*

Sam and I rode his motorcycle to Tomales every other week to visit Robert. I no longer cared if I was a headsucker who couldn't leave my child alone. Lorena and Adrian had split instead of getting a vasectomy, taking Nathanial with them. Two of my babies were gone.

The visits to Robert were awkward. I had to contact the School in advance, like making an arranged court-mandated visit. It was never only Robert and me; I always had to take two or three toddlers along. That was okay; they were all my children. Once, when the kids were about eighteen months old, I took Robert and two other toddlers for a picnic. We walked pretty far for those little legs, spread out a blanket, and ate sandwiches. I beamed, watching them play. Then, as we headed back, they were tired and could barely walk. I ended up carrying two kids, with one straggling behind. I traded off whom I carried, rotating them between my arms. These poor kids were exhausted, never having naps.

Robert always ran up to me with a hug; I never had another painful moment of him in the sandbox ignoring me. Every two weeks, he had grown a little and was more stable on his feet. Not yet talking. Still in diapers. Mom picked him up once a month and drove him to her house for a few hours. She must have thought I was crazy abandoning my child, but she never said a word. She kept our communication open throughout my time in Synanon, as if she knew I might need her one day.

One evening in July while Sam and I whittled in Hobby Lobby, the scuttlebutt was that Teddy, the beloved sculptor who had built the stone fireplace at the Bay (using the rocks my fellow Breeders and I gathered) and who had split some time ago, wanted his sculptures back. He had a gun and was threatening to shoot Synanon members. What? Was Chuck's paranoia justified?

DJ Don and another Director ran upstairs, hands hovering over the guns on their hips.

"I better go," I told Sam, "to see if Don needs me. Maybe I'll have to call a Hey Rube alert." I didn't work directly for Don, but since I was working this week and my counterpart, Corinne, was off,

I felt like I should be on point. My job didn't end at 6:00 p.m.

I followed DJ Don up the stairs.

DJ Don and the Director wore holstered guns. I shuddered. I knew they had guns. After all, every Sunday at Home Place, Chuck hosted a Shoot where the upper echelon and their prized guests, dressed in western attire and practiced shooting. I was never invited.

I cringed, once again seeing the guns up close. My eyes kept straying to the black steel strapped on their hips. Forcing my eyes to Don's, I said, "Let me know what I can do."

I desperately wanted to believe they knew what they were doing with those guns.

DJ Don was on the phone. "Could he be on his way to Badger? We have to protect the Old Man." Furtive conversations went back and forth for at least an hour. I stared out the window, wondering if I would glimpse Teddy sneaking through the trees.

DJ Don glanced at me about midnight, as if noticing me for the first time. "You can go home. We've got this covered." He turned his back on me.

My shoulders slumped as I slinked away.

Sam was waiting for me downstairs. "So what happened?"

"Nothing, I guess." I could hardly swallow. "Don told me to go home."

I'm not part of this management clique. I never will be. I don't want to try anymore.

We walked silently toward our cabin, the stars bright in the waning moon, shining a light into my soul.

Gone were the days when Synanon tried to help people. Once upon a time, if two teenagers had peed on our building, we would have brought them into Synanon, offered them a cup of coffee, and explained how they should be worthy citizens. Once upon a time, we would have tried to help Teddy, not lined up with guns, trying to shoot him on sight.

I tossed and turned, trying to hush my thoughts, my whiffs of doubt. I had spouted the propaganda for so long that I believed it. I believed we were changing the world. I believed nuclear families were the root of unhappiness and drug addiction. I believed larger society had nothing to offer me. I believed I belonged.

But did I?

✳
✳✳

In August, when the heat pushed past one hundred degrees, I welcomed my lunch break after riding the Honda 50 around the complex, my skin filmed with dust from the sun-scorched earth. As Clerk, I was in middle management and attended the Managers' lunches. The facility Manager, Karen, the same Karen I had worked for in Santa Monica, spoke quietly into my ear.

"Now that you're in management, you should take a look at your friends." What did that even mean? Sam and Brody and Myra weren't good enough? What about Elizabeth?

Elizabeth and I had reconnected for the first time since the wedding. She had become known as "The Lady Carpenter," having apprenticed in the Synanon Construction Company after attending Betty D.'s Mudslide Academy in Tomales Bay.

Elizabeth shone as Lady Carpenter, now working with the crew expanding the Strip facilities. She carried herself differently—standing tall instead of folding into her height—and her blue eyes sparkled with the fervor of true belief. I felt a flicker of jealousy at how easily she seemed to belong. Still, after three years, it felt good to be back in the same facility with her.

Unsure what Karen meant by "looking at my friendships," I forced myself to mingle with the other managers and politely declined Elizabeth's offers for lunch or dinner. They weren't my friends; I don't even remember them. I felt like I was at a chamber of commerce meeting, making small talk with people I didn't care about and trying to do what was expected of me.

One afternoon, Elizabeth strode up to me in the dining room, shoulders squared. "I don't even know who you are anymore." She turned on her heel and left. *What the hell was that all about?* I stood gaping at her as she stomped off.

Her words stung, and for a moment I felt like I was becoming someone I didn't want to be. But by then I was an expert at ignoring those feelings, so I shoved them aside.

Meanwhile, Corinne and I had to find housing for everyone moving to the Strip.

When Synanon purchased the property, it was raw land. While the tradespeople and their apprentices built the lodge and community building, they lived in unheated bunkrooms. But now the rooms had heat, and people with more sway clamored to live there.

In September, we ran out of housing.

Karen, my boss, told me she had devised a solution to the housing crisis: we would move the tradespeople out of their bunks in the rustic lodge and into tents on the outskirts of the property.

"Take a few days and come up with a plan. You can make the tent assignments, and then when you figure that out, just call them in and give them their new housing." She looked up from her paperwork. "We can make it fun. Let's come up with an adventure."

I nodded, walked back to my desk, and stared at nothing. How could I do this? It's a hundred degrees in the summer. It would start snowing in a few months. There were scorpions and rattlesnakes. And the workers would have to cross a stream to get to the Shed.

My mom's words from long ago echoed in my head. Stand up for the workers. Look out for the little guy.

My mind began to open. My sense of right and wrong reawakened. While I was terrible at standing up for myself, I could stand up for them. I would not move these residents into tents.

One evening in early `September, after the day's heat had dissipated, Sam and I walked to the Shed, hoping someone had made apple pie. We noticed a group gathered around Kerry, Chuck's daughter, who was talking.

"We want to shrink to eight hundred people. We only want people who are one hundred percent committed to Synanon."

I don't think that's me.

"We officially became a religion a couple of years ago, so we're going to organize ourselves that way. Think of cardinals and high priests and priestesses."

I watched people nodding but stopped listening, imagining DJ Don, the Directors, and Kerry in long robes with pointy hats. I don't know how many residents we had then, but well over a thousand.

I don't want to be part of that.

Synanon had declared itself a religion in 1974. I didn't know anyone who took it seriously; I always assumed it was for tax reasons and the freedom to live how we wanted. Nothing had changed with the religious declaration until now.

Now, Synanon was trying to be a religion. I didn't believe it, but I was already on my way out. I just didn't know it.

Aerial view of the Strip
Photo courtesy of Synanon.com

Chapter 33: Splittee

September 1977, Badger, California

One afternoon in mid-September, I went to the Shed to hydrate before jogging on the trails during my favorite time of day, the afternoon when the sun dipped behind the forest and a light breeze picked up.

Someone in the Shed called me over to the phone. It was Mom. "They told me I can't see him!" She sounded exasperated.

"What do you mean?"

"I mean, I was planning to pick Robert up tomorrow and bring him to my house for the day. Like always. Someone at your school just called and said I can't pick him up." I squeezed my eyes shut, dizzy. "Something about how every time the babies spend time with a grandparent, they get too much unconditional love, and it takes days for them to get used to being in the School again." It was hard to imagine Mom giving anyone unconditional love. She practiced tough love. "They won't even let me drive up to visit him."

I could hardly breathe. "I'll see what I can find out," was all I said. Who would I even call? What would I ask? Synanon was raising my baby as they saw fit.

Now, Mom couldn't even see her grandchild? No wonder I had to take at least one other child with me every time I visited. There was to be no unconditional love for these children. My stomach churned. I needed fresh air. A jog would clear my mind.

I ran, concentrating on my breaths and my steps. I slowed to a walk, cooling down, cherishing the beauty and the scent of the trees, the best smell in the world. As the sun sank toward sunset, I walked in and out of shadows, a gentle breeze blowing across my face.

Jumbled thoughts competed for attention. Why am I letting a bunch of ex-addicts raise my child? What the hell am I doing? Robert will be okay if I only raise him how my mother raised me. Mom had four children, all of whom are responsible, functioning adults. Except maybe for me. Sure, my family wasn't perfect, but at least I had my mom.

I stopped walking and listened to the chirping birds. A squirrel ran up a tree, pausing to look down at me. Even dry in the summer sun, the forest smelled of pine and fresh mulch, the whiff of a rotting tree trunk. The scents that made me happy.

I'm just plain unhappy. I'm basically a happy person. It's this place, not me. No matter how hard I try, I'm not happy.

In a dream state, I silently bid farewell to this magnificent land where I had hoped to find serenity.

I love Robert more than the world—more than this community. I can't bear being away from him. What the hell am I doing here?

I was calm and at peace, perhaps for the first time in my life. I no longer want to be here, this new Synanon that wants to shrink to eight hundred true believers that send the children far away from their parents.

I loved the community when it was vibrant and growing and saving lives, when it was a large extended family. Was it all an illusion? It felt like I knew people so well, but then again, people came and went, and I was moved from place to place. Always a new best friend to make, always a goodbye. Often, there were no goodbyes as friends split. People wove in and out of my life.

I felt like a bubble that had been engulfing me popped. It was as if I drove out of the fog in the Berkeley hills and could suddenly see the stars, the trees, and San Francisco twinkling in the distance, beckoning me.

I was suddenly exhausted from trying to fit in, from being pressured to conform. Do I want to live in a place where, after dedicating years of my life, I can be driven out because I'm not positive enough? Like Cynthia? Where I can be humiliated on someone's whim? Like Bobby? Where I never feel like I do enough and no longer even like myself? Where I can't be part of my son's life?

Like a torrent of water cascading from a breached dam, all my doubts burst forth, roiling down the causeway, destroying the party line, the propaganda.

I began jogging again, kicking up dust on the trail as dusk settled in.

Synanon is no longer a social revolution, and it isn't going back. It has turned against its own members. Unless you follow unquestioningly. I can't do it anymore. Maybe I made it my home because I felt like I had nowhere else to go, but that's wrong, isn't it? That's plain old programming.

I stopped again, hands on my hips, breathing heavily, thinking about what I had been told over and over for years. You're a misfit. There is no place for you in larger society. God, I've been spewing the party line right back in every Game. For eight years. Over a thousand Games.

Looking up at the night's first stars, I admitted the mandates were grueling. Did I do my aerobics? Did I play my Game? Was I friendly at dinner? Was I hanging out with the right people? Was my hair short enough?

I miss my baby!

I could barely see the trail as it grew dark, but I knew it so well. I bent over, breathing, letting my heartbeat slow down, and walked toward the Shed. The locker in my mind sprung open. *My friends are gone. Bobby, Cynthia, Lorena. Elizabeth no longer speaks to me. I missed my baby's first steps. I missed his first words. I don't want to be a visitor—I'm his mom!*

All my doubts and unhappiness bubbled to the forefront. For once, I didn't try to stop the monkey chatter. I relished its truth. Cynthia left, not because it was too hard to put her daughter in the School, but because she was considered deadweight for sounding a little negative. Instead of supporting Cynthia, I joined the bandwagon, caving to the peer pressure of being a Synanon fanatic. And Lorena. That picture of her, arms crossed, trying to stay firm while we all shaved our heads, and finally, giving in. She made it until the forced vasectomies. That was too far.

Bobby was squeezed out after our son was driven four hundred miles away, squeezed out because he wasn't fanatical enough. He wasn't positive enough for me. I needed to be with someone positive who could bolster my zeal as my enthusiasm for Synanon waned. I hadn't thought about leaving; I had only thought about believing once again.

As the locked cupboard in my mind opened wider, I folded my arms and looked down. I was disgusted with myself for silently sitting by as men were forced to choose between the community and sterilization. I was sickened that I sat silently by as women had abortions to live in the community; that I sat silently by as men started carrying guns and holding trespassers hostage; that I sat silently by as teenagers were physically and mentally abused; that I sat silently by as Synanon took my baby from me. All in the name of the community.

No more.

As I reached the Shed, lights ablaze, I knew I had to let go of this place I once loved.

I went into the dining room, smelling apple pie.

"You just missed the pie," someone said. My face fell. "Sugar-free. We can bake another one."

"No, that's okay." *Oh, how I miss sugar! I can't even have sugar!* I thought of homemade cookies after school, of dessert every evening at nine o'clock with my parents. Sugar for home. Sugar for comfort.

I found Sam. "Come, take a walk with me."

He followed me outside. It was dark but starlit.

"I'm leaving."

"I'll go with you." He didn't sound surprised. Maybe he had been staying for me.

"You don't have to." I knew I would be fine on my own. But I said okay. Why not continue this adventure together?

We went to our cabin and packed. We told no one, not even Brody and Myra.

The following morning, we walked to the Clerk's office together. Corinne looked surprised to see me on my day off.

I looked her straight in the eye. "We're leaving."

Her eyes widened. "Leaving Synanon?"

I nodded. "We'd like to get on today's Synacruiser to San Francisco." The next day was my mother's birthday.

Corinne's business persona kicked in. "Of course. I'll get your names on it." I could see the shock on her face. I had never talked about leaving, never uttered a word of negativity. "I can't believe it." She shook her head. "Do you want me to put a Game together?"

"No, I'm good. I don't need a Game." I raised my eyebrows. "*You* need a Game." I admitted to myself how much I hated Games, relieved I would never have to play another one.

"Okay." What could she say? She looked pissed. "How am I going to get all this work done by myself?" I didn't care. Someone else would be rotated. Another body would fill my shoes. We were all expendable. "Come back in an hour, and I'll give you your WAM and collect Sam's motorcycle keys."

We walked to the community room and told our friends, at least the ones we saw. I knew word would spread like wildfire. No one seemed shocked; perhaps we had all become inured to people leaving. Brody wished us well.

"I'll miss you, man," he told Sam, shaking his hand, then hugging him. "You'll do fine."

No one tried to stop us. Another Big Squeeze was on. It's the same old mantra. "If you're not one hundred percent with us, we don't want you." I was no longer one hundred percent, and no longer wanted to be part of Synanon.

My self-revealed distaste for Synanon roiled around my head. What had Synanon become? Where was it going? I no longer had a say—or did I ever? I no longer cared. Was this one big con job? Had Chuck been bamboozling us all along, laughing as he asked more and more of us so we could live in his community, while he amassed property, motorcycles, and airplanes, with unpaid lawyers and housekeepers and cooks and drivers at his beck and call?

More importantly, did I want these people in control of my life? In control of Robert's life? No. Something that once seemed virtuous had turned evil. I was done. I took deep, calm breaths.

I felt free, like the freedom I felt when I rode off with Kevin the night I came home from college. Like the freedom I felt when I hung curtains in my first apartment. When it was all mine.

Sam and I returned to see Corinne and to turn in Sam's motorcycle and helmet. She was back to all business. So many people had split in the last year; I was simply another casualty.

"Here's what's left in your WAM. Thirty dollars." It was like receiving vacation pay after leaving a job.

We handed over the keys to the motorcycle that had defined our fun. It was never Sam's. He had paid to ride it and had to return it to the company like a leased car. We owned nothing, not even the Sony Trinitron TV in our room.

Corinne arranged our ride north on the Synacruiser for later that day and marked us off the Pop Sheet—another statistic.

I called my mom. I knew she would pick me up. Through all these years, she had held out a lifeline, a line I didn't see until I needed it.

I took a deep breath before calling the School. They had no right to keep him, but I was nervous about pushback. Would they try? They couldn't legally, but they could try coercion. I steeled myself for the call. I would be matter-of-fact. Who did I talk to? I don't remember.

"I just want to let you know I am leaving Synanon and will pick up Robert tomorrow at ten."

"Okay, we'll get him ready," the Demonstrator said. I felt weightless. I might float all the way to the Bay Area.

No pushback. Had taking our children out of the School become commonplace? I didn't know, and I didn't care.

My entire body relaxed as if I were finally exhaling a breath I had held for two years.

I split with thirty dollars, a quarter inch of hair, an ex-dopefiend boyfriend, and one suitcase full of clothes between us.

Sierra Foothills

Chapter 34: The Big Wide World

September 1977, Richmond, California

The Synacruiser dropped us off at the San Francisco facility. No one spoke to us on the four-hour ride. No goodbyes. No well wishes. Not even a handshake. We were already ghosts.

Mom and Dad were waiting in their Winnebago. Mom ran out and hugged me like I had escaped from a war-torn country.

"Happy birthday, Mom! This Sam." I had told her about him, but they had never met.

"Best birthday present ever!" She hugged me again. Already, I had received more hugs from her than I had in my entire life.

Dad came out and shook Sam's hand in an awkward welcome to the family. "Come on in; we'll get you home."

My niece, Robert's born-on-the-same-day cousin, was sitting in the Winnebago, sucking two of her fingers and twirling her curly brown hair. She scooched into a corner, staring at Sam with his bushy beard and buzz cut as if he were a grizzly bear.

We drove to Mom and Dad's house, and I climbed the six brick stairs I had stormed down eight years earlier. I was relieved to be home, but didn't really want to be there. I took Sam upstairs, and we put our suitcase in my old bedroom. My window looked out over a vegetable garden instead of a lawn, the rows marked with cobblestones Dad had gathered from the railroad.

The next day, Mom drove me to Tomales, a monthly trip she had made since Robert's move.

Robert ran to me, and my heart leaped. All my fears about him not knowing who I was vanished as he jumped into my arms. God, he must have been compartmentalizing me as I had done with him.

The Demonstrator handed me a bag with a few clothes. No toys. He, like us, owned nothing. There was no sign of the lion my brother had given him two years ago.

"Can I get a copy of his schedule?" I asked. "I don't want to disrupt his life."

I laugh, thinking about this. As if I hadn't disrupted his life fifteen months earlier when I let Synanon take him away from me. I didn't realize that all he wanted was to be back with his mommy.

The three of us drove forty-five minutes back to Richmond, along the winding roads that had transported me into my fairy tale eight years ago, and over the bridge, but this time to Richmond, not Oakland.

I tried to hold Robert's hand as we walked up the brick stairs, but he was Mister Independent, taking each step confidently.

I showed Mom the schedule. "It says he has a walk at ten in the morning… too late for that. I'll do that tomorrow. Let's take it from lunch."

I couldn't stop smiling as we ate tuna sandwiches around the dining room table. Did anyone talk? I think we all sat and watched Robert. I know I did. After Robert finished eating, he picked up his plate and silverware and dumped them in the trash.

"What are you doing?" Mom laughed. Even Dad joined in.

"I guess they taught him to bus his plate." I giggled. "Or maybe they ate off paper plates. I have no idea!"

I retrieved the dishes from the trash. "Okay, the schedule says playtime in the small motor development room after lunch. Then a snack, followed by outside play. Then dinner, bath, and sleep."

"When's his nap?" Mom asked.

"No nap. I think that's how they got them to sleep through the night."

Sam and I sat on the floor with Robert, playing with a few toys Mom had for her two grandchildren: Tinkertoys, Matchbox cars, blocks, and coloring books. My heart swelled watching him. Every breath felt fresh. Unburdened. I laughed for no reason.

Two-year-old Robert didn't sit still for long. He wandered upstairs, looking in all the rooms. He came downstairs dragging a king-size gold blanket with satin edging. He sucked his thumb, rubbing the satin. Then, like a puppy looking for the perfect spot to curl up, he turned around a few times and collapsed on the floor, cuddled in the blanket. We let him sleep in the middle of the hallway for two hours.

I ripped up the schedule.

Now what?

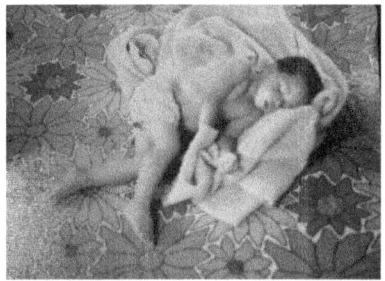

Robert's nap

Mom and Dad

From left to right: The author; Robert; author's mom, grandmother, and sister Julia; Tara

Chapter 36: Clueless

Cults are dangerous, even if they're not putting four-foot-long rattlesnakes in a mailbox or beating people nearly to death. The leaders are unscrupulous, causing deep and lasting damage to their members. They twist our minds to their own ends, whether to become wealthy or merely to bask in the worship of their followers. Often both. Is this what makes them feel important? Successful? Hollow men and women who fill their empty souls with our adoration?

We who follow lose years of our lives, forgo college, give up our children, shave our heads, and work without pay, all because we've bought the bullshit of the snake oil salesman who convinced us his cure-all would heal everything.

Splitting was simple once I made the decision. I thought I was done. I thought I was ready to survive what came next. That was another story, and it was coming fast.

I had no idea how unprepared I was for stepping into a quieter battle to raise a mixed-race child. The world wasn't ready for him, and people could turn against us at any moment, smiling as they slammed doors in my face.

My hair grew long while Synanon echoed through my choices, my silence, my fear.

That story begins in Book 2: Clueless White Mother.

Epilogue

As I finished this memoir, I found a document on Synanon's private website titled Synanon's Tools for Sociometric Manipulation. (See Appendix A.) It was distributed to Tribe Leaders in 1975. Reading it, my blood boiled. There it was in black and white—methodical manipulation, covering everything from the Saturday Night Party, where I'd been recruited, to the systems of reward and punishment that governed our lives. It shattered the last fragile remnants of my hidden belief that Synanon had once been a utopia.

It never was.

It was always Dederich's house, his sandbox, his rules: do things his way or get out.

I've never connected with the word brainwashing. But sociometric manipulation—that fits: the deliberate shaping of relationships, status, and belonging. Shaping who was favored and who was isolated. Dictating how people interacted, and using approval, exclusion, and group pressure to bend emotions, loyalties, even identity.

That describes Synanon perfectly.

I like to imagine the manipulation began benignly—with pressure to stop using drugs. That made sense to me. But I never saw that I, too, was being molded. For what purpose? I still don't know. Dederich had always envied the wealthy oil executives he worked for as a young man. Was I just one rung on his ladder to power and wealth? Or did greed simply swallow him whole as he surrounded himself with sycophants ready to enforce his every whim?

I am still peeling back the layers, piecing together events, shoveling dirt off emotions I buried so deep they barely had names. What exactly had I been part of? And what role had I played?

By staying silent, I sanctioned mass sterilization and abortions. By not paying attention, I allowed children to be neglected and abused. By blindly following, I handed my baby over to the School. Who knows what lasting harm that caused him?

My chest tightens when I think about it now. Was I brainwashed? The word is ugly. Coerced sounds softer. Sociometric manipulation softer still, but it still feels like an excuse. And yet, how else can I explain how mass sterilization or separating mothers from their babies ever made sense to me?

I was intelligent. And still I fell under Synanon's spell. I believed in the communal life we built, the people I loved—the warmth of walking into a dining room filled with fifty friends, the dancing, the hugging, the laughter, the Golden Rule. Character mattered more than skin color. We helped addicts rebuild their lives. We created a community. And I believed my son would thrive in the innovative Synanon School.

The changes were incremental, like that old frog-in-water analogy. Cold water at first: no drugs, no violence. Then warmer: no smoking, mandatory aerobics. Hotter: shaving our heads—uncomfortable, but manageable. No sugar? Fine. But vasectomies? That was boiling water. And I had nearly been cooked alive when I gave my baby to the School.

Technically, you could always split. But for people like Sam, who believed he couldn't survive outside, or for true-believer squares like me, who couldn't imagine life without the community, it wasn't a choice at all.

Even now, I can't fully grasp it. Synanon kept me from my baby. Synanon demanded that men be sterilized. Synanon slid into violence. Into cruelty.

Cruelty seeped everywhere: tearing mothers and babies apart; forbidding parents from holding or even seeing their children; stripping couples of the joy—and the choice—of bringing children into the world; casting people out for daring to speak the truth.

Dederich declared childlessness, denying couples the right to build families of their own. Instead, he brought in wards of the court—the "unwanted children" we were told to raise. Who knew what trauma they carried? Abuse? Neglect? Violence? Did anyone in Synanon even bother to ask what these kids had endured?

There was no tender loving care for them.

And the violence—the child abuse—the silent complicity. What I learned later about the brutality happening while I lived there leaves me mortified and heartsick.

"It happened while I lived there, and I never knew" is not enough. I stayed silent while men carried guns. I didn't question the rumors of violence at the Ranch. I heard that the delinquent teens—the "unwanted children" we claimed to save—were being hit. I felt a twinge. And I stayed silent, convincing myself the leaders knew best.

But the truth was far worse. Spanking the toddlers. Hitting teens with vented paddles and slamming them against walls. Humiliating them by making them wear diapers in front of their peers. Tossing beds that weren't made marine-tight. Forcing bedwetters to hang their sheets for everyone to see.

Some teens reported sexual abuse. They never learned who hurt them.

Child abuse can happen anywhere, I suppose. But it wasn't supposed to happen in Synanon, where we boasted that "character is the only rank."

I knew none of this while I lived there. The Wire fed us only what we were meant to know. What we were allowed to know. But now I wonder what violence Dederich unleashed with those six chilling words: "Sometimes kids need to be hit." Followed by: "Maybe it's time to break some legs."

Now that I know children were neglected and abused, I am horrified that I lived in Synanon while it happened. Did I contribute to their suffering by looking away? By being so consumed with my own crises that I didn't look around? By mindlessly following the leader?

I didn't see. I didn't speak. My silence—our collective silence—condoned abuse. I was afraid of rejection, of being ejected. I clenched my jaw and dug in my heels.

No one was going to run me out.

Today, whenever silence seems like the only way to stay in a community or a job, I stop and ask: Do I want to be part of this? Am I betraying myself just to fit in?

Synanon's story is mine, but it is also a warning: the line between idealism and coercion is thin; the seduction of purpose can blind even the intelligent; and silence can become complicity. I cannot undo the past. But I can bear witness. I can speak the truth. I can remember that character must always outweigh conformity.

I will never close my eyes again.

Appendix A
Synanon's Tools for Sociometric Manipulation

In 1975, Synanon memorialized its tools for sociometric manipulation, encouraging every Tribe Leader (person overseeing thirty or forty people) to use them.

1) Game
2) Haircut
3) General meeting
4) General grill session
5) Newcomer prospect interview
6) Seminars
7) Saturday Night parties
8) Unicept
9) Reach
10) Toys for Thought
11) Job change
12) Rotation
13) Thickened Light tape
14) Massive doses
15) Interthinks
16) Ceremonies, including cop-out, memorials (celebrations of life), marriage, separation ceremonies, Synanon birthdays, rites of passage, retirement
17) Trips
18) Morning meetings
19) The Wire
20) Social Graces
21) Selling the vision
22) Aerobic good health
23) The lifestyle
24) Ability to discriminate
25) Rewards/punishments
26) Money
27) Sex education

Appendix B
Glossary

Act as If: Originally coined by Dederich when he told new residents who came to Synanon to rid themselves of drug addiction that they must act as if Synanon knew what it was doing if they wanted to be cured, and Synanon would act as if the new members were functioning adults until proved otherwise. "Act as if" became a catch phrase, for example, act as if you're happy and you'll become happy.

ADGAP: Synanon-owned business that sold Advertising Gifts and Promotions.

Alfa: My sports car I sold to move into Synanon.

The Bay: The old Marconi property that Synanon bought along Highway One, across from Tomales Bay.

The Beam: Large food service kitchen built to cook food for all facilities, so named when a load supporting beam was placed so low that one couldn't walk under it without ducking.

Betty D.: The wife of the founder, Chuck Dederich.

Bobby: My husband.

Boot Camp: A small, elite group of newcomers (dopefiends in Synanon less than a year), the cream of the crop, who lived at the Ranch. Formed in 1972, the Boot Camp was another experiment in teaching people how to live without drugs.

Breeders: Tongue-in-cheek name for a group of pregnant couples.

Chuck: Founder and Leader of Synanon.

Clumps: An apartment complex across the town in Oakland, California, where most residents slept.

Coffin Beds: Beds for infants and toddlers that sat on the floor—a mattress surrounded by wooden sides.

Connect: The front desk at each facility, which was a connection for housing and transportation.

Contract: One was put on a contract when they broke a rule. It was a shortcut for making a new commitment to Synanon—making a contract with Synanon—to live by the rules. Another use of the word "contract" was keeping a secret with someone about breaking the rules.

Cop out: Admit to doing something wrong.

Demonstrators: Members who worked at the Synanon School. Not only were they the educators, they also looked after the children evenings and nights.

Dog robber: Personal assistant, from the military term for an officer's aide-de-camp. (The aide is expected to rob anyone, including the family dog, to get his general what he wants.)

Dopefiend: General name for anyone who came to Synanon as a misuser of drugs or alcohol.

Glut: Too many personal possessions.

Gracious Dining: Formal dining encouraging long discourse over meals.

Guest Room: A room or apartment that unmarried couples could reserve to spend the night together.

Hatchery: Where new mothers lived together raising their infants, until the babies moved into the Synanon School at six months of age.

Hey Rubes: An elite group of men who wore black berets and attended lessons on how to defend the community against any attack.

Home Place: Wherever Chuck and Betty lived.

Hustlers: The group that hustled up donations for Synanon.

Imperial Marines: A group of men, each in Synanon for several years, who acted as a protection unit for Chuck.

Infant Program: Where the babies age six months to three years old lived.

Jitney: Eight- and fourteen-passenger vans, looking like utility vans with windows and passenger seats.

Lifestyler: Non-substance misuser who moved into Synanon for the community lifestyle.

Love Match: A ceremony allowing couples to live together as if married.

Mobius Loop: An infinity scarf sewn with a half twist so there is neither an inside nor an outside.

Morning Meeting: A daily community gathering before everyone went off to work.

Nylon stocking cap: A nylon (before the days of pantyhose…

before the days of no nylons at all) worn over a woman's head to show she had broken a rule.

Oakland Athletic Club/Athens Club: The Synanon facility in Oakland where I spent my first five years in Synanon.

Pull-up: A verbal correction.

Punk Squad: A group formed in 1972 for teens who came to Synanon as delinquents.

Ramadoulah: Super positive and enthusiastic attitude.

Ranch: One of Synanon's properties in Marin County, California.

Richmond-San Rafael Bridge: Bridge over the eastern San Francisco Bay

Saturday Night Party: Weekly parties where the public was invited to learn about Synanon.

School: The community school where the children lived

Shepherd: A community elder who worked on Synanon Trips

Split: Leave Synanon.

Square: Non-substance misuser.

Stew: A Game lasting twenty-four hours, sometimes unending with people coming in for twenty-four-hour stints.

Synacruiser: Greyhound-size but that transported residents from Oakland to Santa Monica, with a stop at the Visalia airport to pick up residents from Badger.

Synanon bus: a city-size bus that shuttled residents between the Oakland Athens Club and the apartments several miles away.

The Ranch: Property along the Marshall-Petaluma Road in Marin County, California, where Chuck and Betty lived for some time.

The Strip: Property outside of Badger, California, in the Sierra foothills, so named because it had an old landing strip that Synanon renovated.

Tomales Bay/The Bay: The old Marconi property that Synanon bought along Highway One, across from Tomales Bay.

Tribe Leaders: Community leaders who looked after twenty to thirty people.

Trip: A forty-eight-hour experience with little or no sleep.

Tripper: A Trip participant who wore a white muslin robe, with no jewelry or makeup.

Walker Creek: A second ranch property in Marin County.

WAM: A weekly allowance (walk around money)

Wire: In-house radio broadcasting announcements and Games throughout all facilities.

Acknowledgments

I owe a world of thanks to the many people who helped me bring this memoir to life. First, to my husband, Bruce, who stood by me as I wrestled with my emotions and urged me to keep going. Thank you to my Synanon friends who filled in the gaps in my memory and challenged my ideas in our lively Facebook and Zoom conversations. And to the former members who allowed me to interview them—even if your story doesn't appear in these pages, you helped me remember mine. I am forever grateful.

A heartfelt thank you to my developmental editor, Julie Gray, who believed in me from day one and pointed me in the right direction ("Don't forget the zeitgeist of the times"); to my line editor, Dr. Debra Wenzel, Ed.D., who insisted this book needed to be in the world; and to my copy editors, Pam and Michael Rosenthal, who provided a final, thoughtful polish.

I could not have done this without my fellow writers, who patiently listened as I read chapter after chapter and offered invaluable critiques: the OLLI Writers Bloc in Bend, Oregon; the OLLI Writers Critique Group in Eugene, Oregon; and our online Writers Critique Group with members from across the country. I love all of you.

And special thanks to my beta readers and fellow writers—Kate Applegate, Jill Chaffin, Rudy Clark, Cathy Earle, Linda James, Lily Lapin and J. Alex Ruiz. You all rock.

About The Author

Janet Best Dart is a retired paralegal and IT professional living in Bend, Oregon, with her husband, Bruce, and their exuberant Schipperke. A devoted mother and grandmother, she frequently travels to North Carolina to spend time with her son, Robert—who was born in Synanon—and her grandson, Elijah. Her younger son, Christopher, lives close by in Bend.

After retiring, Janet turned her attention to the past she had long kept tucked away: eight years in the 1970s as a Lifestyler inside Synanon, the pioneering drug rehabilitation community that devolved into one of the most dangerous cults in America. The experience inspired her debut memoir, *Tender Loving Care: Escaping from One of the Most Dangerous Cults in America*, which traces her transformation from committed insider to a woman fighting her way out of psychological captivity.

After leaving Synanon, Janet earned a B.S. in information technology and built a life centered on raising her children, pursuing her career, and reclaiming her voice. Today, she remains active in a network of former Synanon residents and children, contributing to Synanon.com, a growing archive of stories and photographs from the community.

When she's not writing, she is hiking, kayaking, sailing, or tending her garden, digging up her lawn, and replacing it with native plants.